# HOTEL DYNASTY

The first Gelardi hotelier was Giuseppe, father of Gustave (Top Left) and Giulio (Top Right).
They were followed into the luxury hotel business by Bertie (Above Left) and Geoffrey (Above Right).

# HOTEL DYNASTY
## Four Generations of Luxury Hoteliers

Geoffrey Gelardi

UNICORN

First published by Unicorn
an imprint of Unicorn Publishing Group LLP, 2021
5 Newburgh Street
London W1F 7RG
www.unicornpublishing.org

Illustrations See Page 9
10 9 8 7 6 5 4 3 2 1

ISBN 978-1-913491-46-8

Design by Martin Derrick and Naomi Waite
Printed in EU

# Contents

(Above): We transformed the original St Georges Hospital building on London's busy Hyde Park Corner into one of the world's most luxurious hotels – The Lanesborough. The Royal Artillery Monument is in the foreground.

# Foreword

On the last day of January 1991 a little snow fell on London and the temperature never got far above freezing. And that was the day on which I turned the key to open the doors of one of the world's finest hotels – The Lanesborough on Hyde Park Corner.

This grand and opulent hotel was created and crafted from what had for over 250 years been one of London's best-known landmarks – St George's Hospital. Where once there had been the pervading smell of disinfectant, hard-wearing but functional linoleum floors, faded paintwork and the hustle and bustle of nurses, doctors, patients and visitors, now there was peace, sophistication, refinement, marble, dark hardwoods and elegant fabrics.

It was a truly astonishing transformation; one that had taken many years to bring to fruition. But in a very real sense, it had actually taken four generations of some of the world's most distinguished hoteliers to get to this point. Because I hadn't literally turned a key to open those doors that frosty morning: there were bowler-hatted doormen to do that. But metaphorically I had turned a key – one that had been passed from my great-grandfather Giuseppe to his son Giulio and from him to my father Bertie and from Bertie to me, Geoffrey Gelardi.

That key was the generations of knowledge, vision, understanding and instinct that are needed to be a hotelier at the very pinnacle of the luxury market: vital attributes that I had gleaned and learned from the experiences of previous generations of Gelardis.

This is the story of a remarkable dynasty, one that has not just witnessed, but been an integral part of the transformation of the hotel industry over almost 200 years.

# Acknowledgements

It's difficult to know where to begin because there are so many people I need to thank. But I suppose my starting point has to be my family – my great-grandfather Giuseppe, my grandfather Giulio and my father Bertie, in whose footsteps I trod during my own career in hotels.

Of them I have to say that Giulio was my inspiration, but Bertie – or Dadsa as we all knew him in the family – was a constant source of love, support, advice and encouragement.

Once I decided to write this history of the four generations of Gelardi hoteliers, it was to my brother Paul that I turned first. Both Giulio and my father left behind massive archives of reminiscences, pictures, menus, tickets and much more. Paul has done an amazing job working on the geneology of the family going back many generations and his research has been absolutely invaluable.

Initially, Jeremy Hughes took up the mantle, ploughing through the archives, and transcribing Giulio's and my father's diaries and historical notes. His work forms the backbone of this book.

And then my old friend Martin Derrick joined the project, adding much new research, editing the material already in hand and doing a great job in terms of picture research, design and layout. We first met when we were twelve years old at school and have remained close friends ever since. It was also he who introduced me to the publisher Unicorn so I have so much to thank him for.

I've also had help, advice and the supply of imagery from many friends and colleagues in the hotel business, most especially from The Savoy and Claridge's. I thank them all.

(Left): Friends for over 50 years! With Martin Derrick, who provided invaluable help in the preparation of this book.

# Illustrations

The vast majority of the illustrations derive from the Gelardi Archives, collected mainly by my grandfather Giulio and father Bertie. Many of the earlier pictures and illustrations are believed to be out of copyright and in the public domain. All of the following are warmly thanked and should any copyright material have been used inadvertently please accept my apologies.

Gustave

# Gelardi Family Members

Giulio

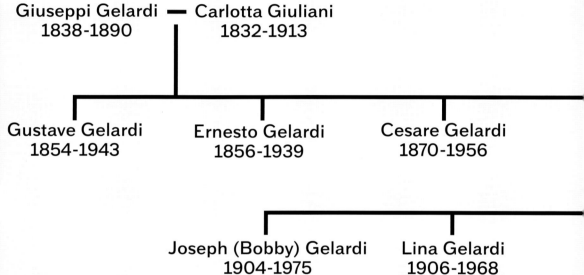

Giuseppi Gelardi — Carlotta Giuliani
1838-1890        1832-1913

Gustave Gelardi        Ernesto Gelardi        Cesare Gelardi
1854-1943              1856-1939              1870-1956

Joseph (Bobby) Gelardi        Lina Gelardi
1904-1975                     1906-1968

Bertie

Peter Gelardi        Michael Gelardi
1946                 1950

Geoffrey

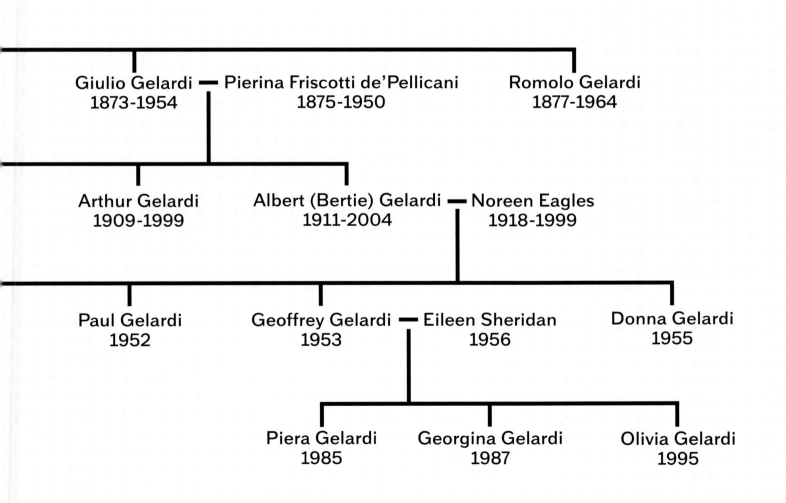

(Above): *A Grand Tour Group of Five Gentlemen*, a painting by John Brown (1752-1787) depicting wealthy British travellers to Rome in the 18th Century.

# Chapter 1

# The Start of the Dynasty

That key that Giulio and Bertie passed to me was actually forged more than one hundred years earlier. My great-great-grandfather Giuseppe Gelardi was the first in the family to work in the hotel business, back in his native Italy where he opened his first hotel in the mid-nineteenth century, at a time when the notion of luxury hospitality as we know it today simply did not exist.

Before this time only the very wealthiest could afford to travel abroad. In the seventeenth and eighteenth centuries young men (very rarely women) from the aristocracy and other grand families had embarked in their early twenties on the Grand Tour – an extended visit to Europe to learn its culture, civilisation and languages. This typically began at Dover and took in Paris and Switzerland before traversing the Alps into northern Italy to visit Turin, Florence and eventually Venice, the climax of the trip.

After months of learning and exploring they returned home with ideas and concepts that would influence art, literature science and political thinking back in the UK.

Those early aristocratic travellers tended to stay as house guests at the homes of upper class contacts on the continent.

But by the turn of the nineteenth century more and more visited Italy, not least the Romantic poets Wordsworth, Byron and Shelley, all of whom were drawn to the country's natural beauty and advanced artistic culture. It was at this time that the first of what we would now recognise as luxury hotels opened to cater for these travellers; a typical example is the Danieli in Venice, created from the magnificent fourteenth century Palazzo Dandolo, home of the Dandolo family, four of whom served as Doge of Venice. The Dandolos had been hosting visiting noblemen for many centuries but it was not until 1822 that their palatial home opened as a hotel.

(Above): Percy Bysshe Shelley was just one of the Romantic Poets who visited Italy to admire its art treasures and natural beauty. Shelley was also buried there, in the Protestant cemetery in Rome, after drowning in the Gulf of Spezzia in 1822. (Below): A white marble sculpture of the dead poet by Edward Onslow Ford was commissioned by his daughter-in-law Lady Shelley in 1893 and presented to University College Oxford where Shelley had studied as a young man.

This was also a time of radical change as the unification of Italy – the *Risorgimento* between 1815 and 1871 – revolutionised both social and political life in the region.

And right in the middle of this political and social upheaval, Giuseppe Eusebio Gelardi was born in 1830 in the small enclave of Brusnengo between Turin and Milan in the heart of Piedmont.

As the middle son of a family of wine producers, he was set to inherit nothing, and success in life would be determined by his own efforts and luck – and Giuseppe was the sort of man who grabbed any opportunities that came his way with both hands. His family sent him to Rome to sell the family wine, and that is where he first encountered the hospitality business.

We know about this because fortunately, his son Gustave left behind some memories of his father written in beautiful cursive script on scraps of paper. He writes that Giuseppe first travelled to Rome in about 1850, where friends in a tavern in the Piazza San Pietro included followers of Giuseppe Garibaldi, the man at the centre of the *Risorgimento*, who contributed so much to the founding of the new united kingdom of Italy.

Gustave's brother Giulio – my grandfather – also left memoirs and from this we know that Giuseppe's first taste of the hospitality industry was working at the Grand Bretagne Hotel in Rome.

While in Rome he married Carlotta, whose family hailed from Velletri, a small commune on the Alban Hills  south of Rome. Her father was a pharmacist and her grandfather a doctor at the Santo Spirito Hospital. Carlotta was a beauty known as the Queen of the *Campo di Fiore*, the translation of which is, romantically, 'field of flowers'.  Gustave recorded that the family lived in or near the Via Degli Artisti but that he himself was born behind Piazza di Trevi at Palazzo Del Drago, the home of Princess Dragone, where by this time in 1854 Giuseppe was a butler.  The butler's job is to run all aspects of the household so in a very real way, the position is not unlike that of a hotel general manager.

It's not certain how Giuseppe came to be major domo in the household of Princess Dragone but one of his duties would almost certainly have

been to take care of visiting English aristocrats taking their Grand Tour.

(Above): No pictures of Giuseppe Gelardi exist and most of what we know about his life and work is thanks to notes left by his eldest son Gustave. Giuseppe was born in Brusnengo in Piedmont, in 1831 as this copy of his original birth certificate attests.

At some stage however he was lured away by a friend, tempted by an opportunity to invest in a hotel in Naples which would have been Giuseppe's first venture into running his own hotel. It was not a happy experience: the business failed and the 'friend' disappeared, so Giuseppe returned to Rome where we know that from 1854, he worked at the Hotel Franz Rössler in Via dei Condotti. He and his family lived in a top floor apartment with an entrance off the Via delle Carrozze.

Franz Rössler's hotel – later known as the Hôtel d'Allemagne – was one of the finest hotels in Rome in the mid nineteenth century. The famous French writer Stendhal stayed there twice and it's rumoured that the Bourbon King Ferdinando II of the Two Sicilies took rooms there after the revolution in Palermo in 1848.

But even for a family with a reasonable income and better accommodation than most would have experienced in Rome at that time, life was not easy. There was no electricity and the only light at night came from oil lamps. Infant mortality rates were high, not least because of the way that diseases were quickly transmitted due to cramped living quarters and the lack of hygiene as we know it today.

In this sense, Giuseppe and Carlotta's life was quite representative of many mid-nineteenth-century families. Their first child, a son, died in infancy. A daughter, Elvera, died before reaching the age of three. Five boys, though, survived: Gustave, Ernesto, Cesare, Giulio and Romolo.

Gustave and his brother Ernesto were sent to a private elementary Dame School, which probably provided a very basic level of education, but it is likely that Gustave's education improved when he became an altar boy at San Carlo church on the Via del Corso, where he would at least have learned the doctrines of Catholicism. He remembered his First Communion and the fringed trousers he wore that day, as well as the feast afterwards.

It's likely that, along with other Catholic children of his age, he would have frequented the Villa Borghese, where there was always the chance of seeing the Pope passing in his carriage; and then the boys would run alongside, hoping for his blessing.

Gustave's education improved further when he and Ernesto moved on to a far better school run by friars in the Piazza Poli close to the famous Trevi Fountain. When the kingdom of Italy was founded as the nation we know today in 1861, illiteracy was near 80 per cent, a rate that didn't halve for fifty years.

So Gustave was lucky that he could both read and write – it is likely that his beautiful handwriting was a result of his schooling in the Piazza Poli. In addition, the boys were taught entirely in French and

(Below): The Hôtel Franz Rössler in Rome where Giuseppe worked, and where he lived with his family from 1854, was later renamed the Hôtel d'Allemagne, when it gained a reputation for being one of the Italian capital's finest hotels.

(Above): The Villa Borghese in central Rome, close to the Spanish Steps, was originally built in the seventeenth century by Cardinal Scipione Borghese who filled its rooms with the finest art of the day. Its parklands now constitute the third largest public park in the city and it was here that Gustave and his brothers came at the weekends, in the hope of seeing the Pope parading in his carriage and managing to obtain his blessing.

allowed to speak Italian only once a week so we can assume that a second language was a boon in Gustave's later career in the hospitality business.

He must have been a good pupil, because not only were his scripts displayed on the walls of his home, but he was also presented with three prizes in his time at school. The Prince Imperial, Louis Bonaparte, who happened to be in Rome visiting his godfather Pope Pius IX, made the presentations and I can only imagine Gustave's excitement and Giuseppe's pride at this great honour. Neither, I suspect, would have dreamed then that this would be the first of many encounters with royalty which Gustave and future generations of Gelardis would experience in the years that followed.

Since his father Giuseppe was running the Hotel Franz and the family were living above the shop as it were, Gustave would have been observing and learning about the hospitality business through a kind of relational osmosis. However, his training was formalised when he left school at the age of thirteen and started work at the hotel. His tasks included fetching and carrying, buffing lamps and cleaning. Later he was entrusted with guests' trays, laden with food and drink and since there were no lifts in those days, he would have had to carry them up and down several flights of stairs.

Life at the hotel was not without its incidents for the young Gustave. On one occasion, after carrying one particularly heavy tray to a room on the top floor, the whole arrangement somehow crashed to the floor, spilling its carefully prepared food and drink. On another occasion, he was sent out to find a taxi for a guest, and while lolling on the back seat enjoying the ride back to the hotel, he managed to stumble out of the door and break his nose.

Around this time, Gustave met Thomas Cook, the travel agent and an innovator of mass travel. Giuseppe was no linguist and at that time could only manage 'my son' when introducing Gustave to English-speaking guests staying at the hotel. And so Giuseppe's 'my son' was called upon to present a bouquet to Cook's wife Marianne.

It might be a surprise to learn that Cook was accompanying a party of Lancashire miners, but with his evangelical beginnings and his first travel groups being temperance campaigners, it is indicative of his belief that travel was spiritually and personally beneficial. His introduction of coupons for Italy's railway system and notes that could be exchanged in the country's banks and hotels was revolutionary, enabling Italians to travel the country and spread that feeling of unity the *Risorgimento* had set out to achieve. Thomas Cook & Son would become an influential feature of twentieth-century British tourism; and Gustave would become the first – but by no means the last – internationally influential Gelardi hotelier.

But that was in the future. For the present, Gustave had to do his compulsory military service. Even though Giuseppe called in favours trying to get Gustave into the smart *Carabinierie Reali*, he eventually joined the *Primo Granatieri di Savoia*, for which the height requirement was five foot eleven. Gustave was six feet tall but despite that, recorded that he was the shortest in the regiment.

According to Gustave's notes his duties included collecting conscripts in Cagliari in Sardinia – all of whom were illiterate – and he vividly remembered the young men's mothers crying when their sons' shoulder-length hair was cut.

Later, he was stationed in the north at the forbidding Forte Castellaccio at Genoa, where he remembered the sounds of convicts' chains as

(Top): The Forte Castellaccio overlooking the port of Genoa where Gustave was stationed during his military service in the *Primo Granatieri di Savoia* – the 'Grenadiers of Savoy', a regiment that still exists to this day. (Above): Gustave was later stationed at the Castel Sant' Angelo in Rome's Adriano Park.

they chinked and rattled to and from their work in the port.

Gustave also spent some time stationed in Rome as we know that at some stage he was on guard at the Castel Sant' Angelo, a towering edifice originally built by the Roman Emperor Hadrian as a family mausoleum, but later used by successive popes as a castle and prison. The family camped on the pavement outside to catch a glimpse of the Pope, but here Gustave's notes become rather patchy. Maybe he just ran out of time. Maybe he wanted to keep some things forever private. Sadly there is a gap of around thirty years, with just pencilled jottings hinting at establishments where he worked, and notes which make us wonder about their meaning, but what we do know is that he ended up in the UK in the mid 1880s.

Giuseppe died one hot and sultry night on 10 August 1890, possibly of cholera which was as much of a danger in Rome as it was in London and all other great cities at that time. It meant that Carlotta was left a widow at the age of fifty-four, looking after Cesare, Giulio and the youngest, Romolo. By this time, the two elder brothers – Gustave and Ernesto – were already in London. Quite how and why Gustave came to cross the Channel remains a bit of a mystery. After completing his military service Gustave was employed as a personal assistant to a Mrs Grisewood who lived on the first floor of a palace overlooking the River Arno in Florence.

(Above): Carlotta Gelardi, wife of Giuseppe and mother of Gustave, Ernesto, Cesare, Giulio and Romolo.

It's possible that 'Mrs Grisewood' is a name used by Gustave to disguise the woman's true identity because his notes include a reference to 'Mirafiori illegitimate son of V.E.'. Could this have been Victor Emmanuel I, Duke of Savoy and King of Sardinia? Or perhaps more likely Victor Emmanuel II, King of Sardinia from 1849 who became the first king of the newly united Italy in 1861? He was known to have had several mistresses and fathered numerous children out of wedlock and it's possible 'Mrs Grisewood' was one of those paramours. In any event, it became clear that her interest in Gustave went beyond the professional so in order to escape, he went to London after asking his brother Ernesto to replace him in the Grisewood residence.

Clearly Mrs Grisewood held no grudges because she provided Gustave with letters of introduction that resulted in a meeting with Frederick Ponsonby, one-time Assistant Private Secretary to Queen Victoria and now aid to Bertie, the Prince of Wales, known as the 'Playboy Prince,' who later was crowned Edward VII on the death of Victoria in 1901. Ponsonby arranged for Gustave to work as steward at Merton Hall, Norfolk, home of Thomas de Grey, sixth Baron Walsingham. 'Steward' meant that Gustave was responsible for the running of the estate, reporting directly to Lord Walsingham and responsible for organising shooting parties. A very keen shot, Walsingham is recorded as having killed 1,070 grouse in a single day on Blubberhouses Moor in Yorkshire on 30 August 1888.

(Below): Gustave and Emily, who met at Merton Hall where both were employed by Lord Walsingham. They married on New Year's Eve in 1885.

More importantly, on a personal level, Merton Hall was where Emily Collins was employed as governess. She and Gustave were married on 31 December 1885 and a daughter Elvera Helen Gelardi was born at 53 Ovington Street, Chelsea, less than two months later

# Thomas de Grey, 6th Baron Walsingham

When Gustave Gelardi arrived in England he was truly fortunate to find work as steward of Merton Hall, Lord Walsingham's estate in Norfolk. It consisted of a fine house and almost 20,000 acres of land.

Walsingham was an interesting man, born in 1843, educated at Eton and Cambridge and becoming the Member of Parliament for West Norfolk at the age of twenty-two and keeping his seat until he succeeded to his late father's title and estates and entered the House of Lords.

He was a first class cricketer, playing for the MCC and Cambridge University and was a keen ornithologist and lepidopterist. He donated his collection of over 260,000 moths and butterflies to the Natural History Museum and apparently shot all the hummingbirds in the Museum's collection.

Shooting was his main interest and he indulged on an epic scale – setting a record solo bag in August 1888 when he shot 1,070 grouse in a single day. Starting at just after 5am, he had two teams of forty beaters driving the grouse over his guns – he had four guns and two loaders to ensure he was always at the ready. The final, 20th drive was at just before 7pm, but for good measure Walsingham bagged another fourteen birds while walking home.

He set another shooting record a couple of years later in 1890 when he compiled a 'most varied' bag of 191 different species, which as well as game and wild birds included a rat, a coot and even a pike!

Walsingham was married three times but died bankrupt and without an heir in 1919. Despite having an annual income of some £10,000 a year from his estates in Norfolk and Yorkshire – which would be around £1 million today – the sheer

Lord Walsingham and his country seat Merton Hall, where Gustave Gelardi first worked for the Baron.

cost of his extravagant shooting and gambling meant he ran up huge debts.

But happily for Gustave, before his financial crash Walsingham entrusted him with the task of transforming his London home into the Walsingham Hotel – and so launched him on his career as a highly-regarded luxury hotelier.

on 23 February 1886. It seems that Emily had been hidden away in a Chelsea boarding house in the months before the marriage – which unsurprisingly was conducted not in a Catholic ceremony but in a Chelsea society church. But why would they have waited until Emily was nearly eight months pregnant before marrying? And why choose New Year's Eve?

Perhaps the answer lies in the libertine lifestyles of some of those whom Gustave would have met while employed by Lord Walsingham. One was obviously Bertie, the future Edward VII, who enjoyed life to the full during the *Belle Epoque*, that time before the First World War when life was enjoyed in a kind of golden haze by the aristocrats of Europe.

He, Walsingham and other friends were epicureans and gamblers, and loved driven shoots. Bertie also had many mistresses including Lillie Langtry, Jenny Churchill (Winston's mother), Camilla Parker Bowles' great-grandmother Alice Keppel, and Daisy Warwick. He even commissioned a *siege d'amour* – a special chair to aid his love-making. Certainly Emily was a very beautiful young lady, which would not have escaped the notice of these two notorious lechers.

(Below): King Edward VII, formerly Bertie, the fun-loving Prince of Wales. Was he, or was Lord Walsingham the father of Elvera?

As the present Lord Walsingham observed, his ancestor the sixth Baron's marital infidelities 'were remarkable, in an age when infidelity was commonplace; though the scandal was for the most part confined to the locality since it seems he usually slept with his housemaids'. It is this behaviour which leads us to conjecture that Bertie or Walsingham might have been the father of Gustave and Emily's daughter Elvera.

Could there perhaps have been an 'arrangement', since there appeared to be no stigma attached to the circumstances of Gustave and Emily's marriage? Could there have been a connection with the Freemasons, as Gustave was a member of the Alfred Newton Lodge which met in Kensington and at that time, the Grand Master of England and the Grand Sovereign of the Order was none other than HRH the Prince of Wales?

We don't know whether the Prince of Wales,

or Lord Walsingham, or indeed someone else might have been the father because Gustave's discretion was beyond question. But we do know that he was promoted to Walsingham's private secretary at around that time and was then given responsibility for converting the baron's London home into the luxury Walsingham House Hotel.

After a childhood watching and learning how his father Giuseppe ran his hotel, his military training and his experience of entertaining Walsingham and Bertie's bacchanalian coterie, Gustave was perfect for the role.

(Below): Walsingham House Hotel on Piccadilly opened in 1888 and quickly established itself as one of the places in London to see and be seen.

The Walsingham House Hotel on London's Piccadilly was completed in 1888, replete with frescos of hunting and fishing scenes in the grand dining room by the well-known Italian artist Cesare Formilli. A contemporary review in *The Artist: an Illustrated Monthly Record of Arts, Crafts And Industries*, was emphatic: 'They are well worth going

to see, and Lord Walsingham and his very able manager, Mr. G. Gelardi, ought to be indeed congratulated upon having emerged from the ordinary decorative routine. Instead of putting this important work in the hands of the ordinary decorator, they have had the enterprise and good judgment to employ the services of a first-rate artist. It is a pity the rubbish one commonly finds, even in an otherwise magnificent hotel, cannot be improved in the same way in the direction of true artistic feeling and expression.'

An advertisement in *The Times* newspaper of 21 October 1889 declared the Walsingham House Hotel to occupy 'the most unique and central position in fashionable London'. It went on to boast that 'the Restaurant and Public Rooms overlook Green Park and command a magnificent view. A charming terrace and garden are also attached to the hotel. Each Single Room and each Suite of Rooms is provided with a luxurious bathroom.'

Despite all this, sadly the Walsingham House Hotel did not exist for very long. Queen Victoria died on 22 January 1901, and it was announced that the coronation of Bertie, Prince of Wales, would take place on 26 June 1902. The route from Buckingham Palace to Westminster Abbey passed the Walsingham House Hotel and the baron, spotting a way of making a great deal of money quickly, sold hundreds of tickets for people to have a roadside view. But just before the big day, Bertie became very ill, and was operated on by his physician, Frederick Treves. There were rumours that the King had cancer. A story also circulated that it was appendicitis and that he underwent surgery on a billiard table at Buckingham Palace. Both are inaccurate. It was an abscess from which Treves drained a huge quantity of pus. The coronation was postponed to August of that year but the delay

(Above and Below): As the contemporary advertising boasted, the public rooms of the Walsingham Hotel were exquisitely decorated.

# WALSINGHAM
## HOUSE
## HOTEL AND RESTAURANT,
### PICCADILLY, W.

**THE MAGNIFICENT NEW RESTAURANT,** with Reception Rooms, Private Dining Room, &c., exquisitely decorated, and perfect in every detail, IS NOW OPENED.

*The Table d'Hôte is now open to non-residents.*

**WALSINGHAM HOUSE** occupies the most unique and central position in Fashionable London.

**THE RESTAURANT AND PUBLIC ROOMS** overlook the celebrated Green Park, Piccadilly, and command a magnificent pastoral view, although in the heart of London.

**A CHARMING TERRACE AND GARDEN** are also attached to the Hotel.

Each single Room and each Suite of Rooms provided with a luxurious Bath Room.

G. GELARDI, *Manager.*

*Telegrams:* "SOIGNÉ, LONDON."

meant ruin for Walsingham – as he had to return the money from the ticket sales that he had already spent on wine, women and gambling.

And so he was forced to sell the Walsingham House Hotel to César Ritz who also bought the Bath Hotel next door, and demolished both to build the luxury Louis XVI-inspired building we know today.

Even though he was about to lose his job, Gustave helped in the negotiations with César Ritz. Oh, how I would have liked to have been there, Gustave hailing from a comfortable though far from wealthy childhood in Rome and César, the last of thirteen children from a Swiss peasant family, discussing enormous sums of other people's money!

(Right): Gustave Gelardi during the time he was managing the Grand Hotel in Folkestone.

# The Life and Times of César Ritz

César Ritz was born in 1850, the youngest of thirteen children brought up in a poor peasant family in the Swiss village of Niederwald. He started as a waiter but soon moved up in the world of hospitality, running the restaurant of the Grand Hotel in Nice when still just twenty-three.

Three years later he was made manager of the Grand Hotel National in Lucerne and the Grand Hotel in Monaco and by this time he had already formulated his recipe for success: insisting that 'the customer is always right'. And he also mandated that a good hotelier should: 'See all without looking; hear all without listening; be attentive without being servile; anticipate without being presumptuous. If a diner complains about a dish or the wine, immediately remove it and replace it, no questions asked.'

In 1888 he opened a restaurant with the great chef Auguste Escoffier in Baden-Baden, where they came to the attention of Richard D'Oyly Carte who invited them to London to become the first manager and chef of The Savoy Hotel.

They left under a cloud in 1898, accused of taking bribes from suppliers but were not held back for long, as the Ritz Hotel in Paris opened that very same year. The Ritz in London followed in 1906 and the Ritz in Madrid in 1910. Ritz's health was failing and he retired in 1907, leaving Escoffier to run the business.

Ritz, of course, was well known to both Gustave and later Giulio Gelardi. Gustave had helped in the negotiations for Ritz to take over what had been the Walsingham Hotel on Piccadilly and Giulio had been told by Ritz that he was not suitable for a career in hotels! Despite this, they became friends: 'I had come to know him well,' wrote Giulio, 'and despite the difference in our ages and my inexperience in the business, he gave me friendship and consideration. When he came

(Above): César and Louise Ritz in 1888. Ritz would have a profound influence on starting Giulio Gelardi upon his career in the hotel business. The friendship that later developed lasted until Ritz's death in 1918.

to London he never failed to send for me.'

On Ritz's last visit to London in 1917 or 1918, he asked to see Giulio at Claridge's. 'When I went into the hall to meet him, I gasped at the sight. The great leader of our business, this man always so impeccably dressed – smiling, alert and commanding in presence – now a shrivelled little figure in ill-fitting clothes, bent and old, his eyes those of a man tired out.'

But Ritz suddenly sparked with new energy as the two moved through the hotel the renovation of which Ritz had planned. 'Claridge's was my creation,' he claimed. Giulio never saw him again, as Ritz died a few months later.

For Ritz, this was a decisive move to restore his damaged reputation. He and his chef Auguste Escoffier had been enticed from their celebrated restaurant in Baden-Baden by Richard D'Oyly Carte, to become respectively the first general manager and chef of The Savoy Hotel which opened in the Strand in 1889. It was next to The Savoy Theatre and was funded by the profits that D'Oyly Carte made from the Gilbert and Sullivan operettas that showed there.

The Savoy was in many ways London's first true luxury hotel featuring electric lighting, lifts and bathrooms with hot and cold running water for most of the bedrooms; sure enough, it attracted the great and the good from the worlds of entertainment, business and politics.

But on 7 March 1898, Ritz, Escoffier (and Ritz's assistant Louis Echenard) were summoned to appear before D'Oyly Carte and members of the board of directors. The hotel's auditors discovered that in the first six months of 1897, £37,549 of wine had been sold yet receipts totalled merely £34,073. The hotel profits had slumped

(Left): Gustave was made general manager of the Cadogan Hotel in 1902 after the closure of the Walsingham Hotel. The Cadogan Hotel in London's Sloane Square opened in 1887. The blue plaque on the front of the building commemorates Lilly Langtry who lived here for seventeen years from 1895. (Below): That same year the hotel became infamous as the venue for Oscar Wilde's arrest for gross indecency with Lord Alfred Douglas.

*Upper Lees, Folkestone*

by more than 40 per cent. The board's lawyer Sir Edward Carson advised that, 'It is the imperative duty of the directors to dismiss the manager and the chef for among other reasons, gross negligence and breaches of duty and mismanagement.' In the event, the two men were not formally dismissed though they left the company by mutual agreement.

Ritz wasn't floored for long. Between the opening of the hotel which bore his name in London in 1906, he also found time to open the Hôtel Ritz in Paris in 1898 – clearly he had been working on this project for some time before leaving The Savoy earlier that same year. Ironically, it was Ritz's customers at The Savoy who persuaded him to open a hotel in Paris, and with funding from Marnier-Lapostelle – who had developed Grand Marnier, a new orange flavoured cognac-based liqueur in 1880 – Ritz was able to acquire a large mansion on the Place Vendôme, once the home of a prince, and over the next two years converted it into a 210-room luxury hotel.

For Gustave, the reality was that he was now out of a job. Happily though he soon was offered the post of general manager at the Cadogan Hotel on Sloane Street, where Oscar Wilde had been arrested in April 1895, and where one of Bertie's amours Lillie Langtree had lived between 1880 and 1897. Like César Ritz, Gustave had quickly bounced back.

(Above): Gustave's next move was down to the south coast, to the fashionable resort of Folkestone, where Cadogan Hotel owner Daniel Baker asked him to open the Grand Hotel. It was positioned overlooking the sea on The Leas, a highly-popular promenade.

(Above): The Palm Court at the Grand Hotel in Folkestone

Clearly Gustave was highly respected and trusted at the Cadogan Hotel because the energetic chairman of the company that owned it, Daniel Baker, also had plans to open the Grand Hotel in Folkestone, the Channel port that was an important conduit to Europe at that time. He duly asked Gustave to help supervise the project, as well as run the hotel on completion.

The Grand was originally built between 1899 and 1900 as residential apartments but it was converted and opened as a hotel in 1903.

Despite having been built right next door to the Metropole Hotel on the marine promenade known as The Leas, the Grand Hotel was an instant success, not least because it was frequently patronised by Edward VII, who by now treated Gustave as both a friend and a confidant. Alice Keppel (great-grandmother of Camilla Parker-Bowles, now the Duchess of Cornwall) and Empress Eugenie, wife of Napoleon III, were regular guests, and there were greats from the theatre – Basil Hallam (who was killed at the Battle of the Somme), Sterndale Bennet and Nelson Keys (who appeared in the 1924 *Ziegfeld Follies*) – and opera: Enrico Caruso (who will appear in Giulio's story later), Antonio Scotti, Giacomo Puccini – described as Italy's greatest composer after Verdi – and another famous composer, Paolo Tosti, knighted in 1908.

Yet another regular was Woolf Barnato, one of the 'Bentley Boys' whose exploits at the Le Mans twenty-four-hour race were legendary. It's also very likely that one of his team-mates, Dr Joseph Benjafield would have stayed there prior to his many trips to the continent. 'Benjy', as he was known, was an eminent doctor and bacteriologist as well as being one of the finest drivers of his day. And the reason why he might well have made the Grand Hotel his base when crossing the Channel? He was one of the family, having married Gustave's elder daughter Elvera in 1914.

According to the local *Folkestone Herald*, 'The Grand Hotel is patronised by the best people and is always full. At this time of year, nothing could be more charming than a weekend in Folkestone.'

To be seen at the Grand was part of a socialite's routine. In fact its heavily glazed frontage was such that locals called it 'the Monkey House,' trying as they did to spot the King and his entourage through the windows. The term 'Monkey Suit' for a dinner jacket was also coined at this time as the Grand Hotel's guests would always dress for the evening.

For Gustave, this was an exciting and a busy time. He seems to have started up a sideline import/export business sometime after the First World War – *Comptoir Général D'Importation et D'Exportation* – which operated out of Folkestone for a while before being wound up in 1922. For the rest of his career he remained in Folkestone running the Grand Hotel though he was also managing director of the Cadogan Hotel in London – and always staying there whenever he visited the capital. He must have had some sort of financial involvement with the Cadogan Hotel, as around 1930 he sold the shares in the company that he owned and resigned as managing director

For the remainder of his career he stayed in Folkestone at the Grand Hotel until the outbreak of the Second World War when he retired and moved to Glossop in Derbyshire, some fifteen miles east of Manchester, where his younger daughter Lola was living. He died there in March 1943 and later was returned to Folkestone to be buried in a magnificent tomb constructed from the finest Italian marble, alongside his wife Emily who had passed away a decade earlier.

(Above): Elvera, Lola and Emily. (Below): Gustave and Emily are buried in a magnificent Italian marble tomb in the cemetery at Folkestone where they spent so many years of their lives.

# Benjafield, Barnato and the Bentley Boys

Bentleys first competed at the 1923 Le Mans 24 Hours race when Frank Clement and John Duff recorded the fastest lap in their Bentley 3.0-litre. They returned in 1924 to clinch the race overall. By 1925 the Bentley company had suffered financial difficulties and was taken over by the debonair Woolf Barnato – by all accounts a regular at the Grand Hotel in Folkestone where Gustave Gelardi would have welcomed him.

W.O. Bentley retained control of the racing team and entered three cars for the 1926 event, the best placed being the car of renowned journalist Sammy Davis and Dr Dudley Benjafield coming sixth. Benjafield was very well known to Gustave, as he had married his daughter Elvera in 1914!

Then in the 1927 race what seemed like disaster turned out to be a precious victory for Davis and Benjafield. As darkness fell a spinning car caused the leading Bentley of Leslie Callingham and Frank Clement to crash into a ditch. Seconds later the second Bentley of George Duller and Baron André d'Erlanger crashed into the same ditch, before Sammy Davis, who was just behind, arrived at the scene of carnage. He just managed to avoid going into the self-same ditch but his car – Number 3 – was seriously damaged with its front wheels out of alignment.

At that time the rules of the race meant that only the driver could work on a damaged car and in just half an hour Davis heroically changed the wheel, rigged up a new headlamp and re-attached the running board. As the race continued it seemed that second place was the best the Bentley drivers could expect but just ninety minutes from the end, the leading car broke down and Davis and Benjafield swept to an incredible victory.

That epic win was later celebrated by a dinner at The Savoy hosted by *The Autocar* magazine and it's a shame that by this time my grandfather

(Top) Dudley Benjafield at speed in his 3-litre Bentley during the 1928 Le Mans 24-Hour race. Celebrations at The Savoy after Benjafield and Davis's victory in 1927 (Above).

Giulio had moved from managing The Savoy to his new role at CIGA Hotels in Italy so he would not have had the pleasure of personally welcoming his niece's husband and the rest of the Bentley team!

Supported by Woolf Barnato's finances, the Bentley team went on to win Le Mans three times in a row, in 1928, 1929 and 1930 and thus was born the legend of the 'Bentley Boys', a group of drivers who were all men of independent means whose hectic lives tended to hit the headlines both on and off the track. As well as Dr Dudley Benjafield, they included the former fighter pilot Sir HRS 'Tim' Birkin, motor sport journalist SCH 'Sammy' Davis, 'born adventurer' Glen Kidston, former Olympic fencer John Duff and of course their leader Woolf 'Babe' Barnato whose fortune derived from the Kimberley diamond mines in South Africa and who famously raced the Blue Train from Cannes to Calais in 1930 for a £200 bet. Not only did Barnato beat the train to Calais – he was actually in his club in London as the train pulled into Calais station and so won the bet handsomely. However, it's reported that the French police fined him far more than his winnings for racing on public roads.

As for Dr Benjafield, he was a serious medical man despite the playboy image of the Bentley Boys. He was born on 6 August 1887, in Edmonton, London, UK and attended the University of London and then received his MD from University College Hospital in 1912. Specialising in bacteriology, he served in Egypt during the First World War and once hostilities finally ceased, he used his expertise to combat the great Spanish flu epidemic of 1918–19. He later worked at St George's Hospital, on London's Hyde Park Corner, in the building which would become The Lanesborough Hotel.

(Above): Dudley and Vera Benjafield. (Below): Some of the Bentley Boys photographed in Mayfair in 1927 before Dudley Benjafield and Sammy Davis's victory. From Left: Frank Clement, Sammy Davis, Dudley Benjafield, Bernard Rubin, Woolf Barnato and Tim Birkin. Barnato would go on to win the Le Mans 24 Hours three times from 1928 to 1930.

The five Gelardi brothers in London around 1898. Standing (Left to Right):
Romolo and Giulio. Seated (Left to Right): Cesare, Gustave and Ernesto.

# Chapter 2

# Five Brothers in London

By this time, as the nineteenth century drew to a close, three of Gustave's brothers had arrived in London. At some point, after the opening of the Walsingham House Hotel, Gustave's brother Ernesto came to the UK from Italy so clearly, like Gustave, he had not remained in Mrs. Grisewood's employ for long.

Gustave - no doubt through the contacts he had been building up - found Ernesto a position as a butler in Ascot. There he met and married Anna Rassier, a wealthy German woman with whom he bought a hotel in Folkestone. When she died, Ernesto married her sister Franziska in 1915. They had two daughters, Berta and Theresa (who we shall meet again in my father Bertie's story). Berta's ambitions were in acting, and she appeared most notably as Esther Summerson in the 1920 film version of *Bleak House*, directed by Maurice Elvey. A contemporary review in the film industry publication *Kine Weekly* praised the film's design: 'The costumes, make up and scenic effects are all excellently modelled on Phiz's drawings.'

Ernesto was not the only brother that Gustave helped. He had earlier also found Cesare a butler's position in Kensington, but there was friction when a relationship Cesare was having with a maid, Hannah Wareham, resulted in her pregnancy. They married when she was three months pregnant in December 1895. Gustave's indignation doesn't make sense, considering that his wife Emily gave birth so soon after they married, which further arouses curiosity about what might have surrounded those circumstances.

Whatever disappointment Gustave expressed towards Cesare, it didn't last - when he took up as general manager of the Cadogan Hotel, it was Cesare he hired as his assistant. Cesare learned from his older brother and acquired the skills necessary to move on and run a high-quality establishment of his own. He did so by emigrating, maybe to establish himself away from Gustave and the relatively small world of

(Below): A still from the 1920 silent film of *Bleak House*, in which Berta Gelardi (though credited with the name of Berta Gellardi) took the part of Esther Summerson.

(Top, Above, Left): The Cadogan in London is now a Belmond hotel. The blue plaque on the wall commemorates Lillie Langtry who lived in this house, and when her home was incorporated into an enlarged Cadogan hotel, she remained in residence, keeping her bedroom for many years. In the early twentieth century after Gustave was appointed general manager, he employed his younger brother Cesare as his assistant.

hospitality in Britain, becoming the general manager of the Windsor Hotel in Montreal. Years later, my father Bertie would visit him there with my grandfather Giulio.

Cesare must have had a fine apprenticeship under his elder brother Gustave's guidance because at that time, the Windsor was the largest and best hotel in all of Canada. It first opened its doors in 1878 as a reflection of the wealth, opulence and opportunity offered by the commercial dominance of Montreal which at that time was Canada's largest and most prosperous city.

Its owners, a group of six Canadian businessmen lead by William Notman - whose photography business had gained an international reputation - deliberately modelled the hotel on the original Waldorf-Astoria in New York on 5th Avenue and 34th Street which was demolished to build the Empire State building - my grandfather Giulio Gelardi would manage the new Waldorf-Astoria on Park Avenue in later years.

By the time Giulio's elder brother Cesare Gelardi arrived in Canada to run the Windsor, the hotel had suffered a devastating fire in 1906 that destroyed much of the building, but this was used as an opportunity to renovate and expand with the addition of a new Windsor Annexe wing, which increased the total number of rooms from 368 to 750.

The hotel welcomed politicians, business leaders, royalty and other luminaries such as writers Mark Twain, Rudyard Kipling and Oscar

MONTRÉAL.—Hotel Windsor.
(Windsor Hotel.)

(Left): Cesare Gelardi emigrated to Canada to run the Windsor Hotel in Montreal – then the country's most prestigious hotel, situated near the station of what at the time was Canada's most prosperous city.

Wilde and film stars such as Sarah Bernhardt, Fanny Davenport and Dolores Costello.

The Windsor sat at the epicentre of Montreal's social scene and as such it hosted both the annual St Andrew's Society Ball and the Winter Carnival Ball for decades. Later in the twentieth century, King George VI and Queen Elizabeth stayed there just before the outbreak of the Second World War in 1939.

Sadly it was yet another fire that put paid to the Windsor Hotel, when in 1957 much of the building was so badly damaged that only the 200 rooms in the Windsor Annexe remained. The hotel never regained its stature, due in part to increased competition from newer downtown hotels, and it finally closed in 1981 to be converted into office buildings.

My grandfather Giulio also arrived in London unannounced during the 1890s, the fourth brother to arrive in the capital. His own memoirs make it quite clear why he hadn't

(Top): The grand Dining Room of the Windsor Hotel with its magnificent rotunda. (Centre): A rare picture of the kitchens and staff. (Above): The prestigious St Andrew's Society Ball was held at the Windsor Hotel in its early years. (Right): It also hosted King George VI and Queen Elizabeth during their state visit to Canada in May 1939.

given advance warning of his arrival: *'My two elder brothers, Gustave and Ernesto, were by now quite well established in England; but feeling that since they had had a bad experience with Cesare when he arrived in England, they might have tried to stop me leaving Italy, I hadn't told them of my plans and was arriving quite unheralded.*

*'When I got to London the reception was cold and reserved, but not unfriendly. Gustave loved me I was sure. He had been proud of my success at school and though rather disappointed that I had not achieved my ambitions to become a lawyer, he believed in my*

*intelligence and my courage to make good whatever career I would undertake... I insisted with my brother that he should try me at some work at once. He relented and put me in the kitchen to work with the Chef. The hotel – Walsingham House – was a big establishment. I worked and learned as hard and as quickly as possible and kept away from the family for some months. Slowly I gained the confidence of my brother and his senior management and was put to work in the office.'*

Sure enough, Giulio gradually won Gustave's trust and worked his way

(Above): The Promenade des Anglais in Nice around 1900. The seven-kilometre promenade was financed by English residents and completed in 1824. Ever since it has been a magnet for visitors, artists and residents to enjoy the Mediterranean sunshine. It also encouraged yet more winter visitors which is why Gustave and Giulio invested in their own hotel project in the South of France.

up in the organisation; he clearly became so dependable that Gustave founded the Gelardi Hotel Company with him, putting all their money into a venture that they hoped would make their fortunes on the French Riviera.

Europe's aristocracy 'discovered' what is now known as the French Riviera in the early part of the nineteenth century when they started decamping to Nice and Cannes for the winter. Many fine second homes were built, including what is now the Musée Masséna, originally built for Prince Victor d'Essling, the grandson of Napoleon's General Maréchal Massena, and the Musée des Beaux Arts in Nice, first constructed for the Ukrainian Princess Elisabeth Vassilievna Kotschoubey.

The British upper classes also made the Mediterranean a winter destination, so much so that they banded together to pay for the construction of the seaside walkway on Nice's seafront – mainly so they might have somewhere to walk without being harassed by the many beggars who had flocked from the surrounding countryside to Nice after successive poor harvests. Work started in 1820 and it became known as the Promenade des Anglais in 1860, after Nice became part of France when Emperor Napoleon III was granted the Duchy of Savoy and the County of Nice by the Kingdom of Sardinia's Prime Minister Count Cavour as a major part of the price for French support for the unification of Italy.

As more people flocked to Nice and Cannes, so larger and more luxurious hotels were opened – in Nice for example, the Excelsior Régina Palace that opened in 1897 and welcomed Queen Victoria through its doors and the Hotel Negresco in 1912; and in Cannes, the Splendid was extended and upgraded in 1905 and the Carlton opened in 1913.

So in the early part of the twentieth century, the south of France was undoubtedly a place of opportunity for hoteliers with vision and funding. No wonder, then, that Gustave and Giulio enthusiastically sought their share of this glowing business opportunity. They had the skills to run a luxury hotel and they managed to bring together a range of investors with the capital to make it all possible.

They included stockbrokers, merchants and 'gentlemen', as well as Lady G. D'Arcy Osborne – a relative of the Duke of Leeds – and also Alan Doulton from the famous Doulton pottery company; perhaps most interesting of all was Amédée de Guerville.

List of Persons holding Shares in *The Gelardi Hotel Company*
Limited, on the ___ 14 ___ day of ___ October ___
the date of the last Return, showing their Names and Address

### NAMES, ADDRESSES AND OCCUPATIONS.

| Folio Register Ledger, containing particulars. | Surname. | Christian Name. | Address. | Occupation. |
|---|---|---|---|---|
| 6 | Loeb | Sydney John | 4 Lancaster Gate, London W | Stockbroker |
| | Plasto | Stephen | Sandringham Hall, nr Norwich | Gentleman |
| 7 | Czarnikow | Horace | Cranford Hall, Kettering | do |
| | Doulton | Alan | The Pyrehill, Stone, Staffs | Potter |
| 8 | Thornton JP | Thomas William | Brockhall, Weedon | Gentleman |
| | Osborne | Lady G D'arcy | Churchill, Hemel Hempstead | |
| 9 | Parke | Mayhew Pittar | 1 Queen Victoria St. E C | East India Bro |
| | Wombwell | Arthur Charles | The Firs, Newbury Berks | Gentleman |
| 10 | Talbot-Ponsonby | A+Brabazon | Langrish House, Petersfield, Hants | Valuer to HM Government |
| | Gillespie | George | Reform Club Pall Mall, S.W. | Merchant |
| 11 | Menzies | John Herbert | Trentham, Stoke on Trent | Land Agent |
| | do | Robert | 17 Victoria St, S W | Surveyor |
| 12 | Gelardi | G E C | The Grand Folkestone | Hotel Manag |
| | de Guerville | Amedee | Valescure & Raphael France | Gentleman |
| 13 | Gelardi | Vera | The Grand, Folkestone | Spinster |
| | do | Emily Bertha | do | Married woma |

(Above): Gustave and Giulio attracted a wide range of investors to the Gelardi Hotel Company

He was elected president of the Valescure Golf Club in 1909 – one of the the very first golf courses to have been constructed in France. Inevitably, it was British visitors passing the winter months in St Raphael who had first established what was then a nine-hole course in 1895. Amédée de Guerville recruited the famous golf architect Harry Colt to extend the course to eighteen holes in 1910.

He also commissioned the British firm Boulton & Paul to build the clubhouse which was fabricated in the firm's works in Norwich before being transported to the south of France and erected in situ – an early example of prefabricated building.

How Gustave and Giulio got to meet Amédée we don't know. However, he clearly knew the St Raphael area and was equally clearly an influential character in the region, so it perhaps comes as little surprise that when it was established in 1911, the Gelardi Hotel Company bought a plot of land covering some 150 acres in Valescure at the foot of the Esterel that bordered the golf course. Given that the area had already attracted many British visitors, on the face of it, this seemed a safe investment. Léon Sergent was appointed as architect for the proposed new hotel and again, this appeared a safe choice as between 1880 and 1919 he built many villas and hotels for the British in the St Raphael area.

(Below): The sad story of the downfall of the Gelardi Hotel Company, as related by the Secretary Ernest Baker to the Registrar of Companies in London.

TELEPHONE No. 97.

GELARDI HOTEL COMPANY, LIMITED.

ERNEST A. BAKER
SECRETARY.

OFFICES—BOUVERIE CHAMBERS,
BOUVERIE ROAD EAST,
FOLKESTONE.

28. July 1917

Dear Sir ,

With reference to your formal Notice of the 16th. inst. requiring the registration of this Company's Annual List of Members for the year 1916 I beg to enclose you such List made up to the 31st. December last together with cheque for 5/- registration fee but in doing so would like to call your attention to the following facts :

The Company was formed in 1911 for the purpose of erecting and carrying on an Hotel at Valescure in the South of France The building was only partially completed when the Company ran short of funds & the Contractor a Paris builder refused to complete the job until further money was forthcoming . This money the Company was unable to obtain & to add to the difficulties the Chairman of the Company a London Surveyor committed suicide in August 1912 . This gentleman had had the whole of the Company's finances under his special charge & his assistant was the Secretary to the Company until November 1912 when he resigned and I was appointed in his place .

Since that date the finances of the Company have not improved the Paris Contractor has stepped in and obtained possession of the property in France and the Company is without funds of any description , in fact I myself have never

GELARDI HOTEL COMPANY, LIMITED.

OFFICES—BOUVERIE CHAMBERS,
BOUVERIE ROAD EAST,
FOLKESTONE.

NEST A. BAKER
SECRETARY.

received a penny for salary since the date I was appointed . The Company has no funds to provide for Liquidation expenses on a Winding up & there is no prospect of finding any money .

I think it well to point out these facts & I should be obliged if you would be good enough to inform me what are the proper steps to be taken under the circumstances .

Yours faithfully

Secretary

The Registrar of
Joint Stock Companies
Somerset House

P.S. The Shareholders & Debenture holders are I believe perfectly aware of the Company's position

A Parisian builder started construction of the new hotel but understandably stopped work when the building was only partially completed because he was not being paid. Presumably the shareholders had put up sufficient capital and had seen the budgets for the project but according to a report to Companies House in 1917 by the company secretary Ernest Baker: 'The building was only partially completed when the Company ran short of funds and the contractor refused to complete the job until further money was forthcoming. This money the Company was unable to obtain and to add to the difficulties the Chairman of the Company (a London Surveyor) committed suicide in August 1912. This gentleman had had the whole Company's finances under his special charge and his assistant was the Secretary to the company until he resigned in 1912 and I was appointed in his place.

'Since that date the finances of the Company have not improved, the Paris Contractor has stepped in and obtained possession of the property in France and the Company is without funds of any description'.

Robert Menzies, surveyor of 17 Victoria Street, London is registered as one of the Gelardi Hotel Company's shareholders so presumably it was he who was the chairman who brought the business down. The Gelardi Hotel Company was struck off the register of UK companies and dissolved on 3 January 1919.

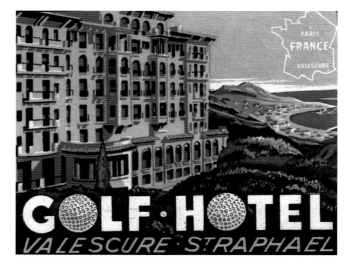

However there is no doubt at all that the project could and should have been a great success were it not for the presumed embezzlement. The site was bought at auction in 1924 by Paul L'Hermite who finished the work and opened Le Golf Hôtel on Valentine's Day 1925. The rollcall of guests in those early years is astonishing: Lord Mountbatten, the Duke of Windsor, King Leopold III of Belgium, Prince Bertil of Sweden and King Umberto of Italy. And then after the Second World War, Richard Burton and Elizabeth Taylor, Laurel and Hardy and many more international celebrities.

The Gelardi Hotel Company had been a disaster but the setback didn't appear to hinder Giulio. As we will see, he was a remarkable man, whose life spanned the greatest changes of the mid twentieth-century, from the First World War and early years in London, to what could have been a very dangerous relationship in Italy with Benito Mussolini, negotiating the real-life intricacies of prohibition in New York and a brush with his own mortality during the German bombing Blitz of London during the Second World War.

All five brothers were united in London in 1899 with the arrival of the youngest, Romolo. At first he worked at the Henry Gaze company – one of the world's first travel companies and at the time a rival of the better-known Thomas Cook company.

He was based at various tourist offices owned by the Gaze House of London: the Strand, Piccadilly, Queen Victoria Street and the Old Bailey; he also worked for a while at their other offices in Rome.

When the company was dissolved in 1903 he was recruited by his brother Gustave to work as controller and help out in reception and general management at the Grand Hotel in Folkestone which opened to great acclaim that year.

Romolo stayed there until 1907 when he moved to Venice as secretary/controller of the Hotel Royal Danieli – then, as still today, one of the finest hotels in Italy. Originally the

(Below): Romolo Gelardi worked at the Henry Gaze company when he first came to London in 1899. By that time it was already a well-established international travel agency and a serious competitor to the Thomas Cook company.

(Above): The Hotel Royal Danieli, overlooking the Venice Lagoon and situated just 200 metres from St Mark's Square, as it was when Romolo took up his position as secretary/controller in 1907. (Left): as it is today.

fourteenth century home of the Dandolo family, the iconic building overlooking St Mark's basin was opened as a hotel in 1824. By the time Romolo arrived it had been transformed and modernised with the adoption of electric lighting, central heating and lifts to all floors. Along with the Gritti Palace and other properties in Venice, the Danieli had also become part of the Compagnia Italiana Grandi Alberghi (CIGA), founded by Count Giuseppi Volpi in 1906 and often described as the first luxury hotel chain in the world – which would later be run by Romolo's older brother Giulio, my grandfather.

Romolo returned to London in 1909 where he married Katharine Neale and was employed for the summer as manager of the Clevedon Hotel at Woodhall Spa in Lincolnshire, where Katharine also worked as a book-keeper.

Later that year they moved to Brussels where Romolo was appointed assistant manager of Wietcher's Hotel, part of the Carlton Group. Two years later he was on the move again, this time heading for Canada and the Windsor Hotel in Montreal where his brother Cesare was general manager. Romolo was chief steward for a while before crossing the border into the United States where he lived in New York City while working at various establishments before retiring to Flushing, New York state. He died in 1964.

As a footnote to that time when all five of the Gelardi brothers were in London, their mother Carlotta also came to England some time early in the twentieth century. The 1910 census shows that she was living with Giulio at that time. She finally died in Bexhill on 16 April 1923 from a combination of gangrene which had infected her foot and congestion of the lungs. At her death she was attended by her son Ernesto.

(Below): On his return from Venice Romolo moved further north in England, to the Clevedon House Hotel where he and his wife Katharine worked for a while. (Bottom): The hotel is now the well-known Golf Hotel, situated right next to the Wood Hall Spa Golf course.

(Above): The Gelardi Family and friends in London about 1900, which clearly shows that some were better than others at keeping still during the long exposures required at that time. Front row, left to right: Gustave; Theresa (daughter of Ernesto); Vera (Elvera) (daughter of Gustave); Renato Bausch (reclining, a family friend who worked at the Walsingham House Hotel along with Gustave); Berta (daughter of Ernesto); and Giulio. Middle row, left to right: Emily (wife of Gustave); Anna Marie (wife of Ernesto); Hannah (wife of Cesare); Unknown though perhaps wife of Renato Bausch; Unknown, possibly Franziska Katherine Rassier, younger sister of Anna Marie and future wife of Ernesto; and Carlotta (Giuseppe's widow and mother of Gustave, Ernesto, Cesare, Giulio and Romolo). Back row, standing, left to right: Ernesto; Cesare; and Romolo.

(Left): Carlotta Gelardi in 1908.

# Chapter 3

# The Leading Hotelier of the 20th Century

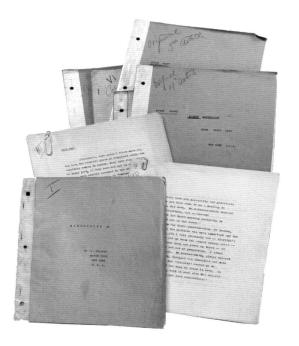

(Above and Below): Giulio's diaries and manuscripts are frustratingly incomplete. They provide so much insight into his personal and professional life, yet there are gaps of years. Was he too busy to write in those times, or have the original documents simply been lost?

My grandfather Giulio was an extraordinary man, not least because he had the astonishing ability to observe the world around him and then to describe what he was seeing and doing in vivid detail. He was undoubtedly one of the world's most influential hoteliers and fortunately for us, he seemed to recognise how important his contribution to the development of the luxury hospitality industry had been because he left behind a treasure trove of writings, cuttings, photographs, caricatures, hotel floor plans, menus and wine lists.

At the epicentre of his archive are half a dozen slim manuscripts, each of about thirty typed pages, on paper so thin that when I turn them, I can see my own fingers through his words, and that's a moving experience. The paper is very similar to that used for airmail letters in the 1960s and 1970s when postage costs were high and always based on weight.

The pale blue card cover of the first of these matter-of-factly asserts: 'MANUSCRIPT #1' along with 'BY G. GELARDI', and the date and location – 'New York, U.S.A'. Giulio's autobiographical manuscripts are supplemented by a C.V., articles from *The Evening Telegram*, Toronto, for which he wrote a series in the mid-1930s, letters of thanks, a radio interview from South Africa in 1952, an enormous black scrapbook from the 1930s, itineraries for liners he sailed on such as the

*Empress of Britain* and *Rex*, telegrams, song lyrics (written by Giulio and set to music by Maximillian Bergere) and *Rockefeller Center Weekly*. A cutting from *New York American* dated October 27th, 1935 with the headline 'Will Mediterranean Be Scene of a New Great War?' interrupts Giulio's everyday concerns and reminds me of his international outlook and facility with languages.

There is also a small green album with a handwritten label, 'Press Cuttings, Book 1' which covers the 1920s and 30s, offering glimpses of Giulio's wider professional horizons and, to some extent, his personal life. And then there are two A5 leather-bound diaries, one red dated November 1950 – July 1951, the other green dated August 1951 – January 1952, in Giulio's careful hand, which are deeply personal and astonishing, since each day's entries are addressed to Piera, his late wife. The first entry reads:

'Dearest Piera, it was not easy to say Goodbye this morning…I felt such a coward running away from you … I tried to pray… my heart beating choked the words in my throat… how I wished it wouldn't break… Through my tears I saw your beautiful face smiling and shaking your head as you used to when hurt, but forgiving… your lips moved: God bless you, Giulio.'

The pages which follow ache with Giulio's love and sense of loss as he sails from Southampton to Cape Town aboard RMS *Carnarvon Castle* in late November 1950. In them he records the daily details of the voyage he and Piera had promised to take together but which he finds himself travelling alone.

That trip to South Africa – to stay with my father Bertie and mother Noreen – took place after Giulio had finally retired from the

(Above): Giulio as a sub-lieutenant in the *Bersaglieri* Corps. (Left): Founded in 1836, their role was as fast-moving sharpshooter skirmishers. They came to prominence in 1870 when they were the first through the breach in the Aurelian Walls close to Porta Pia to take Rome and ensure the final unification of Italy. Their trademark wide-brimmed hats trimmed with black capercaillie feathers are still worn today.

hotel business. So how did he start in the world of hospitality and how did he rise to become the world's leading hotelier by the time of his retirement?

When his elder brother Gustave left Italy for London and the Walsingham Hotel, Gustave was twenty and Giulio just six years old. As he grew, Giulio would have heard about Gustave's successes, and those of his other brother Ernesto's progress in the hotel business because it's fair to assume that both would have written regularly to the family back in Italy; and it's almost certain that Gustave was sending money too, to support his mother and younger brothers.

Yet but for a happy accident, Giulio might not have taken the hospitality route at all, since he was deeply interested in Latin and Greek literature and had taken a degree in law at the University of Rome. It was an innocuous conversation with his batman Giovanni, when he was a twenty-year-old sub-lieutenant in the *Bersagliere* - the sharpshooters of the Italian infantry - that began Giulio's fascination with hotels. Giovanni told him that the son of a poor Swiss shepherd named César Ritz, having started his career as a waiter in a humble bistro in Paris, had just become the general manager of the Grand Hotel, the Albergo in Rome. What seemed to excite Giovanni even more was the fact that he too had been a waiter before joining the army and he could see that opportunities abounded for the right people. Giulio too, clearly recognised the import of this casual conversation: 'Giovanni, of course, did not know that his was the voice of fate in my ear; no more did I'. A seed of some kind had been planted and Giulio resolved there and then to call upon the 'great Ritz'.

Giulio had joined the army in the first instance because it offered 'the only means of guaranteeing [his] daily bread'. And even with a commission of a sub-lieutenant, the pay was so meagre that it was barely enough. At that specific moment with Giovanni, Giulio only had one ambition, and it wasn't professional: 'That was the hope of someday being able to wed the beautiful girl I had first seen one day in church; now it seemed a lifetime ago! I had immediately fallen in love without knowing her name'. That girl was Piera. 'Of this,' he writes, 'there is more to tell.' Even in his dairies, Giulio managed to maintain an element of suspense!

Giulio needed money to live, and certainly if he was to be able to marry and support a wife and family. Giovanni had suggested that there was much to be made in the hotel industry and Giulio, emboldened with the knowledge that he spoke English and French as well as his native

Italian and had studied German and Spanish, he felt the hotel world might be the place to demonstrate his talents. The only suit he owned was his fine sub-lieutenant's *Bersaglieri* uniform, complete with its wide-brimmed hat decorated with black capercaillie feathers. He duly called on César Ritz but the meeting didn't go quite as he had hoped. Ritz looked at his showy uniform and declared: 'Life in a hotel would prove too hard for you'. How could hotel work be too hard for an army officer? Giulio persisted but Ritz said was, 'Go abroad and work in less important houses! You must have experience. And polish up your languages through contact with natives. Then come to see me again.'

(Below): A portrait of Giulio taken in June 1898 at the Harrods Studios in London.

Thirty years later, Giulio found himself working at the very desk from which Ritz had addressed him. As well as coming full circle, his route even followed in some of Ritz's footsteps, working at the same establishments. Ritz told him, at the end of his life, 'When you become manager of Claridge's, remember it was my creation.' This is something of an exaggeration because Claridge's first opened in 1856, long before Ritz came to London.

Originally it was a series of townhouses that were knocked through to create one property, but The Savoy company acquired the whole site in the 1890s, demolished the townhouses and built a brand new hotel that was opened in 1897. Ritz was certainly involved in the planning for the redevelopment of Claridge's that began in 1893, but he would not have been there to see the reopening as he and Escoffier had parted ways with D'Oyly Carte by then.

Nevertheless, Claridge's was, in fact, where Giulio spent 'the happiest days of [his] hotel life', in contrast to his time at The Savoy which he described as 'the most amusing and entertaining'.

But Giulio's involvement in these two London landmarks was to come later in his career. He had been a scholarly youth in Italy and had developed a love of learning and books that became defining characteristics in his life. Even so, in order to pay for his passage to England, he sold his beloved collection of books for 400 lire, an act of great personal sacrifice but also an act of faith in his abilities: he *was* going to be successful in his chosen field.

Taking Ritz at his word, he set off to make his own way in the hotel business. Selling his books yielded just enough for a steerage ticket. He stopped in Genoa and tried to get passage to America but failed, and instead inched slowly towards England on the cheapest trains he could find. At the end of July 1897, he found himself waiting at the Italian-French border at Modane, struck that he was about to leave his country behind. A huge step. A sense of fear. The glittering Alps hiding the plains of the country of his birth. 'Am I a coward?' he wondered.

Reaching the customs house, he recognised a man whose photograph he had seen in the newspapers – Guglielmo Marconi. He had read that he was going to England to continue his experiments in radio transmission. Giulio saw a parallel between them, two men who had opted for voluntary exile in order to achieve their goals. It was when Giulio offered to act as an interpreter for an American woman having difficulty interacting with the officials, that Marconi spoke.

'Very good!' he smiled. 'Where did you learn English?'

In the conversation which followed, Giulio learned that Marconi's mother was English, and he had spoken it almost before Italian. Giulio concluded – somewhat dramatically – that 'he too was leaving to seek other fields of action, for the realisation of his great dream – harnessing the space infinite.' Both men were barely twenty-two.

On 12 December 1901, Thomas Barron sent the first transatlantic wireless message from Poldhu, Cornwall, to Marconi who received it in St John's, Newfoundland. Marconi's ingenuity was one of the greatest contributions of the twentieth century and our lives would not be what they are now without it. Just five years after the event, Giulio was a member of the Italian committee which honoured Marconi with a dinner at Prince's Restaurant, London, and was delighted Marconi remembered him. Their lives were to cross repeatedly on Marconi's frequent visits to Claridge's where he kept a permanent suite, as well as on various occasions at the Excelsior in Rome.

Between that first encounter and Marconi's famous wireless call across the Atlantic, Giulio arrived at Gustave's Walsingham House Hotel,

# How Marconi Changed the World

Guglielmo Marconi was fascinated by both science in general and electricity in particular from an early age and began working on 'wireless telegraphy' in the early 1880s. He decided that the way forward was via radio waves and his early experiments were all conducted with equipment designed and built by himself.

Having made good progress, he approached the Italian Ministry of Post and Telegraphs, seeking funding for further development but got no reply. Later he discovered the minister had simply scrawled 'to the Lungara' on Marconi's letter – Rome's insane asylum was then on the Via della Lungara!

And so he decided to head to England where he felt he had a better chance of finding support than he had in his backward-thinking native country of Italy. It was on that journey that Marconi and Giulio Gelardi first met and their paths were destined to cross many more times over the coming years.

Once established in England, Marconi proved the worth of his new invention. First he sent Morse Code signals across Salisbury Plain; then in 1887 the first transmission over open sea – the Bristol Channel to be precise; and across the English Channel in 1899. That year he headed to the USA where he installed transmitting equipment on the American liner SS *St Paul* which became the first sea-going ship to announce its arrival from sixty-six miles away. And then Marconi turned his attentions to transmitting right across the Atlantic, achieving this epic feat in 1901 when a simple Morse Code letter 'S' sent from Poldhu in Cornwall in the far south west of England was received on Signal Hill in St John's Newfoundland on 12 December 1901.

From that time, progress was rapid and just a year later the first full radio transmission from Glace Bay Nova Scotia was picked up in the UK. Marconi had invented the radio which would transform the whole field of communications and make the world a smaller place.

Giulio was a leading member of the Italian committee in London which hosted a dinner in honour of Marconi at Prince's Restaurant in London in 1902 and at that dinner it became clear that the now world-famous inventor had not forgotten that first meeting at Modane five years earlier.

He and Giulio met again in the USA and they presumably had plenty to talk about some years later when Marconi returned to the UK and lived at The Savoy soon after Giulio had been appointed general manager.

(Top): Guglielmo Marconi's equpment was rudimentary but he proved that with his transmitter on the right and receiver with its paper tape recorder on the left, messages could be sent over long distances. (Left): The ultimate proof came in 1901 when he sent the first transatlantic message from the UK to Nova Scotia in Canada where his associates are pictured setting up the receiving equipment.

where he was set to work in the office, as Ritz had suggested, to start learning the hotel business from the ground up.

As we have seen, Gustave was not entirely happy to see Giulio arrive in London but his support for his family was unstinting, as ever. Furthermore, Gustave provided Giulio with just the sort of grounding he needed, ensuring he understood every aspect of the hotel business.

Initially, at the Walsingham, he started at the bottom, working in all positions within the hotel to better understand how its machine works, as all great hoteliers have done and will continue to do. In what he termed a 'synopsis' of his CV, he says that between 1897 and 1911 he went 'through the mill', but it was hard work that would be invaluable to his later career. After all, who would you want in charge – someone who has sweated a twelve-hour shift in the kitchen and served in the restaurants and carried a guest's luggage to their room and cleaned the rooms and made the beds and understood what it's like to fulfil those specific roles? Or an accountant whose experience goes only as far as interpreting balance sheets and keeping costs in check?

(Below): Giulio's elder brother Gustave gave him a job at the Walsingham Hotel and set him to work learning the ropes in every department – an invaluable and essential grounding for any hotelier.

The ideal, of course, is someone who is a blend of both. But the key is a close understanding of how every aspect of the hotel operates; Giulio learnt that the hard way as did my father Bertie a generation later and as did I later still. Being a successful hotelier is a craft, balancing so many disparate elements within the machine so that everyone is happy – the guests and the people who look after them. Giulio was just such a blend. He was passionate about this notion that his role was to interlock each department into a harmonious whole.

He stayed at the Walsingham until it was sold – ironically to César Ritz – in 1902. He then worked at Claridge's for the first time, still learning the ropes of the hotel business, initially as a cashier but later progressing to the role of assistant manager.

Then in 1907 he went to Marseilles as catering manager for the Anglo-Egyptian Shipping

Company; however he was back in Britain around six months later to start a new job on the managerial staff of the Piccadilly Hotel. Although he only stayed there for two years, his time there might have been a crucially important step in the development of Giulio's own management style.

He truly appreciated Giuseppe and Gustave's achievements, and he certainly learned a lot from them both. But Giulio's genius lay in his ability to take that traditional hotel business knowledge and modify it so that it met the modern clients' different and more demanding requirements. He was quick to note changes in fashion and technology and swiftly respond to them, and there may have been no better training ground for this than the Piccadilly Hotel.

Interestingly, one of the reasons why The Lanesborough was so successful is that my team and I also took careful note of the latest trends in both fashion and technology and applied what we had observed to create what at the time was the ultimate in customer care and comfort.

(Below): The Piccadilly Hotel was one of London's most modern and luxurious when it opened early in the twentieth century. It was equipped with the very latest technologies including in-room telephones, a first for London.

Though from the exterior the Piccadilly Hotel was a classic establishment, designed by the architect Richard Norman Shaw in a neo-baroque style that reflected seventeenth-century English Palladian architecture, by the standards of the day, this new hotel was ultra-modern in its specification. It had its own generator to supply electricity to its 300 bedrooms, many restaurants and meeting rooms and even four Masonic temples. And it also had its own water supply from an artesian well sunk some 400 feet under the hotel; this was important as it meant the hotel did not have to rely on London's unreliable public water supply.

The Piccadilly was not unique in offering such comforts: nor was it the first as the Savoy had three artesian wells under The building to provide water both for the building and for the boilers which generated steam power to produce electricity for both the hotel and the Savoy Theatre next door. The Savoy Hotel enjoyed electrical power but it was the Savoy Theatre that was the first public building in Britain to be completely lit by electricity, when it opened in 1881.

A TWENTIETH CENTURY PALACE

# THE PICCADILLY HOTEL

## AND

# RESTAURANT

# LONDON

## PICCADILLY AND REGENT STREET, W.

### Two of the World's Greatest Thoroughfares

# OPENS EARLY IN MAY, 1908

SCIENCE, ART, REFINEMENT AND PRACTICAL EXPERIENCE APPLIED TO THE LUXURY AND COMFORT OF RESTAURANT AND HOTEL LIFE

There is nothing more striking in London than the Majestic Facades in Piccadilly and Regent Street, while the gorgeous and graceful interior contains the finest exemplification of XVIIIth century art both in England and France.

For beautifully illustrated descriptive volume, write to Manager:

THE PICCADILLY HOTEL AND RESTAURANT, LONDON, W.

Nevertheless, the Piccadilly's importance as a symbol of the modernising of this part of London is clear since the Prince of Wales, later King George V, attended the official opening of the hotel, the first time a hotel had been honoured like this.

Giulio clearly made his mark at the Piccadilly Hotel, certainly enough to bring him to the attention of Sir George Reeves-Smith, the managing director of the Savoy Hotel Group. Sir George had been managing director and the main shareholder of the Berkeley Hotel in Knightsbridge and had been recruited by Richard D'Oyly Carte to replace César Ritz after he left the company. At the same time the Berkeley Hotel became part of the Savoy Hotel Group, of which Sir George remained managing director and later vice-chairman until his death in 1941.

Having seen his potential, Sir George appointed Giulio as assistant

## CLARIDGE'S
### HOTEL, LONDON

We beg to call attention to our very moderate "Out-of-Season" Prices.

"A HAVEN OF TRANQUILLITY AND QUIETUDE," not being directly on a main artery of London's Traffic, its Guests enjoy immunity from Street Noises.

CLARIDGE'S HOTEL, GROSVENOR SQUARE, W. (Brook St.)

The Centre of the most Fashionable Quarter of the West End, within a few minutes' walk of Bond Street, Piccadilly, Regent Street, and Hyde Park.

General Manager          RENAUD PIOVANELLI.

(Above): The original Claridge's hotel, which dates back to the very early nineteenth century, was a series of townhouses gradually acquired and knocked through to make one property. The entire site was acquired by the Savoy Hotel company in the 1890s, and the townhouses were all demolished to allow for complete redevelopment of the site. The present Victorian building was designed by architect C.W. Stephens and opened in 1897.

manager at Claridge's in 1909, but he was elevated to general manager in 1912 when the then-incumbent Renaud Piovanelli was moved to run the Grand Hotel in Rome, at that time still part of the Savoy Group. Giulio stayed at Claridge's until 1920 when he was asked to move over to run The Savoy Hotel.

Thus started a life at the forefront of the luxury hospitality business, a life which, as Giulio recollected, was 'crowded with portraits of Emperors, of Kings, of Princes; of Presidents, Premiers and Statesmen; of Indian Potentates and other Oriental dignitaries.'

Those early days at Claridge's were when, in Giulio's words, 'London was at its very gayest.' Once crowned, King Edward VII re-established the old social scene, including the presentation of debutantes at court – which was traditionally the start of the social season in London – and the Great Ball.

'From the first', wrote Giulio in his journals, 'dinner parties, receptions and balls were given in conjunction with the royal functions, and Claridge's and the Ritz were always booked to capacity during three months of every season. London was livelier than Paris.'

Sadly, it was not to last. 'After those gay and prosperous years, disaster suddenly descended upon London's hotel business due to a national tragedy.' That tragedy unfolded in 1910 when news came first that King Edward was seriously ill, and soon after, that he had died. 'Every single entertainment or engagement for an entertainment was cancelled without hesitation, and the season ended. No function of any sort took place for months, and not even the Coronation of King George V, which brought tremendous crowds to London the following year, succeeded in giving London that quality of gaiety it had enjoyed for the previous eight years since His Majesty recovered his health after his postponed Coronation in 1902.'

One of Giulio's most powerful memories came later that year on a beautiful morning in late October 1910, at Claridge's. The hall was crowded with reporters and photographers awaiting the arrival of King Manuel II of Portugal, who had been dethroned by a military coup and was seeking asylum in England. Giulio had known him when he was a schoolboy, before his father and brother had been assassinated on the streets of Lisbon and he had unexpectedly found himself king at the age of eighteen.

Giulio greeted him and managed to elbow a way to the lift to his apartment. 'Merci, Gelardi,' said the former king, 'sauvez-moi, pour le moment, des journalistes!' Conscious of life criss-crossing itself and recognising a pattern, Giulio links it to the same place just over twenty years later, 15 May 1931. That was when Alfonso XIII of Spain arrived, having escaped at night by speeding car to the coast and a still-loyal ship when the Second Spanish Republic was proclaimed. Manuel was waiting for him too, and when Alfonso arrived, they embraced. They had been neighbour kings, had grown up almost together and had suffered similar catastrophes. And here they are under Giulio's care. 'I am a poor man, cher Gelardi; very poor but I do not mind. The saddest plight of an exile,' King Alfonso told Giulio, 'is the thought of his not being able to go back to the land of his birth and of his fathers.'

(Left): Nine Sovereigns photographed at Windsor Castle for the funeral of King Edward VII in May 1910. Standing, from left to right: King Haakon VII of Norway, Tsar Ferdinand of Bulgaria, King Manuel II of Portugal, Kaiser Wilhelm II of the German Empire, King George I of Greece and King Albert I of Belgium. Seated, from left to right: King Alfonso XIII of Spain, King-Emperor George V of the United Kingdom and King Frederick VIII of Denmark. Giulio would welcome both King Manuel II and King Alfonso XIII at Claridge's after their dethronements - King Manuel in October of that same year and King Alfonso 21 years later in 1931.

Giulio's life is characterised by these meetings and I suppose it is to be expected to some extent, considering his position. Nevertheless, history plays out *somewhere* and I've learned that luxury hotels are where the internationally significant rubs shoulders with the intensely personal, sometimes at the same time.

For example, just weeks after the armistice in December 1918, the commander of the Allied armies in France, Maréchal Ferdinand Foch and his adjutant, General Maxime Weygand, arrived at Claridge's.

Mounted police kept back the crowds gathered in Brook Street and the sounds of trotting Household Cavalry announced the approach of a royal carriage. Foch is small and wiry in his field uniform and stands at salute to acknowledge the hurrahs. Giulio shakes his hand, then Weygand's. Claridge's hall is heaving with privileged welcoming spectators, fizzing with relief and excitement that the war is over and here in their midst is the man who commanded the victorious armies. The Princess of Monaco approaches Foch holding the hand of a shy ten-year-old girl – in her other hand she clutches a bunch of flowers to present to the great man. The little girl curtsies but the words she has rehearsed remain glued to her tongue – the Maréchal puts a finger under her chin and kisses her cheek. The crowd hails his action. Giulio is immensely proud – because that little girl is his daughter, Lina.

(Below): Maréchal Foch, overall commander of the Allied Armies in France before the Armistice in November 1918, came to Claridge's the following month, when Giulio's daughter Lina presented him with a bouquet of flowers.

Foch's assessment of the Treaty of Versailles – 'It was an armistice for twenty years'– proved prophetic. Giulio was again on hand at another important post-First World War event when in late 1924, officers of the German Military Mission arrived at The Savoy to sign the Dawes Plan – an agreement as to the extent of reparations that Germany should pay. In an indication of how quickly communications technology had advanced, a direct line to Berlin from the roof of the hotel was established so messages could be carried between The Savoy, Germany, Whitehall, the War Office and Downing Street.

Giulio had moved from Claridge's to The Savoy in 1920. While Claridge's was the London home from home for the world's royalty and wealthy upper classes, The Savoy was frequented by the theatrical and literary greats of the time, whose names continue to resonate. The American theatre impresario Charles Frohman and the creator of the enormously successful *Peter Pan*, Sir James Barrie, discussed plays they would sketch out on menu cards and leave strewn across their table. When other guests realised, they hung around until the two men had gone and collected what they had discarded on the off chance that it might be a splendid souvenir. Tragically, Frohman went down with the *Lusitania* on 7 May 1915. Barrie, who had created his charming 'fairyplay', liked to surround himself with a group of friends to play cricket, including H. G. Wells, whose novel *Kipps* was adapted into film at the Savoy. Although Giulio doesn't record the date, it was 1921, what he calls 'an overdose of limelight'.

The film makers asked for The Savoy staff to wait at table for a scene in which Kipps hosts a dinner for friends, which made complete sense, as they were the experts, but as soon as the shooting began, the waiter-actors became more and more nervous. The first courses went well, but when the roast was served, the waiter fell apart. Giulio described the scene:

'He left the pantry alright, but after a step or two into the open it seemed to him as if he bore in the great silver platter before him not a mere chicken, but the fate of all England! He grew nervous. Then he began to shake. And suddenly while all were watching him, and the guests at Kipps's table were waiting to be served – the waiter's arm relaxed and the platter, chicken and all dropped to the floor with a crash and spread in various directions. The film director almost had a fit and shouted for the scene to be cut.'

(Above): One of the scenes of the 1921 film *Kipps* starring George Arthur was filmed in the dining room at the Savoy - with mixed results.

The waiter was replaced with a film extra who was rather more used to being in front of the camera.

The Savoy was also used as the setting for *Imperial Palace*, the novel by Arnold Bennett. Giulio writes, 'The great author and I became firm friends.' After a lunch given by Giulio's boss Sir George Reeves-Smith, Bennett spoke to Giulio. 'I'm glad to have talked with you Gelardi, I want to see more of you and know you better.' However, soon afterwards, Giulio went to work in Rome and when he returned five years later, Bennett had died.

The Savoy's original courtyard, which was later converted to The Savoy Ballroom, was the real-life setting for the champagne millionaire George Kessler's whimsical Venetian party. There is also an extraordinary link here to Charles Frohman, since Kessler was also on board the *Lusitania* with him when it was torpedoed, but survived. Kessler was very fond of throwing extravagant parties and his Venetian production of July 1905 was quite incredible. Giulio recorded that Kessler directed the preparations from his suite on the first floor:

'Three hundred workmen were engaged to turn the courtyard of the hotel into a Venetian canal. After certain structural alterations were carried out, the courtyard was flooded and on the night of the party, richly draped gondolas specially built for the occasion (as to transport the real article from Venice would have been impossible) floated up and down Kessler's reimagining of the Grand Canal.'

When The Savoy closed for a £100m refit in 2007, Bonhams held an auction of its contents which included some of the artefacts from that event. Simon Usborne wrote about Kessler's party as an example of the hotel's high life in *The Independent* newspaper: 'A silk-lined gondola, strewn with 12,000 carnations, bobs on a Venetian canal, escorted by pearl-white swans. A baby elephant, groaning under the weight of a five foot-high birthday cake, is escorted on board the gondola, accompanied by Enrico Caruso, who croons '*O Sole Mio*' under a paper moon. The whole of this incredible scene is illuminated by 400 paper lamps.'

(Above): The original courtyard of the Savoy, which became the scene for one of the most extravagant parties ever held at the hotel.

According to his notes, though he was working as assistant manager of Claridge's at the time, Giulio was present at The Savoy as the magnificent event unfolded, as agog with the spectacle as the rest of Kessler's guests, not believing what he was seeing or hearing: 'the golden notes from a voice that could only be possessed by one man… (Caruso is) the greatest singer the world has ever known!' As we will see, a similar, though even more personal operatic performance, was witnessed by Giulio's son – my father Bertie – at the Waldorf-Astoria, New York, some years later, in another of those criss-crossings of my ancestral lives.

There was drama of a different sort some years later when Giulio was running The Savoy. He was called to the Court Suite in The Savoy in the early hours of 10 July 1923:

'Rounding a corner, I come face to face with an amazing scene. Near

# Kessler's Gondola Party

The famous Gondola Party that George A. Kessler hosted in honour of King Edward VII in July 1905, was one of the most spectacular events The Savoy has ever put on. It was held in the former courtyard of the hotel which was roofed in 1910 to create the ballroom known as the Lancaster Room.

For the party the entrances to the courtyard were sealed with putty, after which it was flooded to a depth of three feet. The sides of the courtyard were painted to give the impression of being Venice, while the centrepiece was a massive silk lined boat, decorated with 12,000 carnations, which held the table and chairs for 24 guests.

A bridge linked the boat to the hotel to allow the Savoy's waiters, dressed as gondoliers, to serve a twelve course banquet. 400 hand-made paper lamps provided the lighting, while 100 white doves were released to fly above the guests. Fish were released into the water, and swans were brought in to swim in the artificial lake. Sadly, according to contemporary reports, blue dye was added to the water which turned out to be poisonous for both fish and birds, which then had to be scooped out of the water and disposed of.

Despite this the dinner was a huge success, and the highlight was a five-foot high cake, brought over the bridge to the boat on the back of a baby elephant borrowed for the evening from London Zoo. At the climax of the evening the famous tenor Enrico Caruso appeared and gave a performance of 'O Sole Mio'. Apparently the total bill presented to Kessler for the evening's extravaganza was £3,000 – some £360,000 today thanks to intervening inflation.

the door of the suite stands a woman in evening dress. Seeing me, she frantically, hysterically throws her arms around my neck. She is sobbing and mumbling words in French. I put my arm round her and try to calm her, meanwhile looking at the scene before me. A few paces from us a man is lying on the floor. Near him is a pistol, a small spiral of smoke still issuing from its barrel. Obviously, the man is dead. I have already recognised the pair. The woman sobbing in my arms is Princess Fahmy whom I have seen earlier in the evening dancing in the ballroom – and the dead man is her husband.'

It is uncanny how often episodes in Giulio's life appeared to play out like Hollywood scripts. The woman Giulio finds was not a princess at all. Her original name was Marguerite Marie Alibert, whose life was very much something you might expect on screen.

Alibert's 'career' began as a courtesan in Paris where she was born, learning her 'trade' at a *Maison de Rendezvous* in the city, an establishment specifically for men of high social standing. She met the Prince of Wales, later King Edward VIII, when he was a naïve twenty-three-year-old officer at the Hôtel de Crillon in 1917, a liaison which

(Below): Marguerite Marie Alibert was a courtesan who married and later shot the wealthy Prince Al Fahmy (Opposite Top). In 1917, she had started an affair with Prince Edward, later to become King Edward VIII (Opposite Below). The relationship only lasted about a year but she retained around 20 letters from the Prince, said to contain indiscreet comments about the conduct of the war, insults directed towards his father the King and graphic sexual content. The existence of the letters were made known at her trial at which point, to avoid a scandal, the British establishment closed ranks and the trial Judge Mr Justice Rigby Smith acquitted her of murder on the grounds of self-defence but only after the letters were handed over behind the scenes.

had great bearing at her trial for The Savoy shooting.

Alibert was Edward's first great love. He wrote her letters in which he addressed her as '*Mon Bébé*' and included information about the war and abusive comments about his father. The intense affair lasted a year but its consequences could have been far-reaching.

When her relationship with Edward ended, she threatened to blackmail him with the letters in her possession, all of which she had kept. The establishment couldn't afford for her links to Edward to be made public and some kind of deal was put in place because if the letters reached the public domain, the consequences would have been catastrophic. But after Edward, she found a moneybag in the form of the Egyptian multi-millionaire, Prince Ali Fahmy, marrying in January 1923. Thus, by the time of the trial, Alibert's background as a woman who had borne a child when she was just sixteen herself and had later serviced the needs of many powerful men at a high-class brothel, were hidden behind her new identity as Princess Fahmy.

Giulio describes them on their return from their evening at the theatre, he 'tall, thin and with a tanned countenance and wavy hair, the woman small, supple, her simple but elegant black velvet dress enhancing the paleness of her beautiful face.' Giulio notes that as they dance in the ballroom she looks a little troubled and speculates whether they had had: 'A lovers' tiff – or some small rift in their marital life. There is a loud storm outside, there is rain hard against the windows and thunder is shaking the hotel. It's 1 am. and the hotel is expecting guests to arrive from the *Leviathan* which has docked in Southampton. These guests arrive in the middle of the storm, desperate for a nightcap having sailed from a 'dry' country. Soon the mood is cheery and the storm becomes background noise, another bang-bang-bang and the hotel shaking simultaneously disturbing no one. Yet it is followed by an assistant urging me to come at once.'

'I was mad!' the Princess sobs to Giulio. 'The thunder shattered my nerves. Oh save me!' She continues. 'We had quarrelled. He was leaving my room. Then there came a terrific peal of thunder and I was so frightened. Without knowing how or why, I found a pistol in my hand. I called after him – he said he was going to leave me – I could not bear it. He still kept walking away from me. I followed... I don't know any more...'

Even when the police arrive, the inspector, 'quietly and very courteously... took charge of her and escorted her to a waiting police car.' Giulio regarded the whole event as a couple 'maybe too much in love with each other' and the Princess as 'frail, lovely, in terrible anguish of mind.'

In court the Princess's defence counsel presented her as a wronged Parisian sophisticate, abused by her Middle-Eastern husband. Extraordinarily, the court was presented with an account of her husband's cruelty, claims that he raped her and subjected her to 'unnatural sexual practices'.

The facts are that after an argument she shot him three times, the bullets entering his head, neck and back. Her defence spun a story that she had cracked under what we now know as coercive control. However distasteful it appears today, Prince Fahmy was also described as 'a monster of Eastern depravity and decadence, whose sexual tastes were indicative of an amoral sadism towards his helpless wife'.

She was acquitted of all charges and returned to The Savoy before heading back to France. Before she left, Giulio recalled: 'she took one of my hands in both of hers and with tears in her eyes thanked me for what little I had been able to do for her. I have often wondered if she has been able to blot the memory of that storm-torn night from her mind and found the contentment and happiness which I feel sure she most richly deserved!'

Giulio is not the only person to have been taken in by the Princess, who had been acting different parts all her adult life, the greatest of these as the victim during the trial. She was a brilliant manipulator of people and situations, and this saved her from a sentence of death.

In his book *The Prince, the Princess and the Perfect Murder* author Andrew Rose's assessment of Ali Fahmy's death is unequivocal: 'In my study of the trial, I heard described the shooting as a *crime passionnel*. However it was nothing of the kind. This was murder for gain. An execution. A perfect murder.'

(Below): Giulio described the events in his own words in an article he wrote for the *Toronto Herald* some years later in 1935.

# TELEGRAM, TORONTO, SATURDAY, JULY 27, 1935

# Famed Savoy's Gayest Night Climaxed By Fatal Shooting Princess Found With Pistol

**"Save Me, We Had Quarrel-led," Princess Sobs When Manager Finds Husband Slain**

**JURY CONVINCED STORM TO BLAME**

**Hotel Built by D'Oyly Carte Often Chosen as Scene of Mystery Stories**

### By Guilo Gelardi
(Formerly Manager of Claridge's, the Savoy and the Piccadilly Hotels, London)

The gayest evening ever seen at the Savoy turned out to be a prelude to tragedy. It happened this way: When the evening was well advanced, I made my way to a special observation post from which I could see both into the restaurant and the ballroom, and as I stood smoking a contemplative cigarette I noted with satisfaction that the restaurant was filled with a gay cosmopolitan crowd such as could be seen nowhere else but at this—the greatest hotel in the world. In the ballroom hundreds of couples were dancing to the popular airs played by the world famous Savoy Orpheans.

Idly, I watched a party of young people, coming from the restaurant descend the steps to the ballroom. They are chatting and laughing and obviously imbued with the spirit of the evening. Reaching the floor, they whirl away in the dancing throng—all except one couple—the man tall, thin and with a tanned countenance and wavy hair, the woman small, supple, her simple but elegant black velvet dress enhancing the paleness of her beautiful face.

One of my assistants, standing at my elbow, notes the direction of my glance.

*The Savoy's Famed Cabaret*

mind—lying on a hard bed in a prison cell!

I throw open the windows of my office. The thunderstorm has gone, so has my party of friends. Behind St. Paul's a pale sun is breaking through the clouds. Another day dawning and our cleaning brigade is starting work—making the Savoy's toilet for another day and night. What might they bring?

Such is the bald account of the most sensational shooting affair which I have encountered during my 'hirty years as an hotelier. The details of l'affaire Fahmy are no doubt still fresh in many memories. In due course she stood her trial at the Old Bailey, but, and, I must say to my great satisfaction—and due to the skill of her counsel, the late Sir Edward Marshall Hall, Princess Fahmy was acquitted and returned to the Savoy for a few days before returning to her native France. She was of course a Frenchwoman prior

there (?) Ritz and Eschenard are in charge of the living arrangements!"

Well, I am installed in charge of the managerial chair of London's greatest hotel. At Claridge's, the quiet dignity, the lack of rush and spectacle made me acclimatized to the running of an hotel whose keynote was reticence and comfort. I knew that at the Savoy I should have to tackle an entirely different proposition and frankly I was surprised to find how easily I was able to fit in with the new surroundings. The work was so varied and absorbing. It was kaleidoscopic in the variety of its interests.

Yes, indeed, I am proud that I have managed this great hotel.

**In his next article, Signor Gelardi will tell of some of the spectacular parties given at the Savoy by millionaires and world-famous personalities.**

# Chapter 4

# Hospitality at Sea and in the Air

In the nineteenth and on into the early twentieth centuries, the development of the luxury hotel business went hand-in-hand with the development of international travel by sea. The first regular transatlantic services were started as far back as 1838 when *Sirius* and *Great Western* – both of which were paddle steamers – operated a service between London and New York. The Cunard Line launched a Liverpool to Boston via Halifax, Nova Scotia service in 1840 while the White Star Line – which a few decades later was to launch the ill-fated *Titanic* – was inaugurated in 1871.

Speed was always a matter of national pride so it's no wonder that the unofficial Blue Riband – held by the ship recording the fastest crossing either Eastbound or Westbound – attracted increasing interest. White Star ships *Adriatic, Germanic and Britannic* all held the record at some time between 1872 and 1891 but interestingly, after that time the company gave up on commissioning ships designed to offer outright speed and instead concentrated on offering greater luxury for its passengers, even if it meant an extra day at sea.

(Right): SS *Sirius* was built in 1837, originally intended to ply between Cork and London. However the ship was chartered by the British and American Steam Navigation Company for two transatlantic voyages in 1938. The first of these started in Cork on April 4 and *Sirius* arrived in New York 18 days later – still considerably quicker than the standard crossing time for contemporary packet boats of some 40 days.

And so the transatlantic liners became partners as well as competitors of the luxury hotels of the day, both catering to the needs of wealthy clients who expected nothing but the highest standards of comfort and service. Very soon its competitors followed suit in terms of improving levels of service and luxury – though without losing sight of the undoubted marketing appeal of being the current holder of that elusive Blue Riband.

The great chef Auguste Escoffier was one of the first to see the synergy between great hotels and great liners when in 1913 he found himself supervising the kitchens on board the SS *Imperator*, one of the largest liners of the German Hamburg-Amerika Line. Its restaurant was modelled on Escoffier's dining room at the Carlton in London and Escoffier was asked to oversee an important luncheon for 146 German dignitaries, including Kaiser Wilhelm II during the Kaiser's visit to France. Escoffier duly presented a magnificent multi-course repast which included a strawberry dessert named *Fraises Imperator* in honour of the Kaiser. Apparently the Kaiser was so impressed that he asked to see Escoffier when he announced: 'I am the Emperor of Germany but you are the Emperor of Chefs'.

(Above): When launched in 1912 the SS *Imperator* was the largest passenger ship in the world and one of the most luxurious, which is why the world-famous chef Auguste Escoffier was commisioned to supervise its kitchens and restaurant. She went into service in 1913 on the transatlantic route but just over a year later, when WW1 broke out, she was laid up in Hamburg. After the war the Americans seized the ship as war reparations, then in 1919 it was ceded to the Cunard Line who renamed her RMS *Berengaria* and operated her on the Southampton-Cherbourg-New York route until 1938 when she was decommissioned and scrapped.

LIGNE MARSEILLE - LE PIRÉE - ALEXANDRIE ET VICE - VERSA

ANGLO - EGYPTIAN MAIL LINE ˢ/s "CAIRO CITY„

(Above): The SS *Cairo City* and SS *Heliopolis* (Left) were built to ply between Marseilles and the new gambling resort of Heliopolis near Cairo. Giulio was sent to oversee the restaurant but had an unhappy time with mutinous stokers demanding greater rum rations. He soon decided – perhaps understandably – that he was not cut out for a life afloat.

My grandfather Giulio learned much about life afloat quite early in his career when, after some years at Claridge's, in 1907 he worked for a short while for the Anglo-Egyptian Steamships Company.

He described the circumstances in one of his memoirs: 'About 1906 the Hamburg-Amerika Line introduced something new in ocean travel. It had built the steamship *Kaiserin Augusta Victoria* as the last word in marine architecture, except for speed. To appeal particularly to the wealthier class of American travellers, on her was installed a restaurant de luxe, supposed to furnish the finest food of every sort, turned out by the best French chefs. It was under the management of the Ritz-Carlton Hotel Company.

'Shortly afterwards, Baron Empsin, a Belgian electrical magnate, together with British and Egyptian capitalists interested in a new Egyptian resort called Heliopolis, within 10 or 15 miles of Cairo, planned to attract people of wealth to this high-class resort where gambling was to be featured, by offering them luxurious sea travel.

'Two steamers were built, the *Heliopolis* and the *Cairo City*, beautiful vessels designed to make the voyage from Marseilles to Alexandria in record time.

'The Savoy Hotel declined to take over the installation and supervision of restaurants on the two ships which were intended to be just as fine as the Ritz-Carlton restaurant on the *Kaiserin Augusta Victoria*. I was asked to take charge in 1907'.

For his first voyage on the *Heliopolis*, Giulio stored a fine collection of wines and liquors on board. The English crew seemed satisfied with their lot but the stokers complained of the poor rum ration, since they weren't accustomed to the hot Mediterranean. As the boat sailed through the Strait of Bonifacio, between Corsica and Sardinia, the stokers broke into the ship's stores.

Giulio described the events in an article he wrote many years later in 1935 for the *Toronto Evening Telegram*: 'They were smashing open cases of champagne and knocking the heads off bottles of Cliquot and quaffing the contents from the jagged necks. One hulking brute had a bottle of champagne in one hand and a bottle of Grand Marnier in the other and was taking deep draughts from each alternatively'.

Maybe because of his training as an army officer, despite being armed only with 'the rough side of his tongue,' Giulio confronted the drunken mutineers. They threatened to throw him overboard, but having consumed so much of the storeroom's bottles already, they were incapable of carrying out their threats and were forcefully removed by officers and crew, after which the ringleaders were 'clapped into irons.'

After a brief six-months stint on these steamships, Giulio returned to work on dry land but over the course of his life he made numerous voyages on different liners, no doubt noting and comparing their relative standards of service, luxury and hospitality.

He left behind numerous itineraries for liners he sailed on such as the *Empress of Britain* and *Rex*, and described in detail the poignant voyage to Durban and retirement in late November 1950 on the RMS *Carnarvon Castle*, one which his beloved wife Piera would have shared had she not passed away a few months earlier.

(Below): RMS *Carnarvon Castle*, in which Giulio sailed to his retirement in South Africa.

He described the voyage in his diaries: 'The *Carnarvon Castle* (20,140 tons) is an old ship with a long war record. Refitted and refurbished two

years ago she looks clean and fresh. The cabins, even the best ones, are small compared with the *Rex* or *Île de France*.

'The gangway is lowered, cables are released from the moorings, powerful tugs gather their strength for the mighty push that moves the ship slowly from the dock. It is 4 o'clock sharp. The liner, freed from her shackles, blows her whistle in joyful salutation while the band plays *God Save the King*.

'There is no turning back! The ship, gliding down the Solent to the open sea, shakes and vibrates gently with regular rhythm. I pace the deck and through my mind flash the memories of other sailings from so many ports … from Genoa, from New York, from Bermuda …

'We shall be at Madeira about 6pm and leave at 11pm. I expect Mr Paquot, the Manager of the Reids Palace Hotel, will call for me and I shall be glad to stretch my legs on land.

'From what I have seen of the passengers, they don't look a glamorous lot: mostly colonials, businessmen or commercial travellers with their suburban wives, mixing business with pleasure, and a few oddities like myself.

'I had the opportunity of mixing amongst the Tourist passengers. As usual, they are more natural specimens than the hybrid lot of the First Class. Mostly they are nice looking couples, bright and simple, many with small children – emigrating, ready for adventure and full of hope of a better life and success.

'Atomic bomb: I had just stopped writing to light a cigarette when the ship, quivering painfully, has gone slanting in a nasty lurch as it was hit by a huge wave. All the books, the photographs and small bags are on the floor and I just saved myself from a fall by holding onto the writing table.

'On the deck this morning a group of men and women were listening to a tall man gesticulating and using his pipe as a pointer. As I passed I heard him saying " yes … at Bikini … an atomic bomb can produce it even at thousands of miles away. An officer coming down from the bridge stopped just in front of me. He laughed and said: 'Sheer fantasy: if you were talking about what happened last night I was on watch and saw it coming; a simple common or garden tidal wave, we often meet them in these waters at this season, you know we crossed the Equator on Friday'.

'In Cape Town, we lunch at the Mount Nelson Hotel. The lunch was badly cooked and badly served by a not too clean Indian waiter with a white cap. But the noon edition of the Capetown papers announces, "Most famous International Hotelier arrives in S.A.!"

'Arrived Durban, Natal 9am 19th December 1951
18 days and 15 hours from Southampton
6907 miles
Average daily run 460 miles
Average daily speed 18-19 knots
Stops:
Madeira 6 hours
Capetown 24 hours
Port Elizabeth 34 hours
East London 14 hours'

(Below): The SS *Bremen*, on which Giulio and Bertie sailed to New York for the opening of the Waldorf-Astoria. The German-built liner, with its four steam turbines driving four propellors gave it an operating speed of 27 knots - more than enough for the *Bremen* to take the Blue Riband in 1929 and again in 1933.

Giulio was not the only Gelardi to serve at sea. My father Bertie's first trip to New York was with Giulio when they went for the opening of the Waldorf-Astoria. They travelled on the SS *Bremen* which Bertie recalled was 'one of the largest and fastest luxury liners of its time

and we had a pleasant but rather uneventful trip. We did the usual things that one used to do on steam ships of that era, eat, drink and socialise. Father knew several of the American passengers which meant entertaining and being entertained, and we also attended the Captain's and Purser's cocktail parties, played deck quoits and participated in the auction held in the bar every night of the sea mileage to be covered by the ship in the next 24 hours'.

Soon after, Bertie's return was not as a passenger, but as a crew member, working as assistant purser on the SS *Conte Biancomano* in the spring of 1932. After the opening of the Waldorf-Astoria, Giulio was due back at Claridge's in April and was duly booked on the *Rex* for his transatlantic return to Europe. As for Bertie, he recalled that 'Father thought it would be a very good idea if I were to work my passage back to Europe. There were two good reasons for this – for me, I would get new work experience, and for him, he would not have to pay my fare!'

The *Conte Biancomano* set sail from New York on a cruise to the Mediterranean, calling at Naples, Athens, Haifa, Alexandria then back to Naples and returning to New York. Bertie described his duties, which he shared with the second assistant purser, a Mr Fava, whose father, whom Giulio also knew, was manager of the Miramare Hotel in Genoa: 'we shared a cabin and our duties consisted mainly of ordinary reception work, producing the ship's newspaper, covering for the purser on his frequent disappearances and attending the daily purser's cocktail parties.

(Above): The SS *Conte Biancomano*, on which Bertie served as Assistant Purser on his return from New York in 1933. The experience added to Bertie's skills and experience and saved Giulio the cost of his son's fare back to Europe.

| QUADRUPLE SCREW TURBINE EXPRESS STEAMER |
|---|

**"R E X "**

GROSS TONNAGE 51062 · LENGHT 881 FEET · BREATH 88 FEET
**COMMANDER: GR. UFF. F. TARABOTTO**

| DEPARTURE FROM NAPLES | : | MARCH 20TH, 1934, 4.35 P. M. |
|---|---|---|
| " " GENOA | : | " 21ST, 11.15 A. M. |
| " " VILLEFRANCHE | : | " 21ST, 3-30 P. M. |
| " " GIBRALTAR | : | " 22ND, 9.50 P. M. |
| | WESTBOUND | |

| 1934 MAR. | LATITUDE NORTH | LONGITUDE WEST | MILES | WIND | REMARKS |
|---|---|---|---|---|---|
| 23 | 36°44' | 12°51' | 370 | NW-4 NNE-5 | sea moderate sky partly overcast |
| 24 | 37°43' | 25°54' | 628 | NNE-4 | Passed P.ta Delgada (San Miguel-Azores) at 11.35 a. m. sea rather rough to moderate sky overcast |
| 25 | 38°02' | 19°06' | 626 | Var. 3 | sea slight sky mostly blue |
| 26 | 38°10' | 52°35' | 637 | SE-4-3 NNW-5 | sea slight to moderate sky blue and overcast |
| 27 | 39°16' | 65°32' | 613 | ENE-4 ESE-3 | sea moderate to slight sky partly cloudy |
| 28 | | | 388 | Var. 4-5 | Passed Ambrose L. V. at 5 a. m. |

SEADISTANCE 3262    NAUT. MILES
PASSAGE: 5 DAYS, 11 HOURS, 55 MINUTES
AVERAGE SPEED: 24,73 KNOTS

Serie N.A.    No 6148

# "Italia"

*Flotte Riunite Cosulich Lloyd Sabaudo Navigazione Generale*

ANONIMA CON SEDE IN GENOVA - CAPITALE SOCIALE LIT. 720.000.000 INT. VERSATO

## Contratto per Biglietto di Prima Classe (Servizio di Lusso)

rilasciato alle condizioni indicate a tergo

Da *Napoli*    a *New York*
Pir/Mn. "REX"    in partenza il 20/3/1934

Cabina 328
Lett. e Bagno

a favore de i Signori

| | | Posti | |
|---|---|---|---|
| 1 | Comm. Giulio Gelardi | 1 | |
| 2 | Signora Pierina Gelardi | 1 | |
| 3 | | | |
| 4 | | | |
| 5 | | | |
| | Totale Posti | 2 | |

Rilasciato in seguito a telegramma Direzione Genova del 16/3/34 No 485 -

Roma li 17/3/1934 XII

"ITALIA"
FLOTTE RIUNITE COSULICH-LLOYD SABAUDO-NAVIGAZIONE GENERALE

Head Fancy No 16 pagato

**REX**

PASSENGER LIST

'We had to cover the hours from 5am to midnight between us. However when the ship docked and most of the passengers had disembarked we were at liberty to go on shore too. I was lucky because at most of the ports of call there was either a friend or someone who had worked under my father, who was manager of the best hotel, and I thought it only polite for me to make known my presence in his town.

'Needless to say, I never expected to benefit personally in any way from this gesture and you can imagine how embarrassed I was by the profuse welcome and unstinting hospitality I received!' That hospitality included Bertie being given the Royal Suite at Shepherd's Hotel in Cairo along with trips to see the Pyramids, market places and nightclubs. 'It was three or four days spent in luxury reminiscent of the court of the ancient Pharaohs', Bertie recalled.

Eventually, on the ship's return to Naples, Bertie disembarked and made his way to Rome where he was to meet Giulio after his own crossing on the *Rex*.

It's interesting that both Giulio and Bertie witnessed both the high point of the great liners and their eventual decline as newer and

(Opposite and Below): Giulio and Pierina crossed the Atlantic on the SS *Rex* from Genoa to New York in 1934. The Italian liner held the Westbound Blue Riband between 1933 and 1935 so they travelled in state-of-the-art speed and luxury.

faster forms of transport evolved. At first it seemed that the future of international travel might be the airships as the early Zeppelins were certainly faster than any ships and offered the highest levels of comfort and luxury to their elite passengers. The arrival of one of the Zeppelins in New York was a major social event and their commanders were afforded the greatest of respect. While at the Waldorf-Astoria Giulio remembered welcoming Dr Hugo Eckener, commander of the Graf Zeppelin for most of its record-breaking flights, while on one of his many visits to the USA.

The Zeppelins offered unimaginable luxury, with passengers offered three hot meals a day served in an Art Deco cabin with four large arched windows on each side. Sadly, however, the age of the airship came to an abrupt end in 1937 when the Hindenburg burst into flames on landing at Lakehurst Naval Air Station in New Jersey with the loss of 36 lives.

(Opposite): The Hindenburg disaster heralded the end of the hydrogen-filled airship era. (Left): The kitchens and dining room on board the Graf Zeppelin which was commanded by Dr Hugo Eckener (Below), a visitor welcomed to the Waldorf-Astoria by Giulio.

Giulio was also an early witness of the jet airliner, which marked the beginning of the end of the great Ocean liners. While staying at the Langham Hotel in Johannesburg in July 1951 he was invited to a Press Reception for the crew of the Comet jet which had just crossed from London in 14 hours. At the time this was a near-unbelievable achievement and the sheer speed of this new generation of jets heralded a seismic change in the world of international travel.

The Comet itself, the world's first commercial jet airliner, as is well documented, suffered three fatal accidents after first coming into operation in 1952. The catastrophic break-up of the aircraft in flight was later found to be due to metal fatigue and stress that developed in the revolutionary square windows of the early Comets. Later versions were built with oval windows which solved the problem but because of its reputation the Comet never really enjoyed the commercial success it deserved. But it had proved the potential of jet-powered flight and the aviation and travel industries never looked back.

(Right): Heathrow's central area under construction in April 1955 showing the control tower and the Europa Building. Servicing the needs of Heathrow Airport was one of the keys to the early success of the Forte catering business, and once the Forte Hotels division was established, Bertie took charge of the opening of the Excelsior Hotel at Heathrow.

(Above): This early prototype of the Comet airliner - the world's first commercial jet - clearly shows the large square windows which provided excellent views for its passengers. Sadly the design resulted in stress cracks and metal fatigue of the airframe that caused a number of tragic crashes. (Left): The development of the jet airliner also lead to the construction of bigger airports to cater for the massive increase in air travel, including Heathrow Airport to the west of London with its distinctive runway layout.

# Chapter 5

# Giulio's International Reputation is Forged

(Above): Count Giuseppe Volpi established CIGA in 1906. By the time Giulio arrived in Italy, the Excelsior in Rome, which coincidentally also opened in 1906, had been added to the CIGA group. It remains one of Rome's finest hotels (Opposite page).

Giulio spent four busy and happy years at The Savoy before he was asked in 1924 to move to Italy as managing director of the two finest hotels in Rome – the Excelsior and the Grand. At the same time, he would be Inspector General of all the CIGA Hotels. The Campagnia dei Grande Alberghi (CIGA) had been established by Count Giuseppe Volpi in 1906 to cater for the increasing number of wealthy tourists visiting Venice. At first the new hotel group consisted of five Venetian hotels including the Danieli but other luxury hotels in Italy were added over the following years.

The offer to Giulio was such a significant opportunity that he felt he couldn't refuse it so he asked Sir George Reeves-Smith to release him from his contract with The Savoy. Sir George generously agreed and also told him that he would always be welcome back should he wish to return.

Giulio arrived back in his native Rome in February 1924, walking from the station to the Grand Hotel and to his office where he sat at the very desk once occupied by César Ritz when, twenty-eight years earlier, he had urged Giulio to 'Go abroad and work in less important houses!'

Giulio stayed in Italy until 1928. During that time the family lived at the Excelsior Hotel in

Rome while he busied himself reorganising the Grand Hotel in Rome, the Excelsior Hotel in Naples, the Hotel des Iles Borromées in Stresa on Lake Maggiore, the Excelsior Hotel on the Lido in Venice and the Casino in Rapello. What we do know is that the CIGA hotels were very successful under his direction and supervision; and that he played an important part in promoting tourism to Italy, most especially from the United States.

In fact, the Italian government was so grateful that it decorated him with the title of *Commendatore*, the equivalent of a British knighthood.

That government, of course, was under the direction of Benito Mussolini who had established himself as Prime Minister after the fascist coup d'état in 1922. Giulio first met Il Duce, as he styled himself, in October 1925, at the Excelsior in Rome. Mussolini was entertaining in the grand ballroom, an event for which Giulio was responsible. It was an evening resplendent with beautiful women in their jewels and fine dresses and bright and polished diplomatic and army uniforms in a magnificently decorated room in which the service was perfect. Knowing that Mussolini enjoyed playing the violin, Giulio approached him after dinner.

'Is there anything your Excellency would like the orchestra to play?'

'Something very soft and light.'

Giulio instructed the orchestra to play one of Paganini's pieces for cello and violin. Mussolini was clearly enthralled and applauded warmly. Then near the end of the evening, Giulio suggested the orchestra should play the newly published *Il Canto del Lavoro*. Although Mussolini gave it his full

Fot. V. LAVIOSA
ROMA

(Left): During the First World War, Benito Mussolini served as a Private in the *Bersaglieri* Corps – the very Corps in which Giulio had served out his National Service. (Above): The portrait of the Italian leader was taken in 1927, round about the time when Giulio hosted his private parties at the Excelsior Hotel in Rome.

attention, he didn't appear at all enthusiastic, yet he called Giulio over.

'Please ask the maestro to give me a copy of the song. I should like to try it at home.'

'How do you like it, Excellency?'

'Good music, but impossible to march to!'

Mussolini, who would later be Hitler's ally and end his life ignominiously strung up by his ankles at an Esso service station in Milan, had expressed a side of himself few people saw.

At that first dinner, Mussolini was so impressed with Giulio that he engaged him to oversee all of his private parties. Once, when Mussolini quizzed why he wasn't wearing the fascist lapel badge, Giulio answered, 'In my experience, the hotel business and politics do not mix well,' a response accepted at face value. Giulio never joined the Fascist party and it's interesting to note that despite him having a number of private conversations with Il Duce, he was not pressured to join the party.

By 1928 Giulio had resolved to return to England. His four children had all been born, educated and brought up there and were now for the most part settled in that country. Both he and his wife Piera decided it was time to return to be near the family.

Happily, there appeared to be an important job to return to. The Cecil Hotel, which occupied a site that stretched from the Strand to the Thames right next door to the Savoy, was the world's biggest hotel when it opened in 1896. Not only did it boast 800 rooms but it also had banqueting facilities that could cope

(Right): Giulio was honoured with the title of Commendatore for his work in promoting tourism and the Italian hotel industry.

# Giulio and the Schneider Trophy

A contemporary newspaper cutting reported Giulio's return to the UK from his stint with CIGA in Italy after he had had 'a busy time' at the Venice Lido making arrangements for the visitors who went to see the 1927 Schneider Trophy. 'He was very interested to see and compare the hotel arrangements made in the Isle of Wight for the Schneider race held in 1929.'

Certainly visitors to CIGA's Excelsior Hotel in Venice, which was under Giulio's direction at that time, had a fine view of the proceedings as the start/finish line was positioned right in front of the hotel. International events such

as this encouraged ever-greater levels of travel – and therefore of the need for suitable hotel accommodation – and so it is little wonder that Giulio took a keen interest in the Schneider Trophy race, even if it was not the sleek aircraft that caught his attention.

The Schneider Trophy was first competed for in 1913 after French industrialist Jacques Schneider announced the *Coupe d'Aviation Maritime Jacques Schneider* – an international competition to find the best seaplane and to encourage their future development. Thereafter it became a source of national pride to develop and fly the fastest and

most manoeuvrable aircraft. For that 1927 race, it was the Italian and the British teams vying for the honours.

The British *Supermarine S5* piloted by Sidney Webster won the contest in Venice that Giulio witnessed, at an average speed of 281.66 mph. Two years later, back in Britain at Calshot Spit opposite the Isle of Wight, it was the *Supermarine S6* flown by Richard Waghorn at 328.64 mph that was victorious.

Just a few days later, the same machine was flown at a new outright world air speed record of 355.7 mph.

For good measure, the British racked up a third consecutive victory in 1931, again at Calshot Spit, when John Boothman's *Supermarine S6B* took the honours at 340.08 mph. Having won three times, the British retained the Schneider Trophy outright.

(Left): The *Supermarine S5* being prepared for the 1927 race at the Venice Lido. (Right and Below): The updated *Supermarine S6* that won the Schneider Trophy for Great Britain again in 1929, this time at Calshot Spit.

The
SCHNEIDER TROPHY
Sept. 6th & 7th CONTEST 1929

THE ROYAL AERO CLUB
Official
SOUVENIR PROGRAMME
Printed & Published by
GALE & POLDEN LTD, LONDON, ALDERSHOT & PORTSMOUTH.
PRICE ONE SHILLING

with up to 600 diners in the Great Hall, 350 in the Victoria Hall and 200 in the Prince's Hall.

By the late 1920s it was in need of modernisation and refurbishment and the board asked Giulio to take over as general manager of the hotel with specific responsibility for planning a total interior reconstruction to bring the hotel up to the most modern standards. The costs were going to be between £1-2 million – an enormous sum in those days. Sadly for Giulio, the Shell Oil Company was looking for a site for its proposed new London headquarters and the massive Cecil Hotel site seemed ideal. And so the board was left with the choice between spending up to £2 million or receiving more than double that by selling to the oil giant. They decided to sell and the building was largely demolished in the space of a few short months and a new thirteen-storey office building constructed in its place.

So Giulio's plans for the Cecil Hotel came to nothing but a man of his talents and experience would not remain unemployed for long. Sure

(Below): A rare portrait of Giulio (sitting centre) and staff at the Savoy, taken around 1923.

enough, Sir George Reeves-Smith invited him to rejoin The Savoy company as general manager of Claridge's in 1929 - the only time that any former general manager had been accepted back into the company, which clearly demonstrates the very high esteem in which Giulio was held at the time.

For the next two years, Giulio ran Claridge's with his usual light touch but minute attention to detail. His great skill as a hotelier was to understand his clients' needs and wishes and to put in place a mechanism that ensured the highest standards could be maintained at all times. Giulio refers to this delicate balancing act in his memoirs:

*'The modern hotel differs from the old inn as much as the old chariot from the up-to-date racing car - a complex of machinery, intricate and delicate, which requires careful handling and knowledge, coupled with that subtle understanding of human nature and therefore tact to the supreme.'*

To this he adds the advice that César Ritz had provided so many years

(Above): The Cecil Hotel was prominently positioned right next toThe Savoy. Giulio was asked to take responsibility for its full refurbishment but before he could take up his post, the property was sold to the Shell Oil Company as its London headquarters.

before but which still resonates in the hotel business: 'Treat every client as you would a personal guest in your own home. Smile and make each client feel that he is the most important person in your home.' Recollecting Ritz's qualities in the mid-1930s, Giulio writes that his 'lack of education disappeared behind his polished manners and his great asset, to keep silent when the conversation around him became too difficult, saved him all the time.'

(Below): Claridge's Hotel in the first half of the twentieth century.

Even then, in the early 1930s, Giulio was not just keeping abreast of the latest contemporary innovations which could contribute to a hotel's

day-to-day running; he was also thinking about the future, listing a number of possibilities which are astonishing for their prescience:

*'The first addition that the Hotel of a few decades hence may be obliged to adopt is a landing station for aeroplanes or other flying contrivances on its roof; air-conditioned rooms; heating apparatus, self-regulating to the proper degree; radio; electric bolts; indirect lighting; express elevators; pneumatic tubes; electric kitchen ranges... We may obtain motor power from the rays of the sun; we may start our machines which give us light and power by 'short or long waves' – those uncanny forces the great genius of Marconi has revealed and harnessed... robots may be employed to do the most menial work – wash plates, sweep floors, act as a bartender or cloakroom attendant... Television may allow the manager in his office to watch the different departments at work.'*

Yet he warned that although these might change the modern hotel, 'they must not destroy what is paramount... the personal touch in service.' It was true then and it is true today. In my time at The Lanesborough, when it opened we incorporated cutting edge technology, and we did so again when we renovated. Technology is superseded so quickly that high-quality hospitality must incorporate the latest on offer – it's what the clientele expects.

Giulio's personal and business life was also destined not to stand still because in late 1931, on the other side of the Atlantic Ocean, another great hotel was due to open – the new Waldorf-Astoria on New York's Park Avenue covering the whole block between East 49th and East 50th streets. The earlier Waldorf-Astoria Hotel on the corner of Fifth Avenue and 34th Street was demolished in 1929 to make way for the Empire State Building to be constructed, and this was to be its replacement. At the time the tallest and largest hotel in the world, it was designed as two separate but linked entities: a 2,200-room first class luxury hotel and a slender Waldorf Towers consisting of 100 suites, about a third of which were leased as long-term private residences.

Lucius Boomer, President of Waldorf Astoria Inc., was determined that this new hotel would be the very finest in the world, in every respect. It was taken for granted that the layout, décor and furnishing would reflect the heights of luxury; but what Boomer also wanted was a style of personal management that would not only result in that hallmark of excellence that he was seeking – he also was looking for a figurehead who would appeal to the most sophisticated international clientele.

The man he wanted was Giulio Gelardi, who had demonstrated his peerless skills at some of the finest hotels in Europe. The only difficulty was that Giulio was under contract to the Savoy Company and already had a full-time job as general manager of Claridge's. But Boomer was clearly both a determined and a pragmatic man because he proposed a solution to Sir George Reeves-Smith, the hotel proprietor: Would the Savoy Company consider loaning Giulio to the Waldorf for a specific time period so he could take personal charge of organising the all-important opening of the Waldorf-Astoria and its management for the first few months?

(Below): Giulio set sail for New York on the SS *Bremen* in 1931, taking his son Bertie along as his secretary. At the time it was the fastest passenger ship plying the North Atlantic route, having captured both the westbound and eastbound Blue Ribands on its inaugural voyages in 1929, making both crossings at an average speed of just under 28 knots.

We don't know the intricate detail of the deal between Boomer and Reeves-Smith but the fact is that they did come to an agreement: Giulio would remain general manager of Claridge's but would be managing director of the Waldorf Towers at the same time. The plan was that Giulio would travel to New York to organise the services, furnishing and equipment of the hotel, supervise the opening and then remain at the Waldorf-Astoria for the next five months. He would then return to the UK in the spring of the following year in time for the London season. This dual role arrangement would last for four years

my first voyage to the U.S.A
Sailed Southampton Aug. 27ᵗʰ Monday
arrived N.Y. Saturday 1ˢᵗ Sept. '31

during which time he would retain both his Claridge's and Waldorf-Astoria roles, while keeping in touch with his deputies by telephone while on the opposite side of the Atlantic.

He was the only hotelier ever to have simultaneously managed two first class hotels in two different continents and this new chapter in his extraordinary life began on 31 August 1931, thirty-five years after having first attempted to reach America, when Giulio sailed for New York, accommodated in 'luxurious quarters on a crack Atlantic flyer,' the SS *Bremen*, taking my father Bertie with him as his secretary.

By the time the Statue of Liberty came into view, Giulio had made acquaintance with fellow passengers he could expect as guests: people such as Anita Loos, author of *Gentlemen Prefer Blondes*; Louis Wiley, manager of the *New York Times* and Jules Bache, the banker and art collector, most of whose collection he left to the Metropolitan Museum of Art when he died. When Giulio's reason for being aboard circulated,

(Above): A high-level publicity shot taken during the construction of the Waldorf-Astoria. (Below): the intrepid photographer Charles C. Ebbets.

(Overleaf): How the *Bystander* magazine celebrated the opening of the Waldorf-Astoria.

93

# NEW YORK'S
## *sensational new* HOTEL

*By*
*WILLIAM POWELL*

Our New York correspondent, Mr. William Powell, describes the wonderful new Waldorf-Astoria Hotel which was invaded by eager throngs when it was opened recently.

*New York's Wonder Hotel. The recently opened Waldorf-Astoria on Park Avenue. Forty-eight storeys high, its twin towers afford a wonderful spectacle with the sunlight playing on their white walls*

NEW YORK'S latest hotel is unique in that from the 28th storey up, the space is devoted to apartments. All sorts of apartments—some unfurnished, others furnished. The latter have been decorated by leading decorators in America, England, France, and Sweden. London firms who had a hand in The Towers (which is what the upper portion of the hotel is called) are —White, Allom and Company and Lenygon and Morant. The Towers has

THE sensation in New York these October days is the new Waldorf-Astoria Hotel, which has just opened its doors. It dominates not only the East Side sky-line, between Grand Central Terminal and 59th Street (it is forty-eight storeys high), but it is the dominating topic of conversation wherever people gather. Some speak of the magnificent dining-room which was painted by the famous Spanish artist, Sert—some talk of the apartments designed by Sir Charles Allom; while others are captivated by such minor innovations as the little holes in the bathroom walls where one drops one's razor blades.

IN ever-changing New York, an hotel which has stood in one spot for thirty-four years possesses as much tradition as does a European hostelry which may have 534 years back of it. So, to modern Americans the old Waldorf brings up pictures of a glamorous and romantic era. When speaking of it, people invariably allude to the charity balls which were sponsored by the Astors, Vanderbilts, and Goulds; to the champagne suppers given to Florodora girls; and to the ladies of the leg-o'-mutton sleeves who strolled up and down the famous Peacock Alley.

CONSEQUENTLY, it was no wonder that New York fell all over itself to have a peep at the magnificent new structure occupying an entire block between Park and Lexington Avenues, and 49th and 50th Streets. Although special invitations were sent out for the opening, the crowds eager to see the new Waldorf were so great that the police couldn't control them. They say that of the 3,000 ash receivers which were lying about on the tables not one remained the next day!

The Waldorf-Astoria boasts of being the largest hotel in the world, exceeding even such skyscrapers as the Hôtel Pierre, which opened only a year ago, the Sherry-Netherlands, the Savoy-Plaza, the New Yorker, the Pennsylvania, and the Governor Clinton.

COMMENDATORE GUILIO GELARDI
*The presiding genius of the new hotel; he includes the management of The Towers, which is what the upper portion of the hotel devoted to furnished and unfurnished apartments is called.*

The Bystander, October 28, 1931

for its director Commendatore Guilio Gelardi, for years well known to Londoners who patronise Claridge's and the Savoy. Signor Gelardi will continue to be at Claridge's for the season during the spring and summer, and has already established himself as a prime favourite with New Yorkers.

The first Saturday after the hotel opened I tried to take some guests to lunch at the Waldorf—but I only tried! It being a warm autumn Saturday it never occurred to me to book a table ahead, and I was amazed to find that each of the four dining rooms was completely filled up. Quite remarkable when, besides a warm week-end, the Waldorf had to combat depression and a fast-growing fad for lunching and dining in small, intimate restaurants of the Parisian order, and the smart new speakeasies.

*A corner of one of the residential suites in the new Waldorf-Astoria Hotel. The foyer is of simple architectural character, the walls being covered with an interesting decorative paper in sienna tones with figure groups representing the five senses. The woodwork is painted in pink-brown tones and the floor is tiled in black and white rubber*

with one another, which can be thrown into one large room when required. Of course the Waldorf (as all new buildings in New York) has conditioned air—air kept at an even temperature by a cooling, dehumidifying and humidifying installation.

*The military note in New York's newest theatre. Attendants at the new Earl Carroll Theatre sport very military uniforms whilst on duty in the vestibule*

PERSONALLY, I find the smaller, quiet type of hotel, of which New York has many now, more to my taste—I mean the type you find in Europe. But, fortunately for the Waldorf, there are thousands who like hotels which are large and luxurious. So, just as there is a place in London for hostelries such as Grosvenor House and the Dorchester, so in New York there is a large public who will eagerly welcome an hotel such as the Waldorf-Astoria.

THERE are many modern features about this new structure which will appeal to the traveller of to-day. Guests arriving at the Waldorf by motor may enter the hotel by an underground entrance and, taking a lift right by the door, can be whisked skywards to their rooms without going through the lobby. Being situated near the Grand Central Railroad Station, the Waldorf-Astoria has been able to arrange a private yard so that guests coming to New York on their own Pullmans can have them switched directly into the hotel. But I'm afraid that this winter won't see many arriving in this luxurious fashion!

OTHER features which have been incorporated into the Waldorf-Astoria to make it the dernier cri in hotels are: a ballroom fitted with a movable platform; a roof garden fitted with a movable roof which opens and closes by electricity; an auditorium equipped for television, technicolor, and movietone films; private suites with their own terraces; radios in every room; and a flexible arrangement of suites. For instance, on the Park Avenue side there are nine separate rooms, decorated and furnished in harmony

*The "Water Wagon" invades more or less dry New York. Though "speakeasies" may be found in numbers all round the Earl Carroll Theatre, "Adam's ale" is featured within its doors where the ice-water wagon seen above circulates during the intervals for the benefit of patrons*

he experienced some of the press's attention also. The Waldorf-Astoria was - and still is - a byword for luxury and glamour. The opening on 1 October 1931, was a fine affair. Imagine. What a time to be opening a luxury hotel...

The effects of the Wall Street Crash of 1929 were filtering into global economic catastrophe. The hotel was a blindingly bright light in a gathering economic storm, so important that President J. Edgar Hoover broadcast from Washington to those assembled for the event: 'The opening of the new Waldorf-Astoria is an event in the advancement of hotels, even in New York City.' he declared, 'It carries great tradition in national hospitality... marks the measure of the nation's growth in power, in comfort and in artistry... an exhibition of courage and confidence to the whole nation.'

The *Daily Telegraph*'s correspondent reported that 'Six thousand persons, including the leaders of New York's social, business, and political life, were seated at dinner,' adding that 'the great structure of forty-seven storeys, with distinctive twin towers reaching to a height of 625 feet, cost £8,000,000 to build, and occupies an area of 81,000 square feet.'

(Below): Samuel Goldwyn, one of Hollywood's most important characters during the 1930s, was just one of the many celebrity guests that Giulio welcomed to the Waldorf-Astoria.

Besides air conditioning, which was already virtually standard in any new self-respecting New York building at the time, there were innovations which could be publicised to attract future guests: 'a roof garden fitted with a moveable roof which opens and closes with electricity; an auditorium equipped for television, Technicolor and Movietone films; private suites with their own terraces; radios in every room; and a flexible arrangement of suites.'

It's also interesting to note that the hotel claimed to be the first in the world to offer room service and was also the first luxury hotel in the world to employ women as chefs in the kitchens - presumably both these innovations were thanks to Giulio's forward-thinking attitudes. The British *Bystander* magazine (which later merged with the *Tatler*) described Giulio as 'the presiding genius' of all this. For weeks the hotel had to accommodate throngs of sightseers and organised party tours of the property.

Afterwards, there remained the problem of finding a clientele which was further compounded by a flooded market. Within Manhattan alone, there were more than 500 hotels offering some 126,000 rooms. A number of these hotels would be regarded as large by European standards, and many contained 500 rooms, with half a dozen having

between 1,000 and 2,200. Even in their busiest times, these hotels were less than half-full. Remember, too, that this was the time of Prohibition, when so many people risked speakeasies to enjoy a drink.

In its previous incarnation, the Waldorf-Astoria was the favoured haunt of the extremely wealthy, heads of state and, of course, Hollywood stars. The new incarnation provided those stars with another iconic venue in which to be seen in the finest surroundings, and there is no doubt that in the years following the Great Depression which started in 1929, the silver screen gave the hotel a great boost. Giulio records that at the time, 'the salaries drawn by motion picture folk represented the most money anybody in the United States was making.'

He lists the guests who made straight for the Waldorf-Astoria's inherent glamour: they included Will Hays, responsible for the Motion Picture Production Code, a set of guidelines for film-making self-censorship; the film producer Samuel Goldwyn, Richard Dix, who was nominated for an Oscar in 1931 for his

(Above): Dr Hugo Eckener, head of the Zeppelin company and chief pilot during many of its record-breaking voyages, was a guest at the Waldorf-Astoria. The *Graf Zeppelin*, at the time the world's largest airship, attracted enormous crowds when it arrived in the USA. Although it carried 24 passengers in great comfort, most of the airship's revenues came from the sale of special commemorative stamps for franking the enormous quantities of mail that the airship carried.

(Right): Giulio at his desk in the 1930s.

role in *Cimmaron* and Lawrence Tibbett, a well-known baritone who ventured into film, his first role earning him an Oscar nomination in 1931 for *The Rogue Song*, which also featured Laurel and Hardy.

European guests included two-term French Prime Minister Pierre Laval, and Maréchal Philippe Pétain, both of whom, after France was liberated in 1944, were arrested for collaborating with the enemy. Laval would be executed. Dr Hugo Eckener, boss of the Luftschiffbau Zeppelin company and pilot of most of the *Graf Zeppelin* record-breaking flights, including circumnavigations, was also a guest. Ironically, he was anti-Nazi, yet managed to survive the war despite his opposition to Hitler and all he represented. Winston and Clementine Churchill stayed also. Whereas the Americans guests were predominantly actors and entertainers, the European visitors were players on the world stage, whose roles were much more important in the war than the meretricious glitter of Hollywood.

How strange it must have been for Giulio to look back at his time at the Waldorf-Astoria and recall looking after such a diverse range of famous people when the world was changing so dramatically. It must have felt that the world was spinning around him. Gradually, in spite of the world's economic mess, the hotel would become a significant national and international cultural and political hub again.

(Above): When the Waldorf-Astoria opened it was one of the very finest properties in New York. The foyer (Top Right) featured murals by Louis Rigal. All the public spaces including the Salon of the French Suite, the Ballroom and the Dining Room (Bottom Right) were richly decorated and furnished. The Silver Gallery (Below) was another astonishing example of interior design.

It was my father Bertie who would take it on after Giulio, and to whom much of its future success can be attributed. What Bertie recalls fills in some of the gaps left by Giulio, about his parents' lifelong love and the difficulties and intricacies of balancing luxury hospitality with looking after their family.

Those first four years after the new Waldorf-Astoria opened were understandably exhausting for Giulio and running two leading luxury hotels on different sides of the Atlantic quite simply could not be maintained forever.

It therefore probably came as some relief to Giulio to be offered, in February 1934, the position of managing director of the Park Lane Hotel on Park Avenue. He accepted and Bertie went with him as his assistant.

Giulio introduced a number of new initiatives to boost business. The Park Lane had been an apartment hotel but he started letting to short-term visitors – a two-room suite from as little as $10 a day. He also opened what was trumpeted as 'New York's new outdoor restaurant', the Park Lane Gardens, complete with a brook, water-wheel, trees and flowers. However this was a very difficult time in any area of business as the economies of the western world collapsed into recession; for the hotel business it was perhaps even more disastrous.

(Below): Giulio Gelardi was the first to direct two luxury hotels on opposite sides of the Atlantic. (Opposite Page Above): To celebrate this unique occurence, a fine Luncheon was held at Claridge's in London in August 1931. (Opposite Page Below): The following year, Giulio hosted a banquet for senior management at the Waldorf-Astoria in New York.

'I was earning good money and we were happy in New York where we had made many friends', Giulio recalled. 'But the hotel business in the States had gone from bad to worse: all the new ideas and new stunts I had tried had been ephemeral successes. The company was heading fast for bankruptcy, the fate of many hotels in New York at that time. It was a thankless job and I set my mind to return to London.'

Bertie would stay a while longer in the USA as he got a position at the Rockefeller Center, and Giulio was fortunate that once again, he found his experience and knowledge and international contacts reaped dividends at just the right time: his friend Mr R. Vaughan, a director of the Ritz-Carlton Company in London, stayed at the Park Lane on one of his many visits to New York and it's clear that he and Giulio must have discussed the situation. 'Before he left to return to the UK he asked me whether I would be willing to join their company and I readily agreed', Giulio wrote.

*With Commendatore Giulio Gelardi's Compliments*

*General Manager*

*Claridge's Hotel, London.*

*The Towers, Waldorf Astoria, New York.*

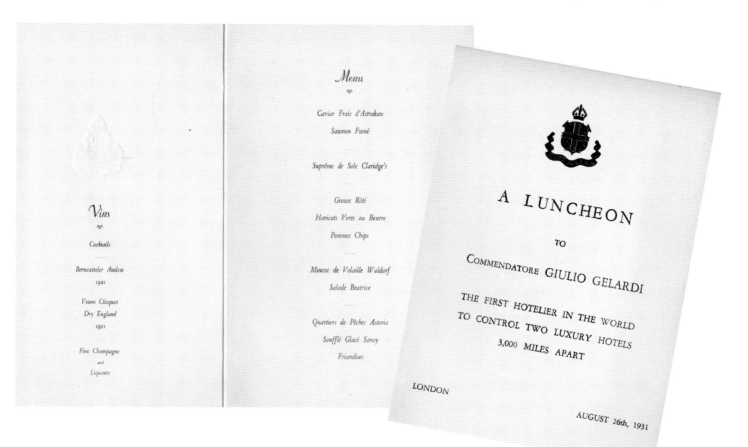

*Vins*

Cocktails

Berncasteler Auilese
1921

Veuve Clicquot
Dry England
1921

Fine Champagne
and
Liqueurs

*Menu*

Caviar Frais d'Astrakan

Saumon Fumé

Suprême de Sole Claridge's

Grouse Rôti

Haricots Verts au Beurre

Pommes Chips

Mousse de Volaille Waldorf

Salade Beatrice

Quartiers de Pêches Astoria

Soufflé Glacé Savoy

Friandises

A LUNCHEON

TO

COMMENDATORE GIULIO GELARDI

THE FIRST HOTELIER IN THE WORLD
TO CONTROL TWO LUXURY HOTELS
3,000 MILES APART

LONDON

AUGUST 26th, 1931

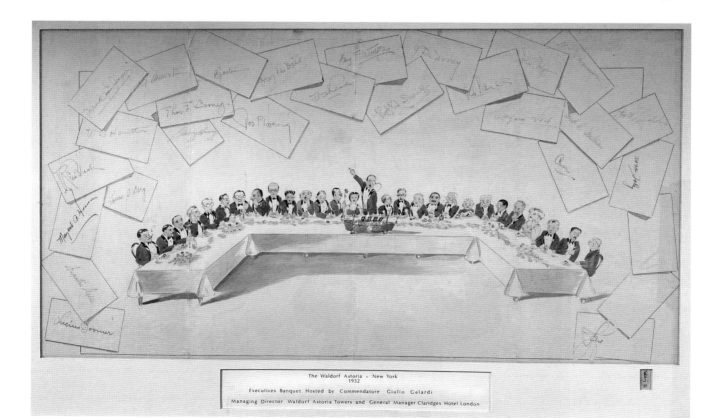

The Waldorf Astoria - New York
1932
Executives Banquet Hosted by Commendatore Giulio Gelardi
Managing Director Waldorf Astoria Towers and General Manager Claridges Hotel London

VANITY FAIR TRAVEL

*Announcing*

COMMENDATORE
GIULIO
**GELARDI**
*as*
*Managing Director*

Commendatore Giulio Gelardi was until recently director of Claridge's, London, and of The Waldorf-Astoria Towers. He is the outstanding hotel figure of Europe. He brings to the Park Lane the highest international standards of service and cuisine.

*Park Lane*

Park Avenue, 48th to 49th
New York

PARK LANE GARDENS
ROUND THE WORLD BAR

LUNCHEON
*given in honor of the*
PRESS
*on the occasion of the
opening of the
Park Lane Gardens
New York*

*May 16, 1934*

(Above): The Park Lane Hotel had 469 rooms. Giulio opened the Park Lane Gardens on the rooftop, which included a restaurant and the Round the World Bar. His arrival at the Hotel was duly recorded in a contemporary issue of *Vanity Fair* magazine (Left).

Sure enough, a few months later, the company's chairman Lord Lurgan offered Giulio the position of general manager of the Carlton Hotel in London and so he returned there in December 1935.

When it opened on the corner of Haymarket and Pall Mall in 1899, the Carlton had proudly boasted itself to be 'The Leading and Most Fashionable Hotel and Restaurant in London'. It was originally managed by César Ritz with his partner Auguste Escoffier as the head chef, then after Ritz's retirement in 1907, Escoffier stayed on until his own retirement in 1920.

By the mid-1930s the Carlton had perhaps lost some of the glitz and glamour of the Ritz and Escoffier years when it attracted many of The Savoy's former clients, but it was still one of London's leading hotels and by all accounts highly profitable for its shareholders.

However these were increasingly difficult times, as Giulio recorded in his writings: '*From 1935 I had watched the world's political situation worsening to a snapping point. The League of Nations ignored or cold-shouldered; the invasion of Japan into China; the Civil War in Spain; the rabid nationalism ... in Germany which has brought about the surrender of the Allies in the Rhineland and the annexation of Austria; the aggressive attitude of Russia; and Communists rampant in the*

(Left): The Carlton opened in 1899 on the corner of Pall Mall and Haymarket. César Ritz and Auguste Escoffier took a 72-year lease on the property which had recently been built to the design of architect C.J Phipps as part of a development that also included the rebuilding of Her Majesty's Theatre. It was an immediate success, attracting clientele from The Savoy and other leading London hotels and paying its financial backers a dividend of 7% in the first year of operation.

HOME OFFICE
ALIENS DEPT.
9 JAN 1936

FORM A.          Crown Copyright Reserved.
FILE No.    CODE

## APPLICATION FOR A CERTIFICATE OF NATURALIZATION.

I, the undersigned, to whom the following particulars relate, hereby apply to the Secretary of State for the grant of a Certificate of Naturalization.

If, at any time before a certificate is issued to me, the accuracy of any of the following particulars is affected by an alteration in circumstances, I undertake to inform the Secretary of State in writing forthwith.

Signature of Applicant..............

Date 4th January 1936

### PARTICULARS RELATING TO THE APPLICANT.

1. My full name in my country of origin was* ...GIULIO GELARDI...............

   †[and I am still commonly known by that name]

2. My present private address is‡ ...2 R. MONTAGU MANSIONS? DORSET STREET? LONDON. W.1.

3. I am by occupation a ......HOTEL MANAGER................
   My place of business is at‡ CARLTON HOTEL, LONDON.

4. I was born on (date) ..4th Aug 1873 at‡ ...ROME ITALY...........

5. At birth I was of§ .........ITALIAN.......... nationality †[and I still am.]

6. My father's full name in his country of origin was* ...GIUSEPPE GELARDI........

   His nationality is (or was at the time of his death)§ .......ITALIAN........
   He is now ‖dead, living at................

7. My mother's full name in her country of origin was* ....CAROLINA GIULIANI...

   Her nationality is (or was at the time of her death)§ ........ITALIAN.........
   She is now ‖dead, living at................

8. I am ‖single, married, a widower, a widow, divorced from my wife/husband.

9. I am of good character, and have an adequate knowledge of the English language.

10. To the best of my belief, I am financially solvent.

11. I intend, if this application is granted, to reside permanently within His Majesty's dominions †[or to enter or continue in the service of the Crown].

12. I have resided for one year immediately preceding this application in the United Kingdom, and for an additional period of four years within the last eight years either in the United Kingdom or in some other part of His Majesty's dominions, as follows :—

| From | To | At‡ | Years. | Months. |
|------|------|------|------|------|
| 1929 | 1930 | CECIL HOTEL, London | 1 | |
| 1930 | 1933 | CLARIDGE'S HOTEL, London | 4 | |
| 1933 | 1935 | 2 MONTAGU MNS., DORSET STREET? | | |
| | | London | 2 | |

13. My total residence in the United Kingdom amounts to THIRTY-FIVE ....years
    †[and elsewhere in His Majesty's dominions to ............years.]

\* Give names in full and in CAPITAL letters.
† Words in [ ] should, if not applicable, be struck out and initialled by the applicant.
‡ Give full postal address.
§ Describe nationality by reference to a *Sovereign State*, e.g. " Russian," not " Russian Pole."
‖ Strike out words which do not apply.

34·9999

(Above): Giulio applied for British citizenship in 1936, as he foresaw that war with Germany was imminent. He was soon to suffer directly from the Blitz over London when he was badly injured after a direct hit on the Carlton Hotel (Opposite Page).

*Balkans were all sure warnings that the 'dove of peace' was winded!*

*'Italy had been following a provocative policy; the conquest of Abyssinia, the intervention in the Spanish Civil War – it was clear that in the event of War, Italy would not be on Britain's side.'*

Giulio's understanding of foreign affairs stood him in good stead because he resolved in 1936 to apply for British citizenship, because the last thing he wanted was to be declared an alien and possibly interned if war broke out.

'I was just in time', he recorded. 'All this, unfortunately for the world, was to come true in less than two years. In 1938 the War was only postponed by the comic agreement of Munich. On Sunday 3 September 1939 Britain declared war on Germany – the date brings tears to my eyes!'

Just over a year later, Giulio learnt first-hand what total war meant. On 22 November 1940, at the height of the Blitz, the Carlton hotel received a direct hit. Two people were killed and seven injured. The bomb 'passed through the roof above the main staircase and fell into the well of the hotel, exploding and wrecking inside rooms. Mr G. Gelardi, the manager, who was talking to a guest in the hall, was buried under debris and suffered a broken arm,' said a contemporary report in *The Caterer and Hotel Keeper*. What the report did not say, is that Giulio's arm was broken in six places.

The damage was so great that the hotel had to close indefinitely though the Grillroom and Bar were untouched and remained open throughout the rest of the war years. Once peacetime returned, Giulio stayed on to look after what remained of the business until August 1950 when he resigned.

By that time, the company had sold the unexpired part of its lease to the government of New Zealand and the hotel was demolished soon

after and the new High Commission of New Zealand was built in its place, now New Zealand House.

Giulio's life had been one of two lifelong loves – Piera his wife and the hotel business – and his was a story of balancing luxury hospitality with some semblance of normal family life. It would be so elegant to complete Giulio's story with him sailing into the sunset with his beloved Piera, but it was not to be as she tragically passed away just three weeks after Giulio had left the Carlton.

## First Pictures of Bombed West End Hotels

FIRST pictures released by the censor of the damage to three famous London hotels which were bombed in recent air raids. Full details were given in " The Caterer and Hotel Keeper " on November 22, but names could not then be given. It can now be revealed, however, that two of the hotels bombed were the Savoy and the Carlton.

These pictures show (above) the Carlton Hotel, where a 500 lb. bomb made an unlucky direct hit on the main staircase, and burst on the roof of the Palm Court ; (top right) the Savoy, which was hit by two bombs which affected several upper rooms, but caused no really serious damage ; (bottom right), a third well-known West End hotel which sustained a direct hit from a bomb which penetrated only one storey.

Further details on page 5.

But she remained as his heart-filling companion, with whom he would share in those private and intimate diaries his most private impressions of the world as he experienced it after her death. Their love produced a family to cherish, and another hotel man to whom to pass the key. My father, Bertie.

(Opposite page): Bomb damage to the Carlton. (Above): Giulio and his beloved Piera planned to retire together to live in South Africa with Bertie and Noreen but sadly Giulio had to make the trip alone after Piera's death.

# Chapter 6

# My Father Bertie

(Above): My father Bertie, photographed while he was in his twenties.

108

My father Bertie had a great influence on me though I never worked directly with him - unlike the early part of his career when he went as assistant to his father Giulio to America and the Waldorf-Astoria. What should have been a great and exciting venture must inevitably have been marred by the times - this was the era of the Great Depression and when they got to New York there can have been no more jarring conjunction than their positions working at the country's grandest and glitziest property while the streets outside became home to numerous beggars - mostly blameless victims of the economic crash that was no fault of their own.

More shockingly, this was a time when suicides were almost commonplace, with many previously wealthy but now ruined businessmen leaping from their office buildings or booking into their favourite hotel to end their lives. Bertie records that 'Several of these suicides took place at the Waldorf as at other well-known hotels.' That must have had quite an impact, to witness the terrible circumstances that so many Americans found themselves in.

I can only guess what that must have been like for him, having been cossetted in Giulio and Piera's love throughout his childhood at Claridge's, and accustomed to an enormous sense of belonging that his parents' marriage had created. 'I had nothing to bawl about,' he says, so got an excellent reputation for being a very good child. Luxury hospitality was woven into the family fabric and Bertie's memories of his early life overlap with Giulio's roles, experienced from a child's perspective.

Born in July 1911, Bertie's memories of his early childhood at Claridge's and throughout the First World War are characterised by a child's vivid recall. They record the gentility of high society alongside occasional periods of unexpected terror. One evening there was a Zeppelin air raid on London when Giulio and Piera were out to dinner. The nanny quickly woke Bertie and his elder brother Arthur and scooted them down to Claridge's cellars in their dressing gowns and slippers, where their parents found them after running back through the city's deserted streets, not knowing if they would even make it themselves.

On another occasion, Bertie remembers a Zeppelin being shot down by a night fighter pilot, William Avery Bishop, whose exploits were documented in the media at the time. He was a Canadian pilot whose seventy-two victories rank him third behind the German Manfred Von Richtofen aka the Red Baron (eighty) and Frenchman René Fonck (seventy-five). But a fighter ace's exploits don't come close to the adventures of Bertie himself, whose fine dappled grey rocking horse he rides in his imaginary world of fantastic adventures:

'It was a bit wild but I could handle it. They say horses know when they have a good rider on their back and I soon established my mastery over the fine, strong animal, who obeyed my every word.

'We went for great rides together to far and

(Above): Giulio and Piera's children, from left: Bobby, Lina, Arthur and Bertie. This charming portrait was taken in 1917, round about the time of the Zeppelin raid over London when the two younger boys were taken to shelter in the cellars.

# Zeppelin Raids Over London

The Zeppelin raids on London during the First World War were most certainly not on the scale of the Blitz during the Second World War. Nevertheless, there were some 51 bombing raids by the Germans involving 84 airships, of which 30 were either shot down or crashed accidentally.

Although most of their effect was psychological – aimed at creating terror amongst the civilian population – in all the bombs killed 557 people and injured 1,358 so Giulio and Piera had every reason to be alarmed, even if the young boys Arthur and Bertie found being bundled down to the cellars of Claridge's to shelter from the danger something of an adventure.

Bertie remembers a Zeppelin being shot down by the fighter ace William Avery Bishop, who later was awarded the Victoria Cross for his exploits on the Western Front. However the first German airship to be shot down over the UK was in September 1916 by William Leefe Robinson who destroyed a Zeppelin approaching London from near Hatfield. For this, he too was awarded the Victoria Cross.

(Opposite Page): The Zeppelin raids over London which were seen as targeting civilians, were used in recruitment campaigns. (Left): William Avery Bishop, one of the most successful fighter pilots of WW1. (Above and Below): Although the raids were mainly psychological in their effect, real damage was done by the bombing campaign.

unknown lands, we suffered hardships, overcame all dangers and emerged ever victorious. Oh, the tales we could tell you, but what is the use, you won't believe them.'

There is something very winning about this, a side of my father's sensitivity during his childhood which acknowledges creative and self-sufficient resources, qualities he would need as a hotel man.

Growing up in Claridge's, he would have known the hotel from the inside out, always understood the best service and recognised it without thinking as he acquired the knowledge and skills he would need later. He was in it. He was part of it. As soon as he was able to recognise the world around him – and what a strange world for a child to be born into – he understood that everything was ordered, everything was carried out in a particular way.

The Dowager Princess of Monaco was a permanent resident in a fine corner apartment at the time and asked Giulio if she might invite his seven and nine-year-old sons Bertie and Arthur to lunch and take them to some form of entertainment afterwards.

The boys were 'properly scrubbed, polished, smartly dressed, hair nicely brushed' before being sent to Giulio for inspection, who told them what and, more importantly, what not to say, how to behave at the table and very importantly, not to forget 'Thank you, Your Highness.' The boys were let into the room by a major-domo who told them to make themselves comfortable.

While they waited for the Princess, Bertie reminded himself that he must not touch her hand unless she proffered it and not to squeeze it but be very gentle, responding to her greeting with, 'How do you do, Your Highness?' Bertie says that when the Princess entered the room, statuesque and smiling, the boys shot off their seats and stood to attention. She extended her hand and Bertie undid all the careful preparation immediately by addressing her as '*My* Highness' and, expecting to be reprimanded for such a faux pas, was rewarded with her laughing instead.

At once the atmosphere for the rest of the afternoon was set and the boys relaxed. The Princess then asked 'What do people call you?' and Bertie's answer as an honest seven year old was 'Fatty'.

The Princess liked children and spoke to them in a light-hearted manner until she received a visitor after lunch, the glass designer René

(Above): The Dowager Princess of Monaco, a permanent resident at Claridge's, who liked children and who took Bertie and Arthur out for treats. One visit by the boys to her suite was interrupted by the arrival of the great artist in glass René Lalique (Right).

Lalique, whose wares appear today on the BBC's *Antiques Roadshow* and cause people to gasp at their appearance and valuations. They took a coffee together and chatted in French before the Princess summoned her car for the next part of the adventure, a ride in her Rolls-Royce – like an ocean liner gliding down the road – to Drury Lane and a screening of *Orphans of the Storm*, starring Lillian and Dorothy Gish, the brightest stars of early cinema: a silent film lasting two and a half hours.

For small boys today it would be unlikely to hold their attention, but then it was enthralling and dramatic, set in the volatile French Revolution with the Gish sisters conveying danger and triumph with their on-screen presence. What an extraordinary afternoon for two little boys in London in 1921, to have ridden on the beautifully sprung leather bench seat of a Rolls-Royce next to the elderly Princess, followed by the wonder of early motion pictures in a plush cinema.

(Below): Field Marshall Haig in France during the War. His Daimler was later bought by Giulio in 1922.

Another car that provided greater adventures was the Daimler which had once belonged to Field Marshall Haig, which Giulio acquired in 1922, along with a chauffeur, Corporal – now Mr – Snow. That the Gelardis had such intimate links to the players of the First World War astonishes me, yet it was merely their lives entwining and continuing. I consider these things now, a hundred years later, wondering how extraordinary it is that the family went about in such a car. Field Marshall Haig was a soldier who had been trained in the cavalry era, consisting largely of men who rode to hounds, and who had to contend with a war in which machines – tanks and early armoured cars – replaced the 'mounts'.

Haig's Daimler is a reminder of the tension which must have played out between the traditional and the cutting-edge thinking of modern warfare, since he began his military service in the same year (1885) that Daimler perfected his internal combustion engine; this would transform the conflict and cause Haig to be known as either the 'Master of the Field' or 'Butcher of the Somme', depending on one's opinion of him as saint or misplaced-faith-in-cavalry sinner.

After the war, what had been his staff car encapsulated the peace of the new world that emerged, and the Gelardis' ability to just get up and go, driving in the Continent *en famille*. Motoring then was still something of an adventure, the roads inconsistently paved and the car's suspension and wheels at the mercy of the various surfaces traversed.

On one memorable trip from Dijon to Paris, they suffered six punctures. Not even Haig's one-time driver, the unflappable Mr Snow, could cope with that. Just a few miles shy of Paris, the family had to trudge behind the car as Snow nursed it to the nearest village where they banged on the door of a mechanic. Although he didn't appreciate being woken so late, he *did* have the tyre required. Snow did the rest, putting the inner tube in the tyre, inflating it and refitting it to the wheel – so unlike the easy off-and-on routine of today. The family continued, undaunted, arriving in Paris at 3am, where Snow had to wake them from collective exhaustion when they pulled up outside the hotel. 'It all added a coat of spice to the journeys which is missing in this perfect world,' Bertie says, 'today such events would be considered disasters – we thought of them more as achievements!'

I wonder what happened to that car. Bertie is so clear in his recollection and, because it belonged to one of the great commanders of the war, I thought it would be fairly easy to trace and I would even be able to visit it and my father's boyish incarnation, touch its upholstery and feel the ghostly presence of my ancestors. But all I managed to find is a black and white photograph of another of Haig's cars, sold at auction, its lot number '29' affixed to its grill, a Rolls-Royce Silver Ghost Open Drive Limousine and, typed in purple across the top of the image, *'La voiture de Douglas Haig mise aux enchères au profit d'une oeuvre de charité.'* (Douglas Haig's car, sold in aid of charity).

What I did discover, though, is that Haig travelled with two cars in case one of them should fail, so the Daimler would have been paired with this Rolls-Royce. I also thought that it must be possible to trace the driver Corporal Snow, but all I could find in the archives is a Private John Smith, Haig's chauffeur throughout the war, several photographs of him standing next to, or at the wheel of, Rolls-Royces (yet another auction lot, in fact, sold at Laird's in Carlisle). There is a chance, of course, that Bertie is merely mistaken when recalling the name, and that Snow could be Smith.

Bertie's education was at Stoneyhurst College in Lancashire, one of the UK's leading Catholic boarding schools. He admits to 'not exactly excelling' on the academic front but proudly notes that he won full colours at both rugby and cricket.

(Below): The Hermitage Hotel in Le Touquet was first opened in 1904, then demolished and completely re-built in 1910. It was later extended with a new restaurant added in 1924. Five years later Bertie would arrive to continue his training in the hotel business.

He left in late 1928 and having decided on a career in the hotel business, he had to get his basic training. My grandfather Giulio had famously been advised by César Ritz to gain experience at lesser establishments but he clearly did not pass this message on to my father Bertie. Although he did start at the bottom, working in each department in turn so that he would understand all the intricate workings of a large hotel, he most certainly did not undertake his basic training at 'lesser establishments!'

His first assignment was as a trainee at the Prince de Galles Hotel in Paris, then a few months later in April 1929 he moved to the Hermitage in Le Touquet, at the time France's most prestigious resort. The full name of this elegant beach town is Le Touquet-Paris-Plage, but it was not just the wealthy Parisians who flocked there. It was also just a thirty minute 'hop' by plane from Shoreham, near Brighton, from where many of its guests flew in their own light aircraft, sweeping away over Newhaven, Seaford, Eastbourne and Beachy Head to the Côte d'Opale, eager to get in a round of golf before an exciting evening at the casino's baized tables.

(Above): The Prince of Wales, the future King Edward VIII, with Wallis Simpson, whom he later married after renouncing the throne. He was a regular visitor to the Hermitage at Le Touquet and was remembered by Bertie as being always polite though often tipsy.

Aristocrats and socialites burned through money at the bar and the roulette table, including the Prince of Wales, the future King Edward VIII, who often flew in for weekends with his one-armed Aide-de-Camp, General Trotter. His behaviour was rather similar to his forbear, Edward VII. But this future king had nearly been undone by his indiscreet relationship with Princess Fahmy and would eventually become a puppet to the twice-divorced American, Wallis Simpson.

At this time, he was a reckless womaniser, a lush, but Bertie says that although he was very often tipsy, he was always polite. Whatever he did, though, was acceptable – he could get away with it because he was the future monarch. Fortified at the bar, he threw away his money at the casino's gaming tables.

(Top): Amongst the glamorous guests at the Hermitage Hotel were the twin sisters Rosie and Jenny Dolly. They had both acted in silent films and were famous for their Vaudeville acts. Both had a penchant for high-stakes gambling and both allegedly had affairs with Harry Gordon Selfridge (Above).

Bertie's other guests were no less glamorous and no better behaved. There was the brilliant retail entrepreneur Harry Gordon Selfridge, by then in his seventies, who had worked his way up through Marshall Field and Company from stock boy to junior partner in a similar way that the best hoteliers gain their knowledge from the bottom up; also the acting and dancing identical twin sisters Rosie and Jenny Dolly, whose greatest gift was, it appears, gambling. For them, Le Touquet was merely an outing.

The sisters' winnings were outrageous even for the 1920s, millions of dollars, accrued from the money that Selfridge and other wealthy socialites had given them in the first place. Both sisters allegedly had an affair with Selfridge, as well as with a variety of other extremely wealthy admirers, (causing them to be known as 'The Million Dollar Dollies'), including King Alfonso XIII of Spain, whom Giulio had welcomed to London after his escape in 1930.

Le Touquet relied on a seasonal clientele, and closed in September; Bertie's next step on his apprenticeship journey was at the Eden Hotel in Berlin. There he frequently found Marlene Dietrich in the bar, the twenty-eight-year-old star who was in the middle of making the film that would define her career, *The Blue Angel*, which includes the smoky '*Falling in Love Again*'. Did she cup her hand around a light he proffered for her cigarette? Did he mix a cocktail and set it on the bar in front of her?

Years later, when she was seventy-seven, Marlene was persuaded to appear in the film *Just a Gigolo*. The writer Rory MacLean says she only agreed to it 'On condition that we brought Berlin to her; German technicians, two tons of equipment and the complete set of the Eden Hotel'. I like to think that, as she remembered her youth, when she had finished

a day's filming at the Babelsberg studios, she escaped Berlin's pre-war gaiety to slip into the Eden Hotel bar to unwind with a cocktail and cigarette in its trademark holder. And there, out of the corner of her eye, my father, the smart hotel man with his pencil moustache and keenly creased suit, the hotel's bright young employee.

It's extraordinary that Bertie should witness Dietrich's leisure hours at that crunch in time when the city's streets were not only gilded by the fashionable, but ratted with Hitler's ideas also, which would lead Dietrich to leave for America. It was where my father Bertie would head, too, but not out of fear of the Nazis and their regime, but to continue his training.

As we have seen, Lucius Boomer, CEO of the Waldorf-Astoria in New York, asked the Savoy Hotel Company to loan Giulio to run the Waldorf-Astoria Towers, the part of the hotel complex that housed luxury apartments. The loan was agreed, and in a spectacular example of nepotism, Bertie would travel to the USA as his father's assistant!

(Above): The Eden Hotel in Budapester Strasse, Berlin where Bertie trained in the early 1930s. The building was so badly damaged during WW2 that it had to be demolished.

Giulio and Bertie boarded the German liner *Bremen* in October 1931 shortly before the Waldorf-Astoria was due to open, leaving behind a Berlin which was descending into the fever of Hitler's National Socialism, the Nazi party having been voted into parliament in the elections just a month before. If I ever thought that my father might not have been aware of what was going on beyond the immediate world of the Hotel Eden, his typescript reminds me that he was both very well informed and under no illusions as to what was going on around him. He devotes pages to Hitler's rise:

'Von Hindenburg was Germany's great war hero and highly regarded at the time as the founder and father of the New Germany created after the war on the abdication of the Kaiser. He was well into his dotage and most probably didn't really know what was going on and relied very heavily on von Papen's advice. Von Papen was convinced that unless something drastic was done the Communists would gain the upper hand and, though he had no liking for the Nazis, he devised a plan by which he thought he, as Chancellor, would be able to control them and, at the same time, remove the threat from the Communists.

(Below): Von Hindenburg was a highly-respected war hero who was President of Germany from 1925 until his death in 1934. He was forced to appoint Hitler Chancellor in 1933 after the Nazi Party had gained a majority in the Reichstag that year. After von Hindenburg's death, Hitler first appointed himself President before declaring himself Führer and transforming Germany into a totalitarian state.

'He would get von Hindenburg to appoint Hitler Vice Chancellor, in that way he would be under von Papen and thereby politically emasculated, or so von Papen thought. Hitler thought differently! So when von Hindenburg offered the appointment to Hitler he readily accepted, as he knew full well that, with the superiority of the seats held by the Nazi party members in the Reichstag over those held by von Papen's Conservative party, the fact that he had a very large share of the popular vote, and that he had at his command a belligerent private army not averse to using force and now, what would appear to the populace as the blessing of the revered President, his appointment to the Vice Chancellery, he would be in a position to control events and not von Papen and not even von Hindenburg!

'All he needed was an excuse. This he could arrange. Set fire to the Reichstag. Blame this on the Communists as a prelude to an uprising making it necessary for him as Vice Chancellor to order his Nazi party to forestall. This enabled him to brutally eradicate the Communist menace with apparent taciturn blessing of the government and at the same time pressurise von Hindenburg to appoint him Chancellor in place of von Papen. A short while later von Hindenburg himself died and Hitler appointed himself President.'

This reveals that, just like his father Giulio had done earlier, Bertie always kept himself well-informed about the serious current affairs of

the day. And he was most certainly very well aware of the dangers of the political situation in Germany: 'If you want to tame a wild animal don't invite it to tea in your house – it might eat you instead of the cakes you are offering,' he wrote.

Just before he left for America, Bertie was working at the Esplanade Hotel in Berlin. He describes it as 'an older hotel, very palatial and with a clientele consisting mostly of the old German aristocracy and other strata of German high society, whereas the Eden had a more commercial and artistic clientele – rather like the difference between Claridge's and The Savoy in London'.

At the Esplanade, he recorded the different allegiances of the foyer staff. Two Nazis, two Communists, one Catholic Party, one Stalhelm, two Socialists, two Conservatives,

(Top): The Esplanade Hotel in Berlin stood on the busy Potsdamer Platz. It first opened in 1908 and the combination of its elegance and high levels of service soon attracted the likes of Charlie Chaplin and Greta Garbo. One of its crowning glories was the magnificent courtyard garden (Above).

(Right): Bertie in his early twenties when he worked at the Eden and Esplanade Hotels in Berlin and observed at first hand the rise to power of Hitler and the Nazi Party.

two other parties. 'Strangely enough,' he says, 'they all got on well together in the hotel, but I imagine not so well outside.' For me, it adds to the machine analogy, that the hotel is an entity of itself, which must be harmonious or it collapses. I think of those times now and marvel at how these different perspectives were left beyond the hotel door and the troubled streets.

There were still guests to look after, too. In the summer of 1931, the Italian tenor Beniamino Gigli was staying at the hotel while performing in the German capital, and when the assistant manager apologised that he hadn't been able to hear him sing, Gigli responded, 'Well you have been very good to me and I can remedy that right here and now. If you permit me.' And he sang an aria on the spot.

'His strong tenor voice reverberated throughout the whole of the ground floor and, in no time at all, the foyer was full of guests and staff. They stood in quiet amazement not believing what they saw and heard – the world's greatest tenor in full voice. Then when the singing stopped, there was a brief period of utter silence. Then rapturous applause broke out, he made a courteous bow, waved his hand in acknowledgement and made a dramatic exit as if he had just appeared on an opening night on the stage of the Scala in Milan.'

Another musical genius also stayed at the hotel around this time – although he was only some nine or ten years old, he was already world famous. That was Yehudi Menuhin, the great violinist who had come to Berlin to give a concert.

But these musical interludes cannot have been more than memories for Bertie as he arrived with his father in New York on the other side of the Atlantic, just three weeks before the Waldorf-Astoria was due to open. 'The building was finished but there was still a terrific amount still to do and it seemed impossible that it could open on time' wrote Bertie in his memoirs, 'but by the super-human efforts of all involved, it did.'

The grand opening coincided with the first anniversary of the Wall Street Crash, and at that time, of course, the city was dry due to Prohibition. The contrast between Berlin's relaxed and decadent night life and New York's was stark. Yet Bertie records that soon after he arrived at the hotel the telephone rang and when he answered, it was to hear a voice that said 'Welcome to New York. I am the supplier of liquor to this part of New York so if there is anything you would like to order, it will be delivered in half an hour.'

'I was rather taken aback by the direct approach', recalled Bertie later, 'but must

(Below): When the great Italian tenor Beniamino Gigli stayed at the Esplanade Hotel while in Berlin for a performance, Bertie expressed regret that he had not heard him sing. The result was an impromptu aria performed in the foyer of the hotel, much to the delight of both Bertie and the hotel's other fortunate guests.

(Top): The Broadmoor Hotel, Colorado Springs where Bertie met the film and opera star Gladys Swarthout (Above). Apparently she greatly appreciated the 'Bathtub Gin' and bootlegged whiskey that Bertie was able to procure for her, despite the restriction of the Prohibition Era.

say I admired the speed of service.' Initially he declined the offer but later did order some Scotch. 'It duly arrived as promised. The price was high but not unreasonable in the circumstances.'

We know that era well from countless Jazz Age movies depicting the underground speakeasies and coded door knocks, dark alleys and nods through grills. New York was a city fought over by gangsters and government agencies. And it spread. The following year Bertie was working at the Broadmoor Hotel in Colorado Springs, and by this time gangsters were as glamorous as Hollywood stars. Bertie discovered that the hotel had its own way of getting around the drinking laws, one that was much appreciated by another great of the opera world – Gladys Swarthout, the Metropolitan's coloratura diva.

'There were always guests arriving who were dying for a drink,' Bertie recalls, and the hotel had a supply of what was known as 'bathtub gin', made from essence of juniper, pharmaceutical alcohol and tap water. With tonic water, lemon or orange juice, it made 'a very acceptable drink'. Bootlegged whiskey was kept for special guests. On one occasion, when Amberto Campione, the Broadmoor's general manager, was away, Bertie was summoned to reception for an evening arrival of a guest who said she just 'had to have a drink'. Bertie took her up to the manager's suite, put a gin and tonic in her hand and sat and talked. It was none other than Gladys Swarthout, who had argued with her husband and wanted a break incognito.

She was so desperate not to be recognised that she took taxis everywhere and, having made friends with Bertie, called on him instead to take her for an occasional outing. They borrowed Campione's car, as he was only too pleased to accommodate a guest. Bertie unwittingly became a great opera star's drinking partner and confidante, as well as a willing student with an encyclopaedic knowledge of opera which he demonstrated throughout his life.

Ironically, whilst they were benefitting from bootlegged liquor, another guest slipped by without raising anyone's suspicions until the FBI turned up and Bertie recognised him as soon as he was shown his photograph: George 'Machine Gun' Kelly, after John Dillinger, the most wanted man in America. Bootlegger and kidnapper. He was

(Left): One of the more interesting guests at the Broadmoor Hotel was George 'Machine Gun' Kelly, whose nickname derived from his weapon of choice while going about his criminal business. Although he left the hotel before the FBI arrived in search of him - paying his bill in full - he was later arrested and he and his wife Kathryn found guilty of kidnapping. Clearly the police were taking no chances as they transferred George from Shelby County Jail to Oklahoma City for the trial that resulted in a life sentence for both George and Kathryn.

staying under a false name, of course, took no visitors and was a model guest. Understandably he did nothing to draw attention to himself because he was on the run. By the time the FBI turned up, he had paid his bill and left two days earlier. However, the FBI did catch up with him in September 1933 after which he was sentenced to life imprisonment, serving much of his time at Alcatraz, before dying of a heart attack aged fifty-nine at Leavenworth.

Bertie had gone to the Broadmoor in the first place to work alongside Alberto Campione – son of the chairman of CIGA hotels for whom Giulio had worked in Italy – when he became the general manager and wanted Bertie as his assistant. The hotel had been built by Spencer Penrose, who owned gold and silver mines as well as a mountain of tin ore, and who lived with his wife in a large house nearby and took a keen interest in the hotel's day to day running. Colorado Springs had been a small place until the 1880s, when doctors advised their patients that to avoid the threat of tuberculosis, they should head out of the cities to more salubrious areas. It was a fantastic place for my father and he was fortunate in the qualities of Campione, an outgoing conversationalist and entertainer, a natural for hospitality and a superb mentor for a young man who was still early in his career.

24 July 1932 began as a normal working day for Bertie, but Campione had other ideas, which characterised his generosity and kindness. At 7pm he called for Bertie to join him in his suite to discuss a function that the hotel was hosting the next day, but when Bertie entered, ten people of his own age appeared with champagne and glasses singing 'Happy Birthday!' It was Bertie's twenty-first, and he believed the cable he'd received from Giulio and Piera would be the only acknowledgement of his special day. Campione had invited the young people who Bertie had only seen coming and going in the hotel. After a couple of drinks, they were all treated to dinner in the restaurant, and Campione left them to it.

While Bertie was at the Broadmoor Hotel in Colorado Springs, a family created great interest amongst other guests because the seventeen and nineteen-year-old daughters were so beautiful and, according to Bertie, the mother even more so. A feature of the hotel's week was a dinner dance on the terrace every weekend, very theatrical when there was a full moon lighting the lake and mountains. As the daughters danced with their father, Bertie engaged with the mother in his professional capacity.

'I asked her the normal sort of questions and got all the right answers and then she asked me if I would like to dance, which of course I was pleased to do. As we were dancing and conversing on the usual banal topics she suddenly said, 'Do you have a yen for me?' I was completely taken off my guard and being very young and untutored in those matters, I answered 'No!'

Embarrassed, Bertie was relieved when the music stopped and he was able to return the woman to her table. 'Sorry to disappoint you, but that's as sexy as it gets,' he wrote in his memoir many years later, adding wryly, 'I don't mind telling you that I have often wondered… but her husband was a mountain of a man!' With typical discretion, Bertie's notes do not reveal the name of the lady, nor her daughters.

It reminds me, too, that beneath the immaculate attire – the fine suit, the light leather shoes – there is an individual who is emotionally charged by what happens when interacting and looking after guests, that a young sensitive man would have been flustered by being addressed as himself rather than his professional self. It would have been like reaching through to the person wearing the 'costume' of a hotelier. Ultimately, the circumstances and the interaction would have contributed to his knowledge, to be filed under, 'How to behave when a guest comes onto you.'

Thinking of my father in his youth invariably causes me to compare it with my own. Mine was so much easier in comparison. Bertie and Giulio and Gustave were prepared to go wherever it was necessary, travelling to take up jobs so they could provide for themselves and their families. Each set an example for the generation to follow and, even though they often found themselves in challenging circumstances, they appear to have just got on with it. I am profoundly grateful. Whenever I was challenged by a 'shall I, shan't I?' decision in my own professional life, I very often tried to imagine what my father and grandfather would have done.

When the season in the Rocky Mountains ended in late September, only a modest annexe was kept open for the winter. Campione took a position in California and Bertie had lined up an office role at the St Regis Hotel in New York. He bought a second-hand car for $40 – a REO which is no longer a brand that many people remember, but it was one of many car companies set up by Ransom E. Olds, the automotive innovator far better known for the Oldsmobile company that he established in 1897. Bertie's REO was apparently 'a grand presence on the road', and in it he set off with his friend Duane Osborne on the two-day drive, stopping at Chicago on the way, where

(Right): Bertie did not record the exact model of REO car that he bought secondhand for the drive from Colorado to New York but it may well have been a Flying Cloud – which most certainly possessed the 'grand presence on the road' that he clearly remembered.

# Like a Swift Ship on a Summer Sea

Take this distinctly new Reo for a cruise over your favourite roads ; try it out on the hillroad and the rough stretch outside of town. Its smooth riding likens it to a swift craft on a smooth sea. A touch to the accelerator and there follows a rush of power that sends you skimming over the miles —power, smooth at its source, tireless as the trade winds.

The Reo Flying Cloud is named in honour of one of the most beautiful, most famous and fastest ships of the clipper trade. How well it is named you will know when you have had a ride in one, when you have driven one and tested it in your most critical mood. Be sure to try one out.

## REO
### FLYING CLOUD

– much to his father Giulio's disgust – they did not take the opportunity of visiting the World Fair which was on at the city at that very time.

The St Regis was one of New York's established hotels and still fashionable at that time, attracting its fair share of famous and notable people. But that's not a guarantee that Bertie would remember their names when he came to write up his memoirs many years later. There was one guest, for example, whom Bertie obviously likes for her character, the star of a recently opened show on Broadway who became an instant sensation after critics showered her show with rapturous reviews.

'She had become a superstar overnight' and 'remained as she had been before the show opened, never putting on the airs of a star and, in fact, most nights coming back right after the show by herself, asking for her key at reception and just going up to her room.' She was playing the lead in *Roberta*, and sang the show's memorable Jerome Kern song, '*Smoke gets in Your Eyes*' was all Bertie could recall. For the record, it was Tamara Drasin.

Bertie didn't stay long at the St Regis because the following March, after Giulio was offered the position of managing director of the Park Lane Hotel, he wanted Bertie to go with him as assistant manager. 'Another flagrant manifestation of nepotism at its worst', commented Bertie, 'undoubtedly suggested by my mother in such a way that left very little room, if any, for argument'. Bertie chose not to argue with either of his parents: 'I accepted quickly, not allowing any time for second thoughts.'

By then, of course, Giulio realised that apart from Piera, the person he could trust most was his son and they most certainly made a formidable team. Although Bertie saw it as nepotism, hoteliers will always try to recruit the best staff possible and will poach them from wherever to create a machine that works smoothly. To continue the metaphor, hoteliers don't want a noisy engine. We don't want guests to notice that the engine is running. Bertie was, well, both noiseless and priceless.

The Park Lane Hotel, like the Waldorf-Astoria Towers, was a full-service apartment hotel with accommodation let by the day, week, month or even year. It was here where Giulio showed Bertie just how to deal with those guests whose background leaves something to be desired. The apparently perfect credentials supplied by one guest who had reserved a three months' stay turned out to be forgeries, revealed a few days later. He had gangster connections so had to be removed immediately. But how?

(Below): Tamara Drasin, star of *Roberta* on Broadway, who made an impression on Bertie during her stay at the St Regis Hotel.

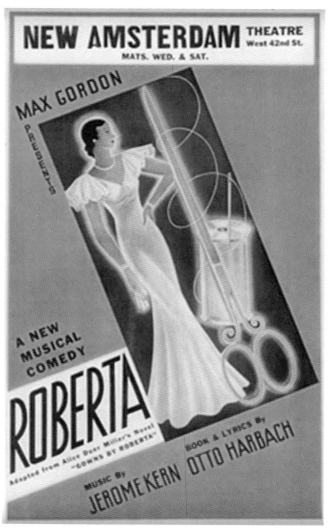

It was Bertie's responsibility but sensing his young son's apprehension, Giulio took charge: 'Come on, we will go now and get rid of him'. Bertie followed him to the suite:

'He took me with him up to the suite, knocked on the door and went in with me tagging a safe distance behind. Without any ado, he merely said, 'I am the managing director of the hotel. I regret to have to advise you that you were booked into the hotel on the basis of credentials which you presented. On checking, these have been found to be unacceptable. You are therefore required to leave these premises by six o'clock this evening. I trust you understand.'

In 1930s gangster New York, it would have been a tense interaction, and a chance that the connected guest might not have wanted to play along. But he would not have wanted the police to have been called and the father and son hoteliers wouldn't have wanted the publicity surrounding such a person staying. As hoteliers we are delighted to welcome and look after our guests, and we aim to provide the best service to each one of them. To us, each is equal. But not every guest is who they purport to be. It was ever thus, and I was later to have my own tricky moments when in the boss's chair.

(Below): The Rainbow Room restaurant at the Rockefeller Center (Opposite) was the scene of lavish entertainment, with fine dining and some of the top stars of the day performing.

Bertie's stay at the Park Lane Hotel was short-lived. J. J. Atkinson had sold the St Regis and acquired the newly opened Rainbow Room Restaurant on the top two floors of the Rockefeller Center and wanted Bertie as his assistant. It would have been reasonable for Giulio to deny the request having what was his greatest professional asset alongside him, but he agreed with no objection. Bertie took up the role of assistant managing director, which involved many late nights because as well as the restaurant, he had the Rainbow Room nightclub as well as a number of private dining rooms to look after.

We glimpse what he was doing from the large black scrapbook in which there is a programme for New Year's Eve, 1934; its cover features a print of the towering Rockefeller Center and it contains a list of entertainers including three orchestras and a ballet ensemble, alongside a menu which begins

with *Canapé Muscovite* and ends with *Bombe Glacé du Nouvelle Année 1935* and *Café des Princes*. This was entertaining on an enormous scale.

Interestingly, at this time Bertie also became publisher of *The Night Club Reporter* – an early form of *What's On* for the world of New York nightlife. I wonder whether he also had some input on the *Rockefeller Center Weekly* publication because he kept a couple of copies in his archive, marked 'Personal Copy of B. Gelardi'.

It would not be long before Bertie's and Giulio's worst fears about the political situation in Germany came to pass. By this time Giulio was back in London at the Carlton Hotel and Bertie re-crossed the Atlantic to return to Britain and go to war

(Right and Opposite): Alongside his role as assistant managing director at the Rockefeller Center, Bertie was publisher of the *Night Club Reporter*. It seems extraordinary today that the lead story of one of the early edition should have been a debate on whether women should be allowed to drink in bars! Bertie was clearly busy at that time because he may also have had a role in the production of the *Rockefeller Center Weekly* (Below).

# THE NIGHT CLUB Reporter

## "The Trade Paper the Public Reads"

Published semi-monthly by:

The Night Club Reporter at 10 East 49th Street New York N. Y. Plaza 3-1125

A. C. GELARDI, *Publisher*

**Barbara McKrell** *Editor*

**George Lowther Peter Dean** *Associate Editors*

Subscription $2.00 a year Single copies 10 cents Printed in U. S. A.

SPECIAL FLORIDA EDITION

**TALENT**

Our roster of agents and artists will aid operators in planning new shows and in the location of unusual novelty acts and other talent.

# THE NIGHT CLUB Reporter

**ARTISTS**

We are constantly receiving enquiries for new talent. Tell us who your agent is so that we may communicate with him!

**VOL. 1. NO. 5**          NEW YORK, FEBRUARY 15-28, 1937          **TEN CENTS**

# CAN *ALL* WOMEN SAY "WHEN"?

## Drinking At Bars Controversy Still Wages Fast and Furious!

It is almost impossible to pick up a newspaper now without reading some opinion or solution of the "Should Women Drink in Bars" question. The controversy is liable to be loud and prolonged in any gathering — masculine, feminine or mixed.

Now Senator Edward J. Coughlin, Brooklyn Democrat, has announced that the bill he introduced in the Albany Legislature on January 29 was "shot in speedily" and should be amended. The original bill provided that any female who "stands at or in front of a bar in any club, hotel or restaurant licensed to sell alcoholic beverages" would be guilty of disorderly conduct. It seems that this left a loophole, because women could *sit* at these same bars and be entirely within the law. The amendment will read "Drinking in front of, or at, a public bar."

The staff of *The Night Club Reporter* has, since the publication of the leading article in the January 15 issue, paid particular attention to the drinking habits of the fair sex. For one of them who takes her drinks too fast and frequently there are hundreds who know where to draw the line between "orderly" and "disorderly." And for the most part the straight mahogany bar, with brass rail and no seating accommodation, is not favored by women. Where the bar is of this type they apparently prefer a table.

The bill is obviously ridiculous. To book a sedate, middle-aged woman who orders a dry Martini at the bar as a preface to a quiet luncheon, on the charge of "disorderly conduct" is unthinkable, yet if the bill became law that is exactly what it would mean.

The Senator himself is not very optimistic that the bill will go very far. "There's too much opposition," he says. His reason for introducing this bill is to protect "young janes under twenty-one from getting loaded at bars." Which is just as silly as censoring all movies in case a young person should see or hear something which would endanger his or her morals. If legislation goes on like this everyone will have to drink milk and read Mother Goose Rhymes!

### Madeleine's

Madeleine, who used to run a grille-door spot in the Fifties during the dry era, has opened a new night club at 121 East 52nd Street, to be called Madeleine's, where she will act as hostess. Recalling the good times we had there when everything was done *sub rosa*, the new venture should have a convivial atmosphere.

### Stork Club Kids

"Some of New York's most beautiful kids—white, black and colored—will be given away every evening. Are you interested?" reads an announcement from Sherman Billingsley. Well, who wouldn't be? But there's a catch. The kids are made of leather—in fact, they're shoes. Every evening at the Stork Club each of the five most smartly dressed guests will be presented with a pair of kidskin shoes, presented through the courtesy of Altman, Bergdorf-Goodman, Bonwit-Teller, Jay-Thorpe, Lord & Taylor, Milgrim, I. Miller, Saks Fifth Avenue and Slater. Prominent fashion authorities do the judging at one a.m.

### Sabbath Diversions

"Sunday Night Diversions" presented by Mrs. Allen Hulbert at the Guard Room of the Park Lane have appealed to many prominent people around town. As the name indicates, these "Diversions" are given on Sundays and begin promptly at nine p.m. The minimum charge is $1.50, which includes supper, and the program is changed every week. The entertainment is very varied—Eric Zardo, pianist; Dario Shindell, well-known on the dramatic stages of America and England; Ann Freschmann, dancer; Marie and Antoinette Bergere, modern dancers; Irving Fisher, musical comedy star and many others will appear on these programs from time to time.

Drinking in the Modern manner at the new Milk Bar of the Chateau Moderne. Photo McNutt.

### General Lodijensky

General Lodijensky, who has been associated for so long with the Russian Eagle of the Sherry-Netherland, is now acting as the suave host of the Trianon Room of the Ambassador. Perhaps this is the beginning of a Russian Room at this Park Avenue hotel, since the General has so many friends among the Russian nobility.

### Medrano & Donna

Medrano & Donna, internationally known dance team, have just returned from a vacation in Florida, and are dancing in the Iridium Room of the Hotel St. Regis.

### Future N. C. Celeb.

Congratulations to Joe Fernandez of Mon Paris, who became a proud father last week. Best wishes also to Mrs. Fernandez. And may the small Fernandez grow up to be a big name in the night clubs!

*"THE TRADE PAPER THE PUBLIC READS"*

# Chapter 7

# To War and Beyond

When Bertie arrived back in Britain, because of his Combined Cadet Force experience whilst at Stonyhurst College, he joined the army as a second lieutenant on 3 May 1940 on an 'Emergency Commission'.

Fortunately, my brother Paul has researched this part of our father's life. The yellowed 'Army Form B-199A', which records dates of postings, training and promotions, as well as Bertie's facility with French, Italian and German, is a skeleton Paul has clothed with the stories he remembers Bertie telling him. He was stationed in Beverley, Yorkshire, and by October was acting as adjutant captain to the colonel of the East Yorkshire Regiment. Bizarrely, and in true *Dad's Army* fashion, one of Bertie's duties was to source and 'arm' the Home Guard with wooden rifles so that they appeared fully equipped to any U-Boat spies who might be reconnoitring the coast.

In 1942 he was posted to India and assumed a position as a general staff officer (GSO3) and saw 'action' in ways other than what might be expected. He was hospitalised not by enemy action but malaria and, amazingly, woke in his bed to find his cousin Teresa Burton (née Gelardi) at his bedside. She was the elder daughter of Ernesto and had been evacuated from Singapore to India after her husband Charles Frank Burton, a lieutenant-colonel in the Medical Corps, who was sent to set up a hospital in Sumatra in the event that Singapore fell to the Japanese. Unfortunately, the ship he was on with the other medical staff that were with him to set up the evacuation hospital, was bombed by the Japanese and

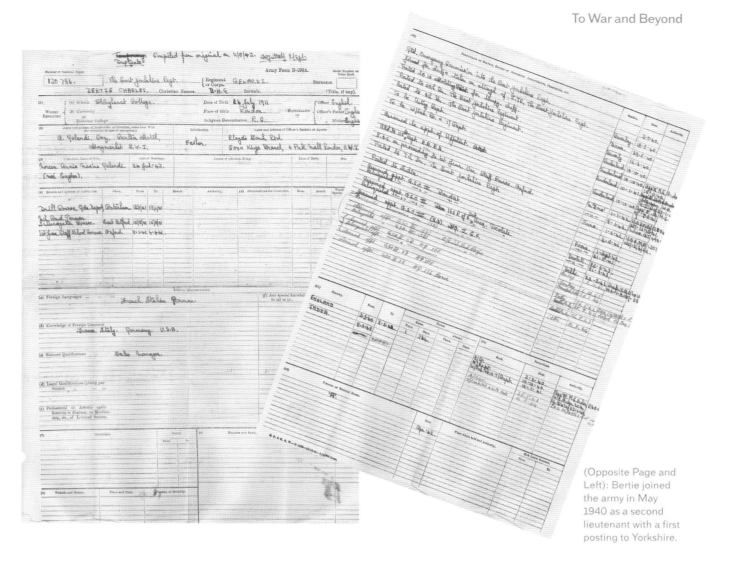

(Opposite Page and Left): Bertie joined the army in May 1940 as a second lieutenant with a first posting to Yorkshire.

was lost at sea. Teresa had volunteered to help out at the Bombay hospital after her ship had docked. The first blood sample she was given to analyse said 'Gelardi' and she went straight to Bertie's side. How extraordinary that the two displaced family members should meet so far from their homes and be brought together by blood!

Bertie's first posting was to Poona, where he found himself 'guarding' Mahatma Gandhi, who had been urging on his followers at Gowalia Tank Maidan on the 8 August 1942; he was arrested within twenty-four hours for declaring 'Here is a mantra, a short one, that I give to you. You may imprint it on your hearts and let every breath of yours give expression to it. The mantra is: Do or Die.'

(Above): Mahatma Gandhi pictured with Sarojini Naidu in 1942. A strong supporter of Gandhi, Sarojini Naidu was a poet and political activist for civil rights and women's emancipation and one of the leading figures in India's struggle for independence.

It's a speech based on pacifist principles rather than a gung-ho sabre rattle, and when I first discovered it, I wondered how I might connect it to the greatest impact on my father's life during his time there – whether he would 'Do or Die' when it came to love.

Malaria is a disease that re-occurs so since Bertie could not rejoin his regiment on active duty, he was then attached to Force 316 which was the super-secret Chindits force – a guerilla warfare outfit under Major-General Orde Wingate – that operated deep behind enemy lines. It was here that he was given charge of the Map Room to ensure that Chindits were supplied with the best maps that could be found or produced for the area into which they would be parachuted.

Noreen Eagles had just joined the WAC-I (Women's Auxiliary Corp - India) as a second lieutenant and found herself in that same map room, reporting to Captain Bertie Gelardi. I think he was smitten from the get-go. Of course, nowadays this would be considered an inappropriate liaison as today to make advances to a subordinate would be deemed sexual harassment. But this was wartime in a very different era and there was Noreen. My mother. A contemporary studio photograph shows her in a polka-dotted dress with a string of small pearls, a gentle smile and warm expression, and I can understand why Bertie would have found her so lovely: she looks so kind and so at ease. Was there immediate mutual attraction?

Although there might have been, my mother was in a position many women found themselves in – she was actually betrothed to a man in the forces from whom there had been no word for a long, long time. His name was Malcolm and it later transpired that he had been captured by the Japanese in Singapore. Word came from him eventually but it's believed that he died, as did so many, in a POW camp or on the Burma railway.

But at that time, people moved on quickly – or it certainly seems that way – with the government stressing that individual losses and sacrifices had been for the greater good and should be borne privately. Whatever my mother might have felt, she and my father married in Srinagar, Kashmir on 24 July 1943, less than a year after meeting. Bertie had taken her to celebrate their joint birthdays at the Dal Lake when he proposed, a fantastically romantic setting, the surrounding hills reflected perfectly in its still waters, and Noreen agreed provided that he could arrange it immediately. He did so within twenty-four hours, taking witnesses from the street for the ceremony itself. 'Do or Die' indeed.

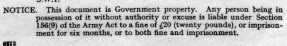

(Above): Bertie in India, where he met and later married Noreen Eagles, a second lieutenant in the Womens Auxiliary Corps of India (Top Right). Bertie was demobbed early in 1946 by which time he had attained the rank of major (Right).

Army Form X212

## RELEASE CERTIFICATE
### EMERGENCY COMMISSIONED OFFICERS—REGULAR ARMY
### (CLASS "A" RELEASE IN U.K.)

(1) T/Major. B.C. GELARDI. (130786)

East Yorkshire Regiment.

The above-named has been granted (2) 97 days' leave commencing 11 Nov 45 and is, with effect from 16 Feb 46 released from military duty under Regulations for Release from the Army, 1945.

Uniform may be worn during leave, except in Eire, but will not be worn after leave has expired, except as may be specially authorised.

As an officer holding an Emergency Commission in the Regular Army he will be placed on the Unemployed List from the effective date of release, with liability to recall to military duty until the end of the present emergency.

During the continuance of the emergency officers will notify in writing any change of permanent address to the Under Secretary of State, The War Office, to whom applications for permission to leave the United Kingdom will also be made.

By Command of the Army Council,

The War Office
AGI (Officers, D)
16 JAN 1946
initials

IF FOUND. Please enclose this certificate in an unstamped envelope and address it to the Under Secretary of State, The War Office, London, S.W.1.

NOTICE. This document is Government property. Any person being in possession of it without authority or excuse is liable under Section 156(9) of the Army Act to a fine of £20 (twenty pounds), or imprisonment for six months, or to both fine and imprisonment.

6273

By the end of the war, Bertie had been promoted to the rank of major. He returned to England where he was demobbed early in 1946 and then he set about finding a position again. Thousands of men were returning to civvy street after years away, links had been broken, the employment market was in spasm. Everyone needed work but picking up where each person had left off was impossible. Even a man with Bertie's experience couldn't just walk into a prominent role.

The Britain to which Bertie returned was a very different place to that which he had left some years earlier. Radical social changes were on the way, spearheaded by the Beveridge Report of 1943 which called for the establishment of a welfare state, and a National Health Service. The General Election of 1945 saw Winston Churchill – the man who had led Britain to victory against the Nazis – rejected in favour of a Labour Government under Clement Atlee. Clearly there was a post-war desire for a more egalitarian society which meant that the luxury hospitality sector found itself distinctly out of kilter with the prevailing concerns of a society which was rebuilding and renewing its outlook. The austerity of the war years would continue and rationing wouldn't end until 1954. The country had to nurse itself back to health.

(Below): Bertie first worked at the Edward Hotel in Durban in 1947 where he started as a cellarman. Soon he was promoted to assistant manager and later, after a spell at Luthje's Langham Hotel in Johannesburg, he returned to the Edward as general manager in 1955.

But there was more for Bertie to consider. Noreen didn't want to make a life in Britain! Her experience of the colonial British in India caused her to baulk at the idea. Instead, she and Bertie had discussed beginning married life in a country with opportunities, such as Australia, but Bertie didn't have the required qualifications for emigration there. However, on his return to England from India he had

stopped off in South Africa and realised that it was a country that not only offered similar opportunities, but which would welcome them with open arms. Their minds were made up.

The plan was for Bertie to prepare a home there for his wife and baby Peter, and he did so, buying a piece of the desert in Little Karoo, a region north of Cape Town. Farming wouldn't be that much of a stretch for an ex-army officer and hotelier, surely? A four-wheel drive Land Rover was a necessity for the rugged land, which Bertie acquired by borrowing money. This in itself was a post-war innovation, as the principle of borrowing and paying back long term became not just possible, but positively acceptable.

In the six months Bertie was in South Africa alone, Noreen had been trying to acquire a passport. She was eventually granted what is known as an Indian Empire passport on 1 July 1946. It records her and Peter as British subjects rather than citizens. As far as can be ascertained, Noreen didn't possess a birth certificate and her date of birth records her as nine years older than she was. It could have been just be a clerical error, but whatever the reason, it allowed her and Peter to reach Cape Town in late in November 1946.

(Above): Noreen in South Africa in the late 1940s. Sadly not even her charms were sufficient to make a success of a trading venture involving poorly-performing golf balls.

They tried to make a go of the farm and my uncle Arthur, also demobbed, set up a business trading in goods difficult to source after the war. These included, of all things, golf balls, and Noreen was persuaded to sell them. Rashbrooke Golf Balls. If the photograph of her is indicative of her charm, she certainly had more than either Bertie or Arthur, so they were half-way to success. That is, until the moment came to prove the product itself, when a potential buyer compared his own golf ball to the Rashbrooke by bouncing them both off a stone floor. The real golf ball bounced perkily three feet into the air whereas the Rashbrooke merely rose a leaden six inches. Noreen's charm wasn't enough to save the day and the event was memorable for her burning, tense embarrassment. When Bertie was tracked for loan repayments for the Land Rover, the farming project fizzled out too. There was nothing else to do but move on.

(Top): Proof that Bertie's knowledge of the hotel business and innate abilities were appreciated as early as 1948 came when he was promoted to assistant manager at the Edward Hotel. (Above): A contemporary Edward Hotel luggage label.

My grandfather Giulio, ever resourceful, rescued them, and it seems so obvious to us now that it should be so. Of *course* it was the answer. Bertie was a hotel man and he needed to exploit his years of experience. Giulio wrote to a friend who owned the Hotel Edward in Durban and he in turn wrote to Bertie. Although he wasn't able to offer him a position similar to what he had been accustomed to before the war, he could offer him something: cellar man. Bertie didn't have the luxury of waiting around for the right job – he had to support his family and so he gladly accepted the lowly role. In the event it turned out to be absolutely the right thing to do because not long after, the assistant manager position came up and Bertie was there to take it immediately. It allowed him to buy a place just outside Durban and he and Noreen were on their way, so to speak.

The intervening years had been hard but Bertie was back in the business he loved and he never looked back. Now he was settled, he implored Giulio and Piera to join him in South Africa, where they could enjoy their retirement and grandchildren, those that had been born and those yet to be, including me.

Sadly that imagined life in the South African sun and the joy of sharing a gradual twilight, wasn't to be. As romantic as Giulio and Piera's beginnings had been, their truly magical bond was tragically broken when Piera died in September 1950. I don't know quite how difficult it was for Giulio to make the decision to join Bertie and his family alone, but after Piera's death, he carried her in his heart for the rest of his days.

The way he 'talks' to her in the diaries he wrote as he sailed on the *Carnarvon Castle* in November 1950 to South Africa is deeply affecting. So soon after losing her, too. No

(Left and Above): Giulio sailed to South Africa to spend his retirement with Bertie and Noreen. But when he fell ill in 1954 he returned to London to ensure he would be laid to rest alongside Piera in the Brompton Cemetery.

wonder he should write that he 'felt such a coward running away' from her, and that his heart's beating 'choked the words in (his) throat'.

And, as if to stress the strength of love Giulio and Piera shared, when he was taken ill in 1954, Giulio asked to return to London and be buried with her in the Brompton Cemetery. United always and forever. Giulio had spent the final three and a half years of his life with his son's family and Piera had lived the whole time through him too.

By the time I was born in 1953, Bertie was running Luthje's Langham Hotel in Johannesburg. In Madden Cole's slim *Room in the Inn: The Story of Johannesburg Hotels*, the cover of which replicates an advertisement for the verandaed Heath Hotel, it is described as 'stately but conservative' and its gracious atmosphere made it popular with wealthy farmers whose wives and daughters 'stayed there during their shopping expeditions to the city.'

A little later, Bertie returned to the Edward Hotel after he was appointed general manager and the family moved back to Durban, now with my sister Donna added in December 1954, to a large single-storey apartment on the second floor of the hotel's annexe, with balconies over Marine Parade and the beach recreation grounds. The Hotel Edward was a return to what Bertie had been used to pre-war.

(Below): Bertie in his office at Luthje's Langham Hotel in Johannesburg.

There were themed rooms: The Causerie was a dinner-dance ballroom where guests were entertained by Mr Loni's Orchestra; The Penny Farthing would be a showcase for the pianist and raconteur Peter Maxwell; Bill Williams performed in *The Hansom Cab*.

Having managed two of South Africa's finest hotels, Bertie became director of the Amalgamated African Hotel Group, which also included The Dawson in Johannesburg, The Elizabeth in Port Elizabeth, Deal's Hotel in East London and The Riviera in Vereeniging – some of the very best hotels in South Africa.

Not content with those responsibilities, Bertie threw himself into three new ventures at this time. The first of these was the unimaginatively named 'Langham-Edward Group Hotel Representation Scheme' of which he was appointed director. Its purpose

(Top, Above and Left): Luthje's Langham Hotel in Johannesburg was opened by W. Luthje in 1906, then extended in 1916. When Bertie was there in the early 1950s it was one of the finest hotels in the city.

was to provide 'a service both to the South African travelling public and to the travel organisations of Southern Africa' by offering the hotel's clientele information on and recommendation of hotels 'of the highest standing overseas.' The scheme was known as '*The Leading Hotels of the World*'. The organisation that Bertie set up was designed to boost business within the South African hotel group but also to recommend selected overseas hotels to its clients – presumably in the hope and expectation that those overseas establishments would, in turn, recommend the Langham-Edward Group hotels to their own clients. This was remarkably long-sighted, though not unique, as a group of European hotels including the Negresco in Nice, the Mena House in Cairo and the King David Hotel in Jerusalem had formed a group of thirty-eight members in 1928 known as *The Luxury Hotels of Europe and Egypt*.

It was not until 1978 that the organisation acquired the name by which it is still known today, *The Leading Hotels of the World*. Now it represents some 430 independent luxury hotels right around the globe.

Bertie's second innovation was launching the first Salon Culinaire of South Africa, an event aimed at boosting the image of South African

(Above): After being appointed director of the Amalgamated African Hotel Group, Bertie was involved in a number of innovations including setting up a Hotel Representation scheme known as the Leading Hotels of the World, organising a light-hearted Waiters Race Meeting in support of charity (Opposite Page Above) and launching the first Salon Culinere to boost the image of South African Cuisine (Opposite Page Below).

cuisine through a new series of awards. Bertie headed the organising committee and hosted the event which was held at the Carlton Hotel in Johannesburg in November 1960.

And the third? This was a little more light-hearted, as Bertie took up the role of Chairman of the Organising Stewards of the annual Durban Waiters' Race meeting, put on by the Hotel Association of Durban and District to raise funds for the Cato Manor Appeal Fund, a local charity. A parade ring, members' enclosure and track along Durban's Lower Marine Parade were set up and an official programme printed.

Four races were held, culminating in the prestigious Waiters 'July' for the Athlone

Supplement to "The National Hotelier", March, 1961

*Salon Culinaire, 1960*

The South African Breweries Limited has pleasure in sponsoring this supplement, which includes sixteen full-colour pictures of a selection of dishes exhibited at the Salon Culinaire presented in Johannesburg recently by the South African Institute of Hoteliers.

The Salon Culinaire was an outstanding success and reflected great credit on the organisers and exhibitors. It fully achieved its objective in enhancing the reputation and prestige of the South African hotel industry.

Although it was a national event and attracted exhibitors and visitors from many major centres, unfortunately there were hundreds who were not able to attend. For the benefit of these, and for the hotel industry as a whole, the Directors of the South African Breweries Limited have decided to sponsor this supplement and hope it will be of interest, benefit and encouragement to all South African hoteliers.

*Sucking Pig Garnished—Section of Collective Cold Buffet.*

Floating Trophy, in which waiters had to race carrying a tray with an empty bottle and a full glass of water. The rules were simple: No bumping and boring. No holding the glass or bottle with the free hand and contestants had to finish with enough water in the glass to reach a prescribed mark.

Bertie threw himself into these varied roles at a time of a great changes within the country's history – changes which the ever-observant Giulio had predicted some years before.

Apartheid was about to culminate in the Sharpeville Massacre of 1960, when crowds gathered outside a police station without the pass books they were legally obliged to carry. The tension between the crowd and the police exploded when the police opened fire, leading to the deaths of sixty-nine people, with hundreds more injured. Clearly South Africa was now becoming a dangerous place to live.

Three separate pieces of legislation had contributed to the instability: the Prohibition of Mixed Marriage Act (1940), the Immorality Amendment Act (1950) and the the Population Registration Act (1950), which categorised people broadly as 'Black', 'White' 'Coloured' and 'Indian'. My mother Noreen and Bertie realised that it was untenable for them to bring up their children in such a rigid and authoritarian environment.

Escape would be to a position for Bertie at the Fontainebleu Hotel in Miami Beach. He stopped off in London to visit family and, attending a cocktail party, was introduced to Charles Forte, who at this time owned a number of restaurants and cafés. Bertie continued to Miami and stopped off in London again on his way back, by which time Forte had developed a business idea which needed my father's expertise.

Forte had already taken his first steps into the hotel world with the acquisition of the Waldorf Hotel in London in 1959 but he wanted this side of the business to grow – and for that he needed someone with a solid hotel background to help him chart his expansion route. That man was my father, Bertie Gelardi, who would move from South Africa to London and forego – for the time being – his planned life in the United States of America.

Looking at photographs of my father and Forte, I'm struck by how alike they are apart from the obvious difference in height – my father was six foot while Charles Forte was just five foot six inches. But both had swept back hair, neat moustaches, and strong noses, and I wonder

whether they might have seen a little of the other in themselves.

Forte's entrepreneurial drive had started in 'milk bars' in London, and moved into catering and hotel businesses, culminating with the purchase of the Café Royal in 1954. The message Bertie sent from the Langham Hotel, Johannesburg to Forte at the Café Royal is an 'Overseas Telegram - Buitelandse Telegram' English/Afrikaans form, capitalised 'ACCEPT POSITION AS OFFERED WRITING REGARDS GELARDI' and signed loopily in fountain pen ink.  To which the reply is 'YOUR 3 LETTERS RECEIVED STOP GLAD APPOINTMENT ACCEPTED WRITING REGARDS CHARLES FORTE'.

One of the letters to which he refers, dated 26 January 1961, is an insight into the very early thoughts Bertie was formulating, after his success in South Africa:

(Above): The Fontainebleu Hotel on Miami Beach, where Bertie had planned to start a new life after leaving South Africa. In the event, he met Charles Forte in London while on his way to the USA and that meeting would lead to a job offer (Below).

# Sharpeville Massacre Affects the Family

It was the Sharpeville Massacre of 1960 that first started my father Bertie and mother Noreen thinking that South Africa may not be the best place to be bringing up a family. The infamous events started to unfold when the Pan-Africanist Congress (PAC), which had split from the African National Congress (ANC) organised a series of demonstrations against apartheid in general and in particular, the Pass Laws, which required citizens to carry reference books ('Passes') at all times. Some 20,000 congregated near the police station at Sharpeville, south of Johannesburg.

The police claimed they were stoned by the crowd so they opened machine gun fire, killing 79 and injuring some 180 including 50 women and children. As a result, international condemnation of apartheid increased and a state of emergency declared in South Africa, with both the PAC and ANC outlawed.

Nearly 10 years earlier, back in 1951, Giulio's diaries show us once again just how knowledgeable and observant he was of the world around him. 'White man has discovered but has not conquered Africa – it still belongs to the native Africans', he wrote. 'Its earth; its diamonds; its gold – white men of many tongues have exploited its soil and its mines and have built up gaudy towns, turned huts into pretentious mansions, run fast in flashy motorcars and dressed in clumsy clothes. Their women, decked with

sparkling stones flock to the opera and wine and dine in vulgar inns, attended to and humbly served by the black man.

'But they are ten to one stronger, the sons of Chaka, Dingaam and Cetawayo, and they are no longer dreaming of the Great Fish River. They are biding their time, building up a national conscience which may well spell the death knell of apartheid'.

In many ways the Sharpeville Massacre did herald the beginning of the end of apartheid, in that it resulted in widespread condemnation around the world and the increasing isolation of South Africa. Eventually, after Nelson Mandela's release from prison on Robben's Island in 1990, he and President F.W. de Clerk negotiated the final abandonment of all apartheid laws in 1994. It was no coincidence that newly-elected President Nelson Mandela chose to sign South Africa's new constitution into law at Sharpeville.

(Left): 79 were killed and many more injured during the infamous Sharpeville Massacre. It started as a protest against Apartheid (Right) and the hated Pass Laws. Many years later Apartheid's abolition was agreed between Nelson Mandela and F.W. de Klerk seen here at the World Economic Forum in 1992.

(Right): Meeting Charles Forte in London was to radically change Bertie's career, as instead of moving to Miami as planned, he accepted Forte's offer to head up a new division of the Forte Group to develop a motor lodge business to serve the needs of the increasing number of car owners in the UK.

'The idea was simplicity itself and arose from the fact that we had an unproductive area – a lounge which was not being used – in a good position in the Edward Hotel, Durban.

'I converted this lounge into a speciality room decorated – by our maintenance crew – in an old London style, circa 1890. A good piano entertainer was engaged from London and he sat at the piano and sang speciality songs, popular songs, cracked jokes, commented on the affairs of the day, led community singing and generally entertained the guests. He had instructions that he had to be at the piano from 8pm to 12 midnight with only a couple of short breaks in order to keep the atmosphere of the room alive. There was no dancing.

'As far as food is concerned, we only served plain and simple dishes in tune with the atmosphere of the room, such as fish and chips in the *News of the World*, chicken in basket, sausage and mash, etc. The waiters were dressed in short sleeves. There were checked tablecloths on the tables and the room was lit by candlelight. There was no cover charge but prices of food and drinks were inflated. This room was so successful that it is still running now five years later and we have, as artists of the right type became available, opened rooms of this character in our hotels in Johannesburg and Cape Town. Often we have all three rooms in Durban, Cape Town and Johannesburg functioning at the same time.

It might seem somewhat strange that fish 'n' chips and bangers 'n' mash should be so popular in genteel surroundings, but why not? I have no doubt that they would have been very good manifestations of those dishes, rather than the ubiquitous versions in pubs throughout the UK in the 1960s and 70s.

The letter continues: 'We have at present under contract a really top rate entertainer for this type of work who is packing the room full at the Edward every night'. Bertie doesn't name him, endorsing him instead and outlining the threat of losing him to someone else:

'You are most probably wondering why I am wasting your time mentioning this to you now, when it could easily wait until I joined your organisation. The reason is that I have just heard that Vic Oliver (who was appearing recently for us in Durban at the Edward) has heard him and so has Henry Sherek who was staying at the Edward, and they were both so impressed that they are considering opening a special room for him in London'.

And here is the crux: 'I have this entertainer under contract with our company until June, so if you could let me know whether you would consider starting a room of this sort I could contact him immediately and discuss terms. We are paying him £300 a month plus room and

(Below): We do not know for certain but it is very likely that the entertainer that Bertie suggested should come to London was Peter Maxwell. He first performed at the Edward Hotel in 1958 and was still entertaining there until 1996.

*The One Hundredth Performance in the "Penny Farthing" — The Edward, Durban, 1959*

It is with much pleasure that we welcome Peter Maxwell to the Causerie for his "Farewell Performance" prior to his world tour.

Peter's career in South Africa started here at the Edward and it is perhaps fitting that his farewell performance should be held in the same venue.

A lot of water has passed under the proverbial bridge since he first opened here. Peter has gained a few pounds in weight, a new whistle and flute, and a host of friends throughout the length and breadth of South Africa.

We know that we are expressing the sentiments of his friends gathered here this evening when we say:

"Thank you, Peter, for the many hours of fun and entertainment which you have provided. Our best wishes for the success which we know will come your way . . . and hurry back to Durban soon !"

O L A Y !

**Programme**

*Dining and Dancing*

8 p.m. to 11 p.m.

*Peter Maxwell*

11 p.m. to midnight

*Dancing*

Midnight to 12.30 a.m.

*Peter Maxwell*

12.30 a.m. to 1.30 a.m.

*Dancing till Dawn*

Fresh Orange Juice and Bacon and Eggs will be served from 2 a.m.

full board but I think he would want more like £500 - £600 in London or else a salary of say £400 plus a commission on takings'.

Bertie is merely bringing success with him, noting the competition and stepping in before they can make a move. Although the entertainer isn't mentioned by name, Peter Maxwell seems to me the most likely man, whose antics were noted for keeping the room musically and comedically engaged.

Using Vic Oliver and Henry Sherek to endorse him would have really pushed Forte to act. Oliver was a fantastically popular actor at the time, married to Winston Churchill's daughter Sarah, and so well-known at the time that he was the first guest on Roy Plomley's *Desert Island Discs* on the 29 January 1942. Sherek, meanwhile was a theatrical manager responsible for producing T. S. Eliot's plays, *The Cocktail Party*, *The Confidential Clerk* and *The Elder Statesman*. Bertie couldn't have found better references.

Bertie's move is reported in a whole page spread of the *National Hotelier*, March 1961, the 'official organ of the Federated Hotel Associations of southern Africa and the South African Institute of Hoteliers'. Headlined 'LEADING S.A. HOTELIER TO JOIN FORTE GROUP IN BRITAIN', it gives his full name Albert Charles Maria Gelardi and describes him as 'one of the most experienced hoteliers to work in South Africa since the war'.

In the accompanying photograph, Bertie is distinctly proud and happy, immaculately turned out with a perfectly straight polka-dotted tie and three-peaked handkerchief in his suit pocket. He looks set for the move. Whilst it would have been an upheaval for Bertie, he would not have been as worried or apprehensive as the rest of his family. London was familiar to him. Britain was familiar to him. For the rest of the family, though, it was a big step into the unknown, but again the Gelardis put on their coats for another adventure.

The article goes on to describe Bertie's new venture, heading up a new division of the Forte Group, 'branching out in hotels and motor lodge hotels'. The plan was that he would start with a three-month preparatory trip to America 'studying the running of this new type of hotel' before establishing such premises 'outside London and Coventry'.

This was the time of the birth of motorways in Britain: the first section near Preston, now part of the M6 had opened in 1958 while the first

The National Hotelier, MARCH, 1961

# LEADING S.A. HOTELIER TO JOIN FORTE GROUP IN BRITAIN

**M**R. ALBERT CHARLES MARIA Gelardi, one of the most experienced hoteliers to work in South Africa since the war, leaves early next month to fill an important post with the Charles Forte Group in Britain.

Operational Manager of the Amalgamated Hotels Group, he relinquishes this post along with chairmanship of the Transvaal Branch of the South African Institute of Hoteliers, the vice-chairmanship of the S.A.I.H., and executive membership of the Hotel Association of the Transvaal.

Mr. Gelardi came to South Africa in 1946 to manage the Grand National Hotel, Johannesburg, for Mr. L. P. Morelli but, on arrival, found that Mr. Morelli had sold the hotel to African Caterers Limited. However, there was a proviso that Mr. Gelardi would be manager for at least one year.

At the end of this period he joined the Amalgamated Hotels Group as assistant-manager of the Edward Hotel at Durban. After two years he was appointed assistant to Mr. David Lister, General Manager of the group, and then became operational manager.

### Early Training

Mr. Gelardi was mostly based at the Langham Hotel, Johannesburg, but spent a further period at the Edward Hotel while it was being modernised.

Born in London, Mr. Gelardi had his early training in Paris (Prince de Galles), Le Touquet (Hermitage), Berlin (Eden and Esplanade), London (Savoy and Claridges) and New York (Waldorf-Astoria).

While in America he was appointed assistant-manager at the Broadmoor Hotel, Colorado Springs, and went on to hold the similar post at the Park Lane Hotel and Ambassadors Hotel, both in New York. He left America to join the British Army and came to South Africa at the end of the war.

His late father retired in South Africa after being General Manager of Claridges

Mr. Dino Tommasini, manager of the Carlton Hotel, Johannesburg, bids bon voyage to Mr. A. C. M. Gelardi, operational manager, Amalgamated Hotels Limited. Mr. Tommasini succeeds Mr. Gelardi as chairman of the Transvaal Branch of the South African Institute of Hoteliers.

and the Savoy in London, and the Waldorf Towers in New York.

The Charles Forte Group, which Mr. Gelardi is joining, is the second biggest firm of caterers in Britain, and they hold the catering concession at London Airport. They are now branching out in hotels and motor lodge hotels.

For the group's Motor Lodge Development Company, Mr. Gelardi will initiate motor lodge hotels outside London and Coventry. Beforehand he will spend about three months in America studying the running of this new type of hotel.

The motor lodge hotel has become most popular in America and most of the big groups are operating in this field.

Sited on the outskirts of cities, the hotels pay cheaper taxes and can offer better value for money than the city establishments. Most hotels are handy to public transport and motorists do not take their cars into the crowded cities.

The hotels to be built near London and Coventry will each have more than 100 rooms and restaurants, bars, etc. Depending on their popularity they may be the first of a Forte chain.

### Farewell Message

Mr. Gelardi said that this type of hotel would be sited at Wynberg (about seven miles on the Pretoria side of Johannesburg) if built in the Witwatersrand area.

In a farewell message, Mr. Gelardi, who was largely responsible for the success of the Salon Culinaire held in Johannesburg last November, said that he hoped that the S.A.I.H. would make a regular feature of such events in view of the interest raised and prestige gained from the first exhibition.

(Right and Below): Alongside the opening of the first motorways in the UK came the development of motorway service areas, providing fuel, restaurants and lodgings for motorists. Charles Forte was one of the first to recognise the opportunities, which lead him to develop the impressive Newport Pagnell Services on the M1 motorway.

full motorway, the M1, opened in 1959. Motorways and the rapid increase in car ownership provided a new freedom to travel and Forte's new hotels were visions of this future, planned to be built on sites just outside city centres where people would be close to public transport and would have no need to take their cars the final mile into crowded city centres.

After seeing for himself how these motel-style establishments operated in the United States, Bertie returned to England and started surveying possible sites for Forte's new British Motor Lodges. He also organised a mock-up room to be constructed, furnished and decorated for the board's approval and then went on to open the first Motor Lodge near Oxford.

Effectively it was a massive service station with a motel attached – the Excelsior Motor Lodge which sported a drive-through covered reception area and a swimming pool. Also on site was an Autogrill restaurant, 24-hour café and 350 parking spaces. In many ways it was very similar to the motorway service areas that Forte was also developing, but the Oxford site near the A34 was nowhere near any motorways at the time it was built.

Bertie did not appear to spend long on the Motor Lodges project because soon after he joined Forte's the company started a rapid expansion into hotels – and this is why, I suspect, that Charles Forte persuaded Bertie to join his company. There was immense mutual respect between the two men, so much so that at meetings, Forte would introduce my father as 'Bertie Gelardi, the greatest luxury hotel man in the world'.

Interestingly, that reputation never faded within the Forte family, as many years later, after Lord Forte's passing (he was first knighted and later made a Life Peer), his son Sir Rocco Forte told my brother Michael 'Your father taught me more about the luxury hotel business than anyone.'

One of Forte's early hotel acquisitions was Alveston Manor near Stratford-upon-Avon. The historic old house boasts in its gardens the famous 'kissing tree' where William Shakespeare was supposed to have enjoyed his first kiss. It's also believed that *A Midsummer Night's Dream* was first performed in those gardens too.

Alveston Manor was turned into a hotel in the 1930s, then was used by the Canadian Army and Air Force during the Second World War before reverting to a hotel once hostilities ended. By the 1960s however, it was tired and in need of major rehabilitation, which Bertie oversaw to transform the building into a four-star hotel.

One of its attractions was that it hosted live performances of *A Midsummer Night's Dream* in the gardens each summer – and this provided me with perhaps my first ever experience of working in a hotel. Lots of casual (and inexperienced) labour was required to set up and run these alfresco performances and for a number of years my elder brothers were roped in to help out. And when I was old enough, I too went along, helping out where I could as part of the team that set up all the lights.

Now began a period of rapid, some might say breath-taking expansion for the Forte hotels division. As we have seen, Charles Forte anticipated the massive increase in travel that greater affluence in the post-war years would bring about. He already held the major catering concessions in the Heathrow Airport terminals and now he planned his first airport hotel. Having bought a site on the busy Bath Road directly opposite the entrance to the tunnels into Heathrow's terminal area, Forte delegated Bertie to plan, fit out, furnish and open the Excelsior Airport Hotel – soon to be followed by a second Excelsior Airport Hotel, this time in Manchester in the north of England.

(Below): One of Bertie's early responsibilities after joining Charles Forte was to oversee the renovation of the Alveston Manor Hotel.

*THIS is Britain's foremost jet-age hotel — standing at London Airport's main entrance on the motorway to London — welcoming the traveller with comfort, elegance and fine cuisine.*

The Excelsior was revolutionary in design because the plan from the outset was to attract passing motorists looking for a meal as well as to fill the 300 bedrooms. The architectural concept of what was originally planned to be called Fortes Airport Hotel – some of the original marketing materials still exist – was to have the catering and residential wings of the building almost entirely separate, though interconnected. It would have a twenty-four-hour restaurant and coffee shop service, a shopping area, car hire service and – this sounds quaint in today's world of mobile phones – a row of public phone booths in timber-clad cubicles!

As for the residential part, each room boasted its own bathroom – with an extra vanity unit in double rooms so two could wash at the same time when rushing to catch a flight – and a control panel operating the lighting, radio, television, background music and air conditioning. This doesn't sound special now but in 1964 in the UK it was quite something.

By this time, the Forte hotel group consisted of five properties – the Waldorf, Alveston Manor, the Forte Motor Lodge at Oxford and the two Excelsior hotels at Heathrow and Manchester. By 1970, just seven years later, following the merger between Forte and Trusthouse Group to form Trusthouse Forte (THF) there were nearly two hundred hotels in the UK including ten luxury hotels in London, plus eight Motorway Service Areas, fifty-two Little Chef roadside restaurants, three Excelsior Motor Lodges, thirty-six Henekey Inns, thirty-nine

(Above): Early marketing materials describe the new venture at Heathrow Airport as Fortes Airport Hotel but by the time the all-new 300-bed hotel opened in 1964 it was as the Excelsior Hotel Heathrow.

(Above): The Excelsior Hotel at Heathrow was opened in 1964 on a prime site on the Bath Road, directly opposite the twin tunnels leading to the airport's Terminal Buildings.
(Right): The Topping Out ceremony which Bertie took part in. Having planned what was then an ultra-modern hotel and overseen its construction, Bertie was then delegated to fit out and furnish the establishment.

Kardomah Coffee Houses and numerous other restaurants and businesses. For good measure there were also some twenty-eight luxury hotels overseas operated by Trusthouse Forte International Limited.

How could this extraordinary expansion have happened so fast? Even before the Forte-Trusthouse merger in 1970 Forte had been expanding rapidly, using its healthy profits from the catering side of the business to grow its hotel portfolio.

Bertie was at the forefront of the operation, taking over and operating the Frederick Hotels Group and rehabilitating the properties; taking over the Phoenicia and Imperial hotels in Malta and again organising their renovation, and then, in a move that astonished the hotel world, buying three of the finest hotels in Paris - the George V, the Plaza Athénée and the Hotel de la Trémoille. It was a truly audacious acquisition and one that initiated Forte's collection of five-star luxury hotels around the world. Bertie is characteristically modest about his role: 'I played a major role in the rehabilitation and operation of the George V and somewhat less of a role at the Plaza Athénée,' he said.

After that, Bertie was kept busy with further acquisitions in Mauritius and three hotels in Bermuda - the Bermudiana, The Belmont and Harmony Hall - each of which required renovation which was 'very successfully accomplished'. Bertie made it sound, well, simple. I wish such programmes of work could be completed in the time it takes to write those few words because in my experience, these were no small undertakings.

After the Trusthouse Forte merger, it was initially agreed that the UK division would be overlooked by Trusthouse and the

The rate of expansion of the Forte hotel business was breathtaking; Bertie was involved in the acquisition of the Hotel de la Trémoille in Paris (Top), and the Phoenicia overlooking Valetta in Malta (Centre). He also opened the Apollonia in Cyprus - here pictured with Charles Forte (Above).

international division by Forte; Sir Charles Forte as he was by then appointed Bertie joint director of the latter. Now he was also in control of the Sandy Lane in Barbados, Dona Felippa in Portugal, Reina Cristina in Spain and Vilamil in Majorca. More hotels were built or purchased, including the Excelsior in Hong Kong, the Apollo in Amsterdam, the Pegasus in Jamaica and Guyana, and the Pegasus Reef in what was then Ceylon. Although I realise that Bertie would have been delegating a great deal (he was *very* good at delegating!), each of these is a huge undertaking in itself and I am astonished at the multiplicity of skills he drew on to complete whatever tasks he had set for himself and others.

As so often happens, the THF merger did not go entirely to plan. Allied Breweries Limited, a British brewing conglomerate, launched an aggressive takeover attempt in 1971. It appeared that the majority of the THF board who were originally from the Trusthouse side were in favour of the Allied bid, including the then Chairman Lord Crowther, whom Charles Forte's son Rocco later claimed had actually encouraged Allied to make the bid. Forte was determined in his opposition: 'Now one thing I don't like is a hostile bid,' he said in an interview with the *New York Times* some years later in 1979. 'I've never made a hostile bid, so I resented one made against my company.'

Forte bought millions of pounds' worth of THF shares leaving himself financially strapped. It was an enormous – though calculated – risk, as had the share price fallen, Forte would have been ruined. In the event,

(Below): The Board of Trusthouse Forte in 1971, just before Allied Breweries made an aggressive takeover bid for the company. Charles Forte mounted a successful defence and the end result was the departure of the directors who had come into the merged business from the Trusthouse side, which left Forte in full control of the business.

(Above): One of Bertie's most notable achievement was the renovation of the Pierre in New York, transforming it into one of the city's most prestigious hotels.

his instincts and business acumen saw him through and his shareholding, now at 28 per cent, was enough to keep Allied, which had 21.4 per cent, at bay.

The end result was the mass resignation of the former Trusthouse directors, leaving Charles Forte at the helm of a new hotel and catering giant. At this time the company managed some 26,000 hotel rooms – but this was just the start.

While all these boardroom manoeuvrings were going on, Bertie was keeping busy in the international division, most importantly when in 1973 the company acquired the management contract of the Pierre Hotel, New York, as 'an excellent springboard to expand into the luxury hotel grade in the United States'.

Bertie moved to New York as president of the property, charged with making it into the top luxury hotel in the city. Imagine being instructed to go into a place and change it. Where does one start? A great deal of it would have been worked out beforehand, just as he had set out his ideas in that letter to Charles Forte when he was recruited to London.

By now, Bertie was *the* man to entrust with the undertaking. Just as he had refurbished The George V and the Plaza Athénée, Bertie set about a similar programme to transform the tired and neglected fabric of the Pierre into the luxurious surroundings which would make people want to visit and stay there. And again, my father modestly describes the process as being 'very successfully carried out'.

In a later note, however, it's clear that Bertie was well aware both of the success of the Pierre and of his part in that triumph: 'I need hardly dwell on the performance of the hotel since it came under my direction', he wrote. 'It is common knowledge that it rose to be one of the most prestigious hotels in the world and produced profits well beyond that anticipated when we took it over. It brought prestige to our company in the United States and is the reason why Trusthouse Forte was able to develop as rapidly as it has done in this country.'

A similar renovation was directed by Bertie at the Westbury on Madison Avenue, 'a middle-of-the-road-hotel when we took it over. It is now recognised as one of the very best and is being patronised by the highest-class clientele,' he wrote. As the company was busy on so many other projects in New York, the restaurant and shopping areas of the Westbury were not renovated until sometime later. However, predicted Bertie, 'When completed to the plans and scheme that I have devised it will be an outstanding hotel and extremely successful'. In fact, it is now no longer a hotel, but an apartment building.

One of Bertie's signature projects was the conversion of 'an old residential hotel on 69th Street and Madison Avenue' which had to be 'completely gutted and rebuilt'. This was to be New York's Plaza Athénée: 'In order to turn this into a luxury hotel, it would not suffice to refurbish and rehabilitate, it had to be completely gutted internally and rebuilt. This again was successfully carried out and the property is now a small exclusive top-class deluxe hotel'.

(Above): Bertie at work in New York. (Below): Plaza of Americas in Dallas. THF had the management contract to run the hotel side of the $100 million development and Bertie arranged for me – his son Geoffrey – to be appointed hotel manager, working under Paul Margetson who had been Bertie's PA at the Pierre Hotel.

He was responsible for a similar renovation at the King Edward Hotel in Toronto, after which it too became one of the leading hotels in the city. Other hotels in North America that he improved were the Plaza in Philadelphia, a 'second rate hotel when we took it over', the Tulsa Excelsior which 'has gained a good reputation' and the Pavillion in Miami, 'a magnificent hotel'.

As well as these renovations, Bertie had responsibility for the newly-built Plaza of Americas in Dallas, which, he said, 'has gained an excellent reputation since it was opened'. There is also an interesting

(Right): The Tulsa Excelsior was just one of the many hotels that Bertie was responsible for renovating as the Trusthouse Forte business in the USA expanded. By 1977 Bertie was appointed President of Trusthouse Forte Inc. (America), the position he held until his eventual retirement in 1984 at the age of 73.

note, presumably written in the late 1970s in which he refers to the Miami Springs Villas and the Travelodge International at Kennedy: 'These two hotels were handed over in disgraceful condition with reputations which discouraged business as they had been squeezed dry for the sake of profits over the last few years.' It demonstrates that the hotel business is not always an easy one. As Bertie dryly observed: 'It takes a long time to pull such hotels up and costs a lot of money.'

In 1977 Bertie was appointed president of Trusthouse Forte Inc (America), an appointment he held until his retirement in 1984. He was then seventy-three years old.

We celebrated his eightieth birthday at Claridge's on the 24 July 1991, and there are the family's signatures on the signed menu card, curling around the *Meurault Limozin, 1987* and the *Chateau Pichon-Longueville-Baron, 1981* vintages. A decade later the family again assembled at Claridge's to celebrate his ninetieth – two very Happy Birthdays indeed, in the hotel in which he'd spent his earliest years. Bertie had come around a full circle.

He had lived through most of the twentieth century, met and looked after some of the most notable people of the age, witnessed wonder and horror, and instilled into the family a powerful work ethic and determination to carry on, whatever life throws at you. I remember this now as I take stock of my own life and thank him for all the wonderful times we spent together in and out of hotels. Thank you Bertie for passing me that key.

(Top Left): Bertie and Noreen back in the UK following Bertie's retirement. (Left): Geoffrey and Bertie being welcomed back to Claridge's for Bertie's 80th birthday celebrations by then general manager Christopher Cowdray. The family would return ten years later for his 90th birthday.

## A LUNCHEON

TO

COMMENDATORE GIULIO GELARDI

THE FIRST HOTELIER IN THE WORLD
TO CONTROL TWO LUXURY HOTELS
3,000 MILES APART

AUGUST 26th, 1931

LONDON

---

### Vins

Cocktails

*Berncastler Anslese*
*1921*

*Veuve Clicquot*
*Dry England*
*1921*

*Fine Champagne*
*and*
*Liqueurs*

### Menu

*Caviar Frais d'Astrakan*
*Saumon Fumé*

*Suprême de Sole Claridge's*

*Grouse Rôti*
*Haricots Verts au Beurre*
*Pommes Chips*

*Mousse de Volaille Waldorf*
*Salade Beatrice*

*Quartiers de Pêches Astoria*
*Soufflé Glacé Savoy*
*Friandises*

---

### Vins

*Meursault Limozin, 1987*

*Château Pichon-Longueville-Baron, 1981*

### Menu

*Escalopines de Saumon Fumé*
*Tièdes en Salade de Premiers*
*Primeurs à la Moscovite*

*

*Consommé de Légumes aux*
*Lamelles de Champignons Sauvages*

*

*Filet d'Agneau de Lait Poêlé*
*Parfumé au Romarin et à l'Ail Douce*
*Haricots Verts Fine Fleur*
*Carottes Nouvelles*
*Pommes Nouvelles Rissolées*

*

*Gâteau d'Anniversaire*

*

*Café*
*Mignardises*

---

*Claridge's    Wednesday, 24th July, 1991*

### Wine

*Puligny Montrachet,*
*Gerard Chavy 1999*

*Nuits Saint Georges*
*Domaine de l' Arlot 1998*

### Menu

*Roast fillet of sea bass*
*with tomato and olive compote*
*scented with basil*

*Lamb cutlet soufflé Belle Epoque*

*Peas and broad beans*
*Fondant potatoes*

*Vanilla sponge birthday cake*
*with seasonal berries and coulis*

*Coffee, tea and herbal infusions*
*Petits fours*

Claridge's

---

Three luncheons at Claridge's, 70 years apart. (Top): In 1931 the lunch that was held in Giulio's honour when he took control of both Claridge's and the Waldorf-Astoria; lunch to celebrate Bertie's 80th birthday (Centre) and 90th birthday (Right).

# Chapter 8

# My Early Years in the Hotel Industry

I suppose it was inevitable that I would go into the hotel business – if only because my time at school was so similar to my father Bertie's. In his memoirs he admitted that while at Stoneyhurst he was never in the first division academically, but he had excelled on the sports fields – at rugby and cricket. If I'm honest, that just about sums up my time at St George's College, Weybridge where I never came top of the class but was a serious player in both the rugby and tennis teams. Despite my father's love for the game, cricket wasn't for me – it always seemed to be too slow and take too long, a bit like golf, which is perhaps why I've never seriously taken up that sport either. And in any case, I'm convinced that I'm still too young for golf!

(Below): My schooldays mirrored my father's: We both excelled more on the sports fields than in the classroom

It had been drummed into my grandfather Giulio by César Ritz that he had to get proper training and in turn he too had insisted that my father started at the bottom to learn every aspect of the hotel business. Now it was my turn and Bertie was a senior executive at Forte – which was precisely why he insisted I looked elsewhere for my basic grounding.

And so I found myself at the Sonesta Tower in Knightsbridge – now the Carlton Tower – where I started on the princely salary of £13.56 a week. My first job was stewarding, which meant washing dishes though I did have a more important role – ensuring that for each banquet function there were the right number of plates, knives, forks, glasses and all the rest. I was working late shifts so the evening before I would set up what is called a Queen Mary trolley, complete with everything required for the following day's events.

Needless to say, if anything was missed there was serious trouble and I admit that one day I forgot the gravy jugs for a very important function. It wasn't noticed by the chef or the head waiter until the last moment and the problem was that the gravy jugs were locked in the silver room and it took a good half hour to locate whoever had the key and get the jugs sent up to the kitchen. It messed up the function royally and I got all kinds of grief because of my mistake – and rightly so. But that is what happens when you put a seventeen year-old in charge!

(Below): The Sonesta Tower, where I first started my training, was not an elegant building but it was superbly positioned on Cadogan Place in Knightsbridge, close to Hyde Park and Harrods. It later became the Hyatt Carlton Tower and is now the Jumeirah Carlton Tower.

It just goes to show that it is the people in the back of the house that really make things work (or can really mess things up!) in the hospitality business. That is why a good manager has to know his or her stuff and has to learn to take care of those people because they are the ones who oil the cogs that make the machine work. Without them doing their job right first time and every time, things don't function. My early blunder was part of an essential learning curve for me – though very embarrassing at the time.

From stewarding I was moved into the kitchens, first in the hot kitchen and later into the cold kitchen. As the new boy I was given jobs such as turning potatoes. What this meant was that I was presented with a sack of potatoes and told to carve each into shapes with exactly seven edges – no more and no less.

I had been working on this for five or six hours before a large German sous-chef came over and on finding that not every one of my rather amateurish efforts was seven-sided, tipped the whole lot into the mashing machine. And I was told to start again. One learns quickly this way! You don't go home until it's done, and don't even think of asking for overtime!

(Below): The Chelsea Room was the best restaurant at the Sonesta Tower and in time I became responsible for its dessert trolley.

It was a costly lesson in attention to detail, but not all my training was quite so negative. I spent some time working with Robert Mey, who was a great pastry chef. My first job in his domain was to make five gallons of fresh fruit salad every morning, as well as the Chelsea buns, the Mont Blanc and the Black Forest cake, but once that basic work was done I'm grateful that he taught me how to pull sugar, how to work with chocolate and much more.

I worked twelve to fourteen hours a day, sometimes six days a week and never got overtime or time off in lieu. But I was learning all the time and working for a guy like that who really knew what he was doing was a great experience. Most importantly, I was having fun whilst also gaining invaluable knowledge.

The top restaurant at Sonesta Tower was the Chelsea Room, and in time I would be responsible for making everything on the dessert trolley. When I was working as commis waiter there, they usually put me on the dessert trolley: I already knew what was involved having made all the desserts while on the pastry team – and knowing your product enables you to sell it.

Sadly, knowledge does not protect you from practical jokers and I can't imagine what the clients must have thought the day I walked out into the restaurant with a live lobster attached to the back of my jacket – just one of the pranks that were regularly played on the most junior on the team!

(Below): The Grand Hotel et Tivollier in Toulouse. After a disaster in the kitchens I was moved to work in the bar.

I stayed at the Sonesta Tower for about a year, spending time in many departments including valet, bar, engineering and housekeeping, before moving to France and the Grand Hotel et Tivollier in the Rue de Metz, Toulouse. Again this was an interesting and important learning experience for me. The owners of this family owned hotel were known to a

colleague of my father's, which is how the connection was made. I had accommodation in the hotel and initially was put to work in the kitchens, on split shifts every day, which meant I would work in the mornings, go away for two or three hours and then return for the evening shift.

The chef was a hot-headed and sometimes aggressive man who thought nothing of throwing pots and pans across the floor at your ankles if he was unhappy with his underlings. On one occasion when especially unhappy with something I had done or failed to do, he actually punched me in the stomach. Not the sort of behaviour that would go down well today, but at the time I suppose it was par for the course. A slap on the back of the head was very common – and he didn't always need a reason for delivering it.

I will never forget the time that chef had been working on a pair of spectacular decorated salmon for two days. It was one of the staff's birthday and in between our shifts that day I suppose we may have had a couple of Ricards too many during our break. When we returned to the kitchen chef asked me to take the now completed salmon downstairs to the fridge and in my slightly tipsy state, needless to say I went flying.

Luckily the sous-chef who was a really nice guy came over and took charge. First of all, he sent me home: 'Go,' he urged. 'Chef will hurt you. I will take care of it,' and I gratefully took him up on his offer.

The upshot was, chef insisted that I never darken his kitchen again so I was moved to the bar, which was one of the best in Toulouse, managed by a great gentleman called Yves. He taught me how to mix cocktails, and how to deal with ice in the days before ice machines were in common use.

Essentially, what we had were large blocks of ice so bartenders had to use an ice pick to break off a piece, then run it under water to make it gleam and sparkle before putting it in the glass. Not very hygienic by today's standards but that is how it was done and it looked wonderful.

Working on the bar was a lot of fun though my French wasn't brilliant and I made a lot of mistakes, including on one occasion using wholly inappropriate language when talking to the owners' mother. It wasn't deliberate, it was simply that this 'Petit Anglais' as they called me, simply didn't understand the full meaning of some of France's more idiomatic expressions.

Another great thing about working behind the bar was that all the local night club owners were regulars so when we finished we could go to any nightclub we wanted, and never had to wait in queues outside or pay for our drinks, which made for a fine social life for an eighteen year-old.

Before long, however, I was back in the UK to start working at the London Hilton in 1974. I worked my way up from enquiries clerk – basically a mail boy on reception – to *chef de brigade*, responsible for room management.

This was where I first came to grips with the Witney System, a vastly complicated room management system, which fascinated me immediately. How do you know what's happening with this property's 509 rooms? The system was displayed on a wall, each room a slot into which a piece of paper recorded the guests' names. Each was colour coded and had a fold to indicate its status. Information included whether the room was clean or dirty, empty, full-rated, an upgrade, group booking, cash payer or complimentary, all vital information which was needed by accounting and the corporate office. The beauty of the Witney System was that the whole situation could be taken in almost at a glance – no computer screen is able to show this so simply: the bigger the system, it seems, the more difficult it is to find the information you need.

(Right): The London Hilton on Park Lane was first opened in 1963, a concrete-framed building designed by the architect William Tabler. It was not only Europe's largest hotel to be built post-war; it was also the first London building higher than St Paul's Cathedral. 101 metres (331 ft.) tall, it had 28 floors and over 509 rooms, many of them suites. It quickly became a popular venue for visiting travellers and businessmen.

It was while I was working a night shift here that a man in his mid-thirties wanted a suite which he stipulated had to be on a high floor – the twenty-fifth or above. The hotel had twenty-seven. Asked for a credit-card payment, he paid cash for a night-and-a-half in advance, which was recorded on the Witney board. At 3am security informed me that the guest had leapt to his death. It transpired that his plan had been so very deliberate that he had even brought tools with which to jimmy open the window. He landed on the ballroom roof on which his body had exploded on impact. He wasn't that much older than I was and I wondered what could have driven him to such drastic action. It reminded me, too, of Giulio's stories about the men ruined by the Wall Street Crash who had checked into hotels in New York, and jumped.

Other guests left behind different impressions of themselves. Middle Eastern guests often took over whole floors or a wing of the hotel. Some would trash the rooms, including burning the carpets with coals from fires they made in the middle of the rooms to smoke hubbly bubbly or hookahs – which also caused major smoke damage. Incredible as it seems now, they were happy to pay for the complete redecoration on their departure.

The Hilton, prominently positioned on London's Park Lane, was quite a hotel in those days – one of the capital's finest. And it was busy: quite apart from its 509 rooms, there was its fine restaurant and bar on the roof (which is now Galvin's), the 007 nightclub and Trader Vic's restaurant down below. There was never a dull moment working there.

My next move was to America. My father had arranged for me to enrol at the Cornell Summer School for three months and after that I joined the graduate management training programme at the Waldorf-Astoria where the director, Frank Wangerman, took me under his wing. Of course it had been arranged by my father Bertie and because I loathed the connotations of nepotism, I worked that much harder to be better than anyone else to prove that I was there on merit. The other trainees loved watching me mess up,nevertheless, we all did at some point. But I deliberately put myself out there, being gregarious and working hard and often volunteering to do extra shifts – as did all trainees.

Of course for me to be at the Waldorf-Astoria, where both my grandfather Giulio and my father had worked, was a memorable experience and a true privilege. Of the six of us on that year's management training course I was the only one who was not actually a graduate but I found myself in the company of a great bunch of very talented people: David Wilkinson who later became general manager of The Dorchester; Tom O'Connell who was food and beverage manager at the Savoy and then general manager at the Ritz; Richard Tannon, whose father owned the 21 Club; and Sharon White, head of HR for all of the Hyatt Group.

The Waldorf-Astoria was also where I first met Guenter Richter, my long time mentor who was influential in the development of my management style. Originally from East Germany, his was an extraordinary story. He worked on an East German cruise ship and visited many Russian resorts including Leningrad (now called St Petersburg) and Murmansk plus various Romanian and Bulgarian ports and even Cuba. All were communist countries so in Guenter's

**The only bar 007 would be seen dead in**

Merciless cold-blooded murder lurks in the doorway. That bowler belongs to Oddjob; the Beretta belongs to Bond. Don't panic. It's the 007 Room at the London Hilton, and all that lethal gear lies harmless behind a display case. Drinks to match the decor have been specially created for members of the international Bond cult. For example, the Goldfinger Cocktail, a concoction of 007 vodka, Cointreau, lemon juice and—least we forget—Goldwasser. Sip it while leaning against the actual Ft. Knox gold bars you saw in the film. There's eating, drinking, and dancing to a swinging group until 2.30 a.m. So live dangerously—phone Hyde Park 8000 and book a table at the 007 Room.

HILTON HOTELS IN
Amsterdam · Athens · Berlin
Cairo · Istanbul · Madrid · Orly
Paris · Rome · Rotterdam
Tehran · Tel Aviv · Tunis

Ring Hyde Park 8000 to make immediate reservations at any Hilton Hotel around the world or contact your travel agent.

GO INTERNATIONAL — STAY HILTON

(Opposite Page): Trader Vic's restaurant and the 007 Nightclub (Above) helped make the London Hilton one of the capital's most attractive nightspots during the 1970s and 1980s, visited by the Beatles, the Rolling Stones and many other celebrities of the day.

(Above): The Waldorf-Astoria's training programme was second to none and I was fortunate to get on it as I was the only one in my year who was not a university graduate. I found myself learning in the company of extremely talented people – most of whom went on to have stellar careers in the hotel and hospitality business including Bill Flynn (Third from Left), Sharon White (Fourth from Left), David Wilkinson (Sixth from Left), Jody Sclafani (Seventh from Left) and Meluda Shizuyo (Second from Right). I'm there (Third from Right), looking rather serious. Other co-trainees were Tom O'Connell and Richard Tannon.

words 'there was no chance to escape in these places!' However in 1964 a cruise was announced to sail from Gdańsk in Poland to Leningrad, Helsinki, Stockholm, Oslo, Copenhagen and back to East Germany. Once in Scandinavia, he and three other crew members managed to give their minders the slip and went to the West German Embassy to ask for political asylum. 'That sounds very easy but there was a lot of drama and anxiety involved,' he told me.

He had come to the US after graduating in hotel economics from the Hotel Management School in Heidelberg, Germany and then won a scholarship from Hilton Hotels Corporation to join their General Management Training Programme based at Cornell University. By the time I met Guenter, he was food and beverage manager at the Waldorf-Astoria and spoke five languages. Eventually after my own graduation I became his assistant, and he was a seriously tough cookie. He had told me three times not to leave a full ashtray on my desk when I left the hotel to go home at night. I forgot his instruction once again and the next morning my desk was gone – he had put me down in the basement and I had to work from there for the next two weeks. That was another lesson learnt. He was not only a great influence and mentor, but he also greatly helped my career as it was he who later got me into Rosewood. But that story comes later.

The mid-seventies were an extraordinary time to be a young man in New York. On the one hand there was most certainly a high level of crime, despite the fact that the city relied heavily on tourism. Its population was also growing fast every year, which applied yet more pressure to the social fabric of NY.

Yet my life was not at all representative of what was going on around me. I was earning just $96 a week and yet I lived in my father's three-bedroomed penthouse on the twenty-first floor of the Hotel Pierre, with an expansive terrace overlooking Central Park. Bertie was only in New York for three months of the year – the rest of his time he was resident in Bermuda – so I had the apartment mostly to myself. I was living like a king, so for me, life in New York was nothing short of wonderful.

(Above and Left): While training at the Waldorf-Astoria and earning a minimal salary, I was living in a 21st Floor suite at the Pierre Hotel!

I was spending a great deal of my down time with my fellow trainee Richard Tannen, whose father, as I said, was one of the owners of the 21 Club – obviously that was a great place for us to hang out! We also liked to go to Studio 54, founded by Ian Schrager and Steve Rubell. The phenomenon that is Nile Rodgers, the disco king, most accurately described the club's significance: 'Lots of clubs evoke a certain era – the Cotton Club, the Moulin Rouge, the Copacabana – but none of those did what Studio 54 did, where if you got in, you were a star, not just a person.' The great artist Andy Warhol described it as 'a dictatorship at the door and a democracy on the dance floor.' It wasn't a club as such, where once you got in you drank and danced the night away, rather it was an event, a constantly changing theatrical set of which guests were a part. A place where I could all too easily blow my $96 and more in a night and did on far too many occasions.

I was young and a bit wild… The club catered for a clientele who wished to leave the city well and truly outside of its doors. It was a short-lived venture, though, its owners Schrager and Rubell being charged for tax offences and jailed for twenty months. In 2017, when President Obama was pardoning or commuting the sentences of high-profile individuals such as the former intelligence officer Chelsea Manning, Schrager's name was almost unnoticed way down the list. After his life-defining Studio 54, incarceration and release, he became one of the founders of the 'Boutique Hotels' and lived what can only be described as an exemplary life; he is now recognised as one of the great hoteliers of the world.

(Below): Ruci Mazanelli, whom I first met at the Waldorf-Astoria when he was banquet manager. Our paths would cross again later in my career.

And as much as I was loving life in New York, I was still teased by my colleagues for my Britishness, and I was still very junior, and therefore fair game for all sorts of pranks. In other trades the newcomer might be sent to buy striped paint or a bucket of steam or a left-handed screwdriver.

I discovered the equivalent in the hotel business when the Waldorf was expecting a visit from the Queen, and I was assured that she needed her slippers changed by a British page boy, who would have to get down on his knees and use a footstool to perform this task. It was much the same when the Emperor of Japan visited a while later, when management insisted he would need a page boy outside his room twenty-four hours a day. Each time, the story would be sustained by very senior management until it was clear there was no time left to prepare such a thing, and sense would return and in the end I did not have to make a fool of myself though it was absolutely clear that I had already been suckered!

As part of my training, I was rotated through every department, and it was while I was working on reception at the Waldorf-Astoria Towers, that a man in his late fifties or perhaps early sixties introduced himself. 'Hi, I'm Ed Gelardi. Your grandfather Giulio gave me a job here as a bellboy.' It was my great uncle Gustave's son.

He was still there as head porter, having been first given a job there in about 1933-34 when he would have been the hotel boy you see in Hollywood films smartly dressed, a spear carrier behind the main actors. In the seventies he would have known the Towers as well as anyone, better perhaps even than the Secret Service guys who were apparently in permanent residence, engaged in almost constant surveillance. Anyone who was anyone, stayed at the Towers.

I loved my time at the Waldorf-Astoria. Not only did I learn a lot but I also made some great contacts - people whose careers would cross with mine in the future, and people who would become life-long friends. People like Rudi Mazanelli who was the banquet manager, a job almost as important as food and beverage manager at the Waldorf-Astoria (some would say more important!) because of the sheer size of the banqueting operation.

(Below): Banqueting was an enormous undertaking at the Waldorf-Astoria and some of the events it hosted were legendary. Just one example was the annual dinner held by the Explorer's Club, founded in 1904, and a serious scientific society that promoted exploration and field study around the world. its dinners were held to honour accomplishments in exploration and were famous for their adventurous and exotic cuisine.

HORS D'OEUVRES
*WILD BOAR
ELK
NORTH AFRICAN SHEEP
HIPPOPOTAMUS
BEAR
LLAMA
PEACOCK
RATTLESNAKE
VENISON TONGUE
MOUNTAIN OYSTERS
1,000 YEAR OLD EGGS
HARBOR SHRIMP (ASIATIC)
DRIED CUTTLE FISH
DRIED FISH LIPS
SEA CUCUMBER
CONCH
SHARKS' FIN
BIRDS' NEST
MUKTUK
MIPKU
HOUMA-HOUMA-NUKA-
NUKA-WAKA-WALLA

"FOLKS, WHAT WOULD YOU SAY TO SOME BANANAS?"

DINNER MENU

FRESH ASPARAGUS WITH PROSCUITTO VINAIGRETTE

SLICED SIRLOIN OF BEEF SAUCE POIVRE

BRAISED ENDIVE

CORN FRITTERS

RING OF COCONUT SHERBET WITH RHUBARB

COFFEE

The Explorers Club Annual Dinner
Grand Ballroom - Waldorf-Astoria New York - April 9, 1976

Frank Wangerman (seen on the left) got me my first major job in the hotel industry when he appointed me director of food and beverage at the Statler Hilton.

I and the other trainees worked two or three nights a month for him, helping where we could, because at the huge banqueting events another pair of hands was always appreciated. Later he was the man who hired me to work at Resorts International, so here was yet another very good contact I made at that iconic hotel.

By now I was twenty-three and my first 'big' job after training was at the 1,700 room Statler Hilton opposite Grand Central Station on Sixth Avenue where I was appointed director of food and beverage. In those days it wasn't regarded as the best neighbourhood. Frankly, I was out of my depth and I had to work even harder as a result.

Frank Wangerman gave me the position, so to others it just looked like another case of nepotism, though I preferred to believe I got the job because I had demonstrated a willingness to work hard. New York's money troubles and the public sector's constant battles with the unions, created issues within the hotel also.

The unions were a powerful presence and I frequently found myself in confrontation with them. I had many consultations with union leaders but Vido Peter, who was head of the union, was my PA Linda's boyfriend. My approach, for better or worse, was unorthodox. 'Tell Vido to be reasonable,' I'd say to her, 'or I'll get rid of you.' I wouldn't have, of course, but you could say that sort of thing in those days. Especially as we were good friends and she knew I was joking.

When I wasn't working or partying, I was playing rugby for New York. I'd been a fullback in the UK but here I played three-quarter. The team was a mixture of ex-pats and Americans, whose background in American Football meant they hit hard. We'd train on Saturday, play our match on Sunday and I'd turn up for work with a black eye or stitches and be expected to greet guests looking as if I'd been mugged. Since I wanted to be taken seriously at work I had to give up the sport.

My next step was another food and beverage position at the Arlington Park Hilton next to the Arlington Park Race Track, about ten miles out of Chicago, a cosier more boutique-style hotel, headed by a tough manager called Joe Kane. As much as I enjoyed the high life in New York, the move to Chicago was hardly a come down. I was moving on, gaining experience, ascending the ladder – following our family motto of *Avanti, Sempre Avanti.*

I rented a penthouse apartment with a wraparound balcony so I was still living comfortably. I arrived in September and the winter which followed was one of the worst ever, with snow drifts to the top of the balcony door for three months. In a similar apartment in the building opposite lived the rooms division manager, George Harrington, and we became great friends. He had an old 1960s Porsche sports car with only a few inches clearance from the ground, whereas I had an enormous gas-guzzling Cutlass Supreme sedan. Needless to say, during that winter it was the Cutlass that got us about town.

The next rung up the ladder was due to that friendship I had made when I was in New York with Rudi Mazinelli who was banquet manager of the Waldorf-Astoria while I was there. Later Rudi was made executive vice president of food and beverage at Resorts International in Atlantic City.

It was a massive operation and the hotel was being ripped off – thousands of dollars were haemorrhaging out of the food and beverages operation, which is why Rudi called to offer me the position of food and beverage manager.

He recognised that I had the youth, determination and enthusiasm to sort out

(Below): What was the Statler Hilton when I worked there in the 1970s, was built by the Pennsylvania Railroad in 1919 and called the Hotel Pennsylvania. It was renamed the Hotel Statler in 1949 when Statler Hotels bought the property, then renamed again in 1958 to the Statler Hilton after Conrad Hilton bought Statler Hotels. Hilton sold in 1979 when it became the New York Penta, then after major renovations, it reverted to its original name and is now once again the Hotel Pennsylvania.

the situation and make a difference. Rudi was a great politician who knew how to put an operation together and get the best out of people to achieve success. I would often drive him home after work to his wife Marianne, a wonderful Swiss lady who had been housekeeper at my father's Hotel Pierre, and invariably I was invited in for dinner with them both. Happily for me, Marianne was a great cook.

Atlantic City, 60 miles from Philadelphia and some 120 miles south of New York on the Atlantic seaboard, was first developed in the 1850s as a health resort and expanded rapidly during the early twentieth century. But the resort was headed for what looked like terminal decline until in 1976 New Jersey voters approved the legalisation of casino gambling in Atlantic City, making it the USA's first gambling town outside Nevada and a few Native American reservations.

(Below): Rudi Mazinelli and his wife Marianne, whose home cooking I greatly enjoyed.

The Resorts Casino Hotel opened in May 1978 in Atlantic City – the first casino hotel in the city. It was renamed the Resorts International Hotel the following year which is when I moved to take up Rudi's invitation, much to the chagrin of my parents.

I was to be in charge of 1,500 employees and responsible for food and beverage revenues in excess of $38 million. There were 300 staff in the kitchen alone. I was twenty-six years of age which meant that whenever I held a department head meeting, I was invariably the youngest at the table.

What I found was a complete shambles. Costs were through the roof at 38 per cent for beverage and food was at 60 per cent. I needed to act fast and decisively to bring these down, and within three months I had done so, reducing the beverage cost of sales to 20 per cent and the food cost of sales to 30 per cent. I put cameras in all bars and sacked anyone who was caught pilfering – which is putting it politely! Eventually, I was able to get the beverage costs down to 13 per cent and 24 per cent for food. It was an extraordinary turnaround.

The unions hated me and the Casino Control Commission love me. At one point there were twenty-three active union cases against me because of my actions. I was fortunate in my relationship with Bobby Lumio, the union treasurer, who I like to think of now as my union 'fixer', or at least the person who was able to smooth things between the union and what I needed to do for the business to run properly without chancers robbing the place so blatantly. There was more to it than that, though.

After I had been in Atlantic City for a year or so, I began receiving threats on my life in the form of written notes and phone calls saying 'Back off' or 'We know where you live.' My car tyres were slashed and the windows were bricked through on one occasion. All because I was stopping the most blatant rip-offs. I hadn't experienced any kind of intimidation before and I didn't really appreciate how serious it was. It was around this time that Bobby Lumio, who was then the union treasurer, befriended me.

We became good drinking buddies and, because I was an employer and he a union man, we always paid our own bills. It was still a dangerous friendship, as we'd discuss the union cases, which probably wasn't wise.

I think if my last name had not ended in an 'i' so I sounded Italian, I might have been treated differently by the union. Instead, I was

(Below): Atlantic City boomed during the Prohibition era and through the 1930s as a beachside resort which was well served by the railroads. It declined during the 1950s and 1960s but despite enjoying a major resurgence in the 1970s once gambling was legalised, but it could never seriously compete with the allures of Las Vegas.

referred to as *paisano* - a fellow countryman. Even though I considered myself very much English, using my Italian heritage was certainly useful at times.

There was another side to Bobby that I didn't know at that time, which became more apparent when he took me to Pat's Steakhouse in Philadelphia, where they reputedly served the best steak sandwich in America. Outside, everyone was pushed aside for us to enter, which I didn't think much of at the time, Bobby enjoying what appeared to be his popularity with friends. It was my housemate George Donohue, assistant head of security at Resorts International, an ex-state police officer, who told me. 'You don't know who you're dealing with. State police are watching you.'

He was right, I didn't realise what was going on. I thought, oh good, at least someone's taking notice of the threats. I *still* didn't get it. Bobby was connected, big time. He was first cousin to Angelo Bruno, who ran the Philadelphia mafia at that time. *My* drinking buddy, *my* good friend; although I knew he was well connected, I was totally unaware of how close Bobby was to organised crime.

At that time Local 54 was one of the most important unions in Atlantic City. As an official President's Commission on Organised Crime noted later in 1985: 'The history of corruption in this union predates the casinos, but the arrival of casino gambling signalled the start of a new quest for control of the Local.'

When I was at Resorts International, the union leader was Frank Gerace. He was appointed president of Local 54 in 1979 after the previous president, Ralph Natale was convicted and sentenced to thirty years for a variety of offences, including narcotics trafficking.

Gerace, who was later named in Senate testimony as a significant criminal associate of the Scarfo crime family, appointed a number of convicted criminals to prominent union positions, including Frank Materio, who was shop steward at the hotel. He came into my office one day to talk to me about security. I was very unpopular with the unions because of the cameras I'd installed which had caught numerous staff red-handed. So I thought that Frank Materio wanting to chat was just another meeting with a union official about yet another crooked worker. Not this time.

'We're worried about your safety,' he said, 'and I have a gift for you.' He slid a revolver across the desk. 'The cleanest gun you'll ever get. Filed off numbers, taped up handle and trigger so it won't take prints. Two rounds in the chest, walk away and drop the gun.' 'I'm not touching it,' I said. 'It's your funeral,' he replied, as he walked out, thankfully taking the gun with him.

When I reported it to security, they didn't want to create a 'situation' because it was the union. No-one, it seemed, wanted to mess with the union, especially where there was no real proof. And in any case, Frank could or would just deny the incident.

The tension with the union didn't just go away, however, and they tried another tactic to get rid of me. With the chef and the banquet manager, they spread a rumour that I was taking drugs and drinking too much. To make the story more salacious, they added that I was sleeping with some of the 600 cocktail waitresses. They recognised

(Below): When Bobby Lumio took me to Pat's Steakhouse and the crowds were pushed aside for us to enter, I started to realise exactly who I was dealing with – a leading figure in the Philadelphia Mafia.

that Rudi Mazinelli was the political animal and that I was the workhorse, believing that once I was out of the way, he would fall too.

Rudi called me. 'You have to go on holiday, now!' He thought I was about to lose my licence so wanted me out of the way fast. George Donohue knew that the whole story was nonsense and he and David Bellisle – who would become deputy director of security for the US Department of State – set about 'clearing' my name.

It was decided that my room-mate George Harrington and I would drive from Atlantic City to Atlanta and on to Los Angeles, two weeks together in his Datsun ZX, a very pretty sports coupé. Two weeks in any car is a challenge, but two weeks in this cramped car was going to be very challenging. You see, George kept everything immaculate. Everything. He would pin his towels so that they fell just so, had ashtrays you could use and ashtrays you couldn't. The same with his car. He had towels on the seats and the floor-wells, and silver foil on the dashboard to protect it.

'Jeez, George, we're going to be in this thing for two weeks!'

We made it to the west coast, and eventually a call came through that George and I could return to Atlantic City. We headed back to the city where I had had an amazing time, not least because the massive Show

Room at Resorts International hosted the likes of Frank Sinatra, Donny and Marie Osmond, Don Rickles, Barry Manilow, Dean Martin, Johnny Mathis and Diana Ross – the greatest stars of that era. It was a truly exciting time to be a part of the fast-growing resort.

And from a professional viewpoint, I also was responsible for an almost overwhelming food and beverage operation: our buffet restaurant used to do between 3,000 and 4,000 covers a day, and on top of that there were three 'gourmet' restaurants, one serving English cuisine, alongside Cappriccio's, the Italian restuarant and Le Palais, the French restaurant which were both outstanding, each being overseen by top New York chefs.

But it was definitely time for a change and now I was determined to move on, to further develop my career into general management and get out of food and beverage.

(Below): Atlantic City was a great place to live and work in the late 1970s but the time came for a move from the East Coast.

# Chapter 9

# Onwards and Upwards

Atlantic City had matured my management skills. It was the wild west of the hotel industry and there, all people seemed to care about were the casinos and volume of business – rarely about quality though having said that, Atlantic City did have some of the best restaurants on the east coast. In the early days the casinos would bus pensioners in from all over and charge them $5 for entry but a couple of years later with more competition in town, they would give them $5 in quarters, knowing that when they ran out and they would bet the last quarter of their own money. It was really not a pleasant environment watching elderly people lose everything.

I badly needed to get out of Atlantic City and get the Food & Beverage brand off my back and it was my father who helped make it happen. This would be the first and only time that I worked for Trusthouse Forte – Bertie was by then president of its operations in the USA – and he arranged for me to help open Plaza of the Americas in Dallas for which THF had the management contract.

This was one of two jobs I was offered which gave me the opportunity to get out of Atlantic City. One was food and beverage manager at the recently-opened Mansion on Turtle Creek, but I accepted the offer of hotel manager at Plaza of the Americas. I took it because it allowed me to get out of food and beverage and into mainstream hotel management.

Plaza of the Americas was an amazing $100 million complex, on a massive scale, with a skating rink in the middle, two towers and 247 rooms. It was owned by Toddie Lee Wynne, well-known for his share in the Dallas Cowboys, and Clyde Jackson, a great property developer and philanthropist who remains to this day a great friend.

(Opposite Page): Plaza of the Americas comprised two office towers and the hotel where I worked for a short time.

In the September issue of *Texas Monthly*, a full-page advertisement commands, 'Address Yourself to the Americas Tower: Bringing

another half million square feet to an ideal corporate environment of excellence. To one of the most successful multi-use communities ever built. To Plaza of the Americas.'

As hotel manager, I was number two in the operation where my boss was my father's former assistant, Paul Margetson, a chartered accountant. He had been Bertie's PA at the Pierre Hotel and was his right-hand man in his role as president of THF in the USA. Paul was quite the man about town, whose wife Ashley was a beautiful Vogue model. Paul is a great guy and also remains a friend to this day – and in fact a very kind letter from him was read out when I left The Lanesborough so many years later.

(Below): Clyde Jackson and Toddie Lee Wynne display an early model of the Plaza of the Americas. The circular restaurant that was planned for the roof of the hotel was never built.

I didn't stay long at Plaza of the Americas, mainly because I was acutely aware of the whole nepotism thing.

Having earlier been offered a job at The Mansion on Turtle Creek in Dallas, I was obviously aware of this first Rosewood hotel, whose website outlines its beginnings: 'In 1979, The Rosewood Corporation, owned by Mrs Caroline Hunt, purchased the property and transformed it into a world-class restaurant and hotel. The Mansion Restaurant opened to rave reviews and extraordinary national acclaim in 1980. In 1981, Rosewood Mansion on Turtle Creek, the luxury hotel, was added to complement the original residence, with 143 guest rooms and suites designed with an inviting ambience. The hotel opened with a grand gala benefiting the local arts and education communities, an early indication of a strong commitment to philanthropic endeavours.

'Throughout the years, modern design elements have been introduced while preserving historic details. Meticulously restored interiors, hand-carved fireplaces, marble floors and stained-glass windows preserve the estate's original magnificence.'

This does not begin to describe the property

which would become one of the finest hotels in the world at the time, under the ownership of Caroline Rose Hunt and developed by Bob Zimmer, another man who taught me so much – most particularly about the concept of real luxury. He would be the first to admit that he wasn't a hotel man, but he was a superb architect and designer, who made The Mansion on Turtle Creek unique and way ahead of its perceived competition. He hired the 21 Club out of New York to open the restaurant, which was sensational. In fact, it was the probably one of the first hotels in the world to forge its reputation *through* its restaurant.

It was a great concept: The restaurant at the Mansion on Turtle Creek was the place to be seen and what it proved was that if you have a restaurant frequented by influential local people, they would book their business associates to stay at the hotel.

The 21 Club had wanted me to go to the Mansion to manage their food and beverage operation. At that time, it's likely that I could have taken any similar position in the country and this would certainly have been one of the very best. But it wasn't to be because my old boss at

(Below): The Rosewood Mansion on Turtle Creek was developed into a world-class restaurant and hotel. I was offered the position of food and beverage manager but in the end moved to Houston to help open the latest Rosewood property – the Remington.

(Above): Houston, with its busy port in the foreground, was one of the fastest-growing cities in the USA in the early 1980s - the perfect place to open a new luxury hotel.

the Waldorf-Astoria, Guenter Richter, who by now had been made vice president of operations at Rosewood said, 'You're coming with me to open our new hotel in Houston.' The Remington. My stay at Plaza of the Americas was just six months and once again I was to follow the family motto of *Avanti, Sempre Avanti* as I put all my belongings in the trusty Cutlass Supreme and set off once again, escaping the family influence in Dallas, to the fastest growing city in the USA.

Houston was reassuringly different to either Atlantic City or Dallas, and owed its rapid growth to the oil boom. The proposed new hotel was spectacular, with the latest of everything, and its core principle was service of the very highest quality.

This is where Bob Zimmer taught me an important lesson. During my time in Atlantic City, I was taught that efficiency was everything so when I was designing the bar at the Remington I was determined to make it the last word in efficiency, with everything the bartenders might need at their fingertips – or at least within a single step.

I showed Bob my plans and was expecting a pat on the back but instead he put a large line right through them. 'This is terrible', he said, 'there's a cash register I can see behind the bar, make it disappear! That blender, get rid of it. The coffee machine, move it to the back room alongside the blender!' I said we'd need at least one more bar boy to make it work like that and his reply was curt: 'Get two bar boys if you need them. The bartenders are showmen, not efficiency experts so build the stage accordingly.'

'Service, service, service' was my mantra but what Bob Zimmer wanted was ultra elegance along with the service. He was I suppose a modern-day William Morris who said: 'Have nothing in your house that you do not know to be useful, or believe to be beautiful.' Zimmer *exuded* style. He instinctively understood that it was aesthetics and ambience which were paramount to creating an environment friendly to the people in it, something which made them feel good before 'feel good' was fashionable.

(Left): I moved to Houston as part of Guenter Richter's team that opened Rosewood's latest hotel – The Remington. The hotel later became part of the Marriott organisation and is now known as the St Regis Houston.

His aim was to create the most beautiful hotels. Zimmer embodied style over business efficiency, and was aiming the venture at the very highest echelons in society. Once I understood this, we worked together to blend his aesthetic ideals with an element of practicality that made for a sensible working compromise.

The end result was an astonishing hotel where I found myself attending black-tie events three nights a week and escorting important ladies to society functions the other two nights. There was a tremendous amount of entertaining and dancing but all this changed swiftly when the oil market crashed, with housing dropping by almost half in value in less than a year, especially for larger properties. The Remington was conceived when Houston was the fastest-growing city in the USA, but sadly by the time it opened the financial outlook was very different.

As for Guenter Richter, his stylish dress sense more than matched Zimmer's style vision for the hotel. Not only was he a sharp dresser but he had no qualms about offering his opinions to others. 'That tie doesn't really go with your shirt,' he told my colleague Guenter Schnee. Unperturbed, Schnee continued to wear the tie with the same combination. Richter demonstrated his disapproval by lopping the offending tie with a pair of scissors. To be fair, Richter replaced it with a much more appropriate Hermès tie and Schnee got a lesson in style – though this is not something that I could imagine happening today!

Richter became my operational mentor, though I never cut off anyone's ties! I was young and ambitious and, thinking about it now, even though we were good friends, he was undoubtedly my boss. I feel that, occasionally, I might have got on his nerves. The economy had taken a dive and the hotel hadn't opened in the way that had been expected, and perhaps to get me from under his feet, he put me forward for a job which was extraordinary, because I was still only twenty-nine years old.

Caroline Rose Hunt had just bought the Hotel Bel-Air in Los Angeles, where the first general manager had lasted three brief months. To my shock, Rosewood offered me the position. It was Zimmer, ultimately, who was willing to give me the opportunity to rebuild the hotel, a property already reasonably iconic in the USA. It was an enormous undertaking for a young man.

But let's never forget our Gelardi family motto: *Avanti Sempre Avanti* – Forward, Forever Forward. Once again, I packed up my car, this time a Porsche Turbo I had bought from my brother Michael, which

(Opposite Page): Guenter Richter's sense of style was well-known, which was perhaps why a local newspaper got us to model European mens' suits.

# FIT FOR A MAN

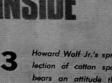
**BY NANCY S. CHISHOLM**
Chronicle Fashion Writer

EUROPEAN MENSWEAR designers have fashioned fit into a precise measurement. Not content with simply measurement in inches, these designers use centimeters to give men a precise fit for spring suits!

"It's a custom fit, right off the rack," says Morris Penner, owner of M. Penner. In Penner's store about 85 percent of the men's clothing is measured in centimeters.

An example of the kind of precise fit from European menswear is a large-chested man who wears an American Size 40 might take a European Size 52, while a smaller-chested man who also wears an American Size 40 might take a Size 50. In the European designs, both men will end up with jackets that are fit for their body shapes. In American fashions, they would have to be content with boxy, fuller jackets.

The same applies for trousers. "A (European) Size 40 pair of trousers translates to a 31½-inch waist pant.

(See IT'S, Page 2)

Photo by Buster Dean, Chronicle Staff

*Two examples of the precise fit for European menswear include a double-breasted cream suit by D'Urban on Gunter Richter, vice president/hotel operations of Rosewood Corp., far left, and a single-breasted Zegna suit worn by Geoffrey Gelardi, manager of The Remington in Houston.*

Photographed in The Remington

turned out to be a complete fake – it looked like a 911 Turbo and it was certainly very beautiful and powerful-looking with its extravagant whale tail and flared wheel arches. It was beautiful, but it was basically a 911 kit car though Michael continued to claim it was a one-off prototype.

Still, I managed to get my belongings into it – I was still single and renting so I didn't actually have that much baggage – and set off to drive 1,500 miles through Texas, New Mexico, Arizona, and into California, parking up for a new life and a new challenge in Los Angeles.

I left behind an apartment in Houston and moved into a large house which the company had purchased next to the hotel. I would not normally have expected to be living in such style as at the time Bel-Air was the most expensive residential real estate in America but the company had bought the next-door house to avoid noise complaints while building the Hotel Bel-Air extension. Sometime after I moved on, *Star Trek* actor Leonard Nimoy bought it and renovated the property to create a fabulous home.

I did arrive at the Bel-Air with great expectations but what I found was a shock: the hotel was a dump and the rooms were nothing less than

(Below): The Porsche 911 that I bought from my brother Michael and shipped to the United States. It looked like the flagship Turbo model but beneath those wings and flared wheelarches was a standard car.

awful. It was in desperate need of renovation to Rosewood standards. The only saving graces were the amazing location and the spectacular gardens with their cascading bougainvillia all over the property.

To get to know the property from the inside out, I stayed in all the rooms. Each of them had that unmistakable and lingering smell of damp. The décor was atrocious. And it wasn't just the surroundings which were old fashioned. Guenter Schnee had come from Houston to help me. He told me: 'I was in my room yesterday afternoon and an elderly woman came in. The poor woman was shattered. I asked if she wanted to sit down, to which she replied, "Yes". I asked her what she wanted. "I'm your maid," she said. She was eighty-seven years old and had been with the hotel for over 30 years.'

The reservations manager, Phil Landon, took the guest book home every night. Not only that, but he was wholly responsible for booking all guests – no one else – effectively policing who was allowed to stay and who was

(Above): The renovation of the iconic Hotel Bel-Air was a major undertaking for a twenty-nine year old but Rosewood trusted me with the responsibility. When I arrived, it was to find that the property was in very poor shape and needed extensive work to bring it up to Rosewood standards.

# History of the Hotel Bel-Air

The Hotel Bel-Air first opened in 1946, up in the Los Angeles canyons, a retreat from the buzz and the noise of the city. The area known as 'Bel-Air', just a mile away from Beverley Hills, had been developed in the 1920s by oil tycoon Alphonzo Bell into an exclusive residential neighbourhood where the likes of Clark Gable bought homes.

Then in 1946 a Texas hotelier, Joseph Drown, bought eleven acres, including the estate planning office that Bell had built right at the start. This formed the basis for Drown's hotel, the first and only hotel in Bel-Air. He built a number of additonal guest rooms and the Hotel Bel-Air opened in August 1946, the perfect venue for privacy-seeking stars such as Audrey Hepburn, Grace Kelly, Marilyn Munroe, Cary Grant and many others.

The hotel was again renovated in the 1970s, then Caroline Rose Hunt bought the hotel and the adjoining property in 1982, which added a further 30 rooms.

It became clear that full renovations would be needed to bring the property up to the standards that Rosewood expected but by the time the work was finished the Hotel Bel-Air was once again one of the finest residential hotels in the world.

(Above): Alphonzo Bell (Left) and Joseph Drown (Right). The Bel-Air estate as it was in the 1930s (Below). The original hotel in the 1940s (Opposite Page Above). Stars such as Cary Grant and Grace Kelly enjoyed the privacy that Bel-Air afforded them (Opposite Page Below).

not! Our guests were the most famous artists, actors and politicians of that time, even though the hotel's design was stuck back in the 1950s while we were now in the 1980s. The property was tired in every sense. Phil Landon had been there for over thirty years. In fact, 30 per cent of the staff had been there for twenty years or more. It was so out of date that I could hardly believe that a hotel with such a reputation had survived. My over-riding priority was to get the existing rooms into a Rosewood-lettable state, through painting and deodorising while trying to keep the character and the characters of the hotel intact.

But the painting and deodorising didn't work. The smell of damp continued to linger. Eventually we discovered the source of the problem – old lead pipework was dripping behind the walls and large-scale remedial work was essential. The property didn't need a lick of paint, it needed complete renovation.

What had started as something of an adventure for Caroline Rose Hunt, was going to be a far larger project than she or Rosewood had foreseen. However she was a remarkable woman, the daughter of H.L. Hunt, the most successful wildcat oilman in Texas, worth billions of dollars. J. Paul Getty, who knew something of such matters, once said,

'In terms of extraordinary, independent wealth, there is only one man - H.L. Hunt.'

Caroline once told me that until she was a teenager she didn't know that the family had money, and was brought up in such a way that she was like everyone else. There was a story that her father was well known for taking his lunch to work in a paper bag. She was the most gracious, down-to-earth individual; universally respected and liked by everyone who met her. I was lucky enough to spend a good deal of time with her, escorting her to different events when she was in LA. On one occasion, I escorted her to a dinner and told her I had to fly to Dallas the next day for a meeting with Zimmer.

'We should travel together,' she said. 'If you fly via Houston, you save $100.' I was expecting to be invited onto a private jet but that was not Mrs Hunt! I flew business class, she flew 'normal'. Her car was ten years old, which perturbed her children so much that one day they took it and replaced it with a new Lexus.

(Below): The hotel's head gardener had worked at the Bel-Air for some 30 years. He loved its gardens but had always wanted to create a herb garden. We made it happen - much to Al's delight, and to the direct benefit of both our chefs and our guests.

Caroline Rose Hunt's acquisition of the Bel-Air in 1982 had been something of a fluke. Joseph Drown, who originally built the hotel in 1946, died before the planned sale was completed, so the probate court stipulated that there had to be a sealed bid auction. By then, much work had gone into a planned $22 million spend for the hotel. But what to bid now? The story goes that Caroline Hunt chose the floor of her new office and her office number as the last six digits of the Rosewood bid. The major opponent in the bidding process was a certain Mr Ivan Boesky, a former American stock trader, who became infamous for his prominent role in an insider trading scandal. He pleaded guilty and was fined a record $100 million. He chose his birthdate for his last six digits – and happily, Caroline Rose Hunt won the bid by a mere $6,000 or thereabouts.

Not long after arriving, Bob Zimmer and Douglas Wells, vice president of engineering, held strategy meetings. They planned to request an additional $7 million to renovate and build a north wing and thirty further rooms. Through discussions and a preparatory budget, it was realised that this wasn't even close to what was needed, a more realistic figure being nearer $15 million. Zimmer told me to come to Dallas to a Rosewood board meeting, at which he was going to ask for double the original budget, in 1981 a previously unheard-of figure of approximately $500,000 per room when the original purchase price was included.

Zimmer, the other executive team members and I devised a presentation for the board, which comprised Caroline Rose Hunt's family, high-flying lawyers, accountants and corporate finance guys. They asked questions. Lots and lots of questions. Mrs Hunt asked if it was absolutely necessary. Zimmer and I were steadfast: 'To do the project justice, absolutely'. Neither of us were accountants, of course, and were viewing it from an aesthetic and operational point of view only. The hotel would eventually run the highest occupancy and average rate in LA and sell for a massive $80 million to a Japanese company just eight years later, an astonishing $869,000 per room. Yet the beginning was an adventure.

To her credit, Caroline Rose Hunt and Rosewood Corporation approved the new budget and so now we had to deliver what we had promised. Zimmer led the renovation and one of his earliest decisions was to divide the property into five different sections, each overseen by a specific designer, which was a ground-breaking concept in itself at that time. The overall idea, though, was to keep the idiosyncratic Spanish hacienda style of the Bel-Air.

(Left): Relaxing with our hard-working car valet staff on one of their nights off. It was not unusual for the Head Valet Ray (pictured left) to drive our celebrity guests such as Gary Cooper home at the end of an evening. His assistant Kevin (right) was an out of work actor who had many small parts in movies and TV series but never quite made it. Gary Cooper is pictured earlier in his career (Below) with Joan Fontaine after they had both won Oscars in the 1942 Academy Awards

(Below): Another regular in the Bel-Air bar was the immensley-talented singer and songwriter Harry Nilsson. His habit of snorting cocaine off the bar caused a certain amount of concern.

There were general stipulations and specifications, too: for example, that Mexican tiles would be used as floor coverings in each ground floor room, and there would be no marble in the bathrooms. All of this would ensure that the Bel-Air DNA was modernised rather than recreated. My role was to ensure that the hotel's culture was retained. I had to change the attitudes of the 'old' staff and demonstrate a better way of doing things. I started by putting a computer in reception. This was the early 1980s, when they were just beginning to emerge as essential components in business infrastructure. For Phil Landon, the 30-year veteran and many of the long-serving staff, it was like putting them at the controls of a spaceship.

The solution I found was to recruit a number of younger people who had no fear of new technology, and have them work alongside the older employees who we needed to retain, both for continuity and guest relations. However, beyond the solution of recruiting new people, I realised as I got to know the guests how much affection and importance the Bel-Air held for them. The milestones of life – christenings, birthdays and weddings – were all celebrated at the hotel. These were all memories that they cherished, making it ever more important that the hotel did not change its DNA. I never had to work so hard to win people over, and to deliver on a promise that it would still be the warm and welcoming home away from home that they had always known. For this was the heart of the old Bel-Air.

Interestingly, the gardening staff had also been part of the establishment for three decades, but they proved to be a surprise as they actively embraced change. When the property had first been built, its original owner Alphonzo Bell had planted the acreage with palms and fabulous flowers. Al Piler was the head gardener when I arrived, who completely disarmed me with his approach. He loved the gardens and knew when every tree was planted. It was quite an experience to spend any time with him because he was so passionate about what he was doing and treated the plants and trees almost as his personal friends. All of my time with him was a joy. He had always wanted to create a herb garden and asked if I would permit it. Of course. Twenty by thirty metres. A gift for him and a gift for our guests.

It proved to be a culinary delight, too, which the chefs Joe Venezia and the overseeing Wolfgang Puck could utilise in thrilling dishes. Puck was at the time the man to make pizzas interesting and extravagant, topping them with salmon and caviar to create gourmet dishes. The Bel-Air was a significant moment in his career – in time he would open over one hundred restaurants including Cut at 45 on London's Park

Lane, my favourite steak restaurant; he is still overseeing the culinary offerings at the Bel-Air after some forty years.

I accomplished what I had set out to do, thanks to the support I received from Zimmer and Caroline Rose Hunt. Together we made the Bel-Air one of the finest properties in the world. Very quickly, its bar was the place to be once again. In its heyday, it had been a refuge for every major movie star of the 1940s, 50s and 60s, who knew that it was a place that could be trusted to maintain their privacy and be discrete. It was exclusive. Gary Cooper, who was part of the Bel-Air neighbourhood, enjoyed and frequented the exclusive bar on a regular basis. Ray, a forty-year veteran who was in charge of parking, would discreetly drive Mr Cooper home on many occasions.

It was very satisfying to see the bar abuzz again, and I became friends with many of the regulars. There was a group of about eight guys in particular who made the place like an episode of *Cheers*: people like the stockbroker and banker Peter Joyce, the family trust expert Leonard Dolsmer, Arnold Lieder, a lawyer who drank like a fish then drove home; Dr Tohme Tohme, a great friend to this day who went on to become Michael Jackson's manager, responsible for bringing him to The Lanesborough some years later; Harry Nilsson the songwriter, a brilliant musician and friend to the Beatles, whose coke habit was such that he'd snort it off the bar counter which got me into all kinds of trouble with our security.

From 9pm until whenever on Friday and Saturday evenings, Bud Herman played the piano amazingly, his fingers virtually deformed from their key-spanning contortions. One summer's evening Julie London, with her sultry smoky voice, came into the bar with her husband Bobby Troupe. They sat at the piano with Bud who graciously stepped aside to allow Bobby to accompany Julie in an impromptu session of song. It was sheer magic! The Bel-Air bar was, once more, a haven for those who had 'made it'. During this time we were privileged to enjoy many guest appearances from famous singers and musicians.

A permanent resident when I arrived was Chatty Wagner, Robert Wagner's mother. She had actually been living at the hotel for years, in the Swan Lake Suite, one of the best offered. Permanent residents are quite usual in the hotel industry – I had a guest at The Lanesborough who lived in the Royal Suite for well over a year. Chatty had been at the Bel-Air for approximately ten. By then she was in her eighties and on occasion I would accompany her around the gardens. The Bel-Air liked to care for its people and she was one of them, a wonderful lady.

I also remember the day I escorted Sophia Loren to her room when she arrived with an entourage. She would have been in her early fifties then, and still bewitchingly beautiful.

'You are the manager?'

'Yes, yes,' I smiled and nodded.

'So young. And so handsome!'

I blushed and excused myself, wondering just how many times she had reduced men to childish versions of themselves.

Actually, I had almost certainly met Sophia Loren many years earlier though I fear I might have been too young to remember. When the family moved from South Africa to England in 1961 we often stayed in the magnificent Wimbledon house that was home to my uncle – Bertie's elder brother Arthur – and his wife Emelia. Arthur had many connections in the Italian movie business and often had weekend guests, including the famous director Carlo Ponti and his lovely wife Sophia Loren. My brother Michael distinctly remembers seeing them, but as I was only 8 or 9 at the time I was probably more interested in climbing the huge cedar tree that grew in the garden outside.

With so many high-profile guests, we had to ensure that security at the Bel-Air was second to none. Most of our security detail was made up of off-duty police officers. They were terrific. They could handle themselves and had permission to carry firearms if it were ever necessary. One night there was a call from a guest at about 11pm.

'It sounds like someone is being murdered in the next room,' we were told. He reported the sounds of crashing furniture, screaming and shouting.

I met the on-duty security, knocked on the door and tried to enter – it was locked, from the inside. It was now so quiet that it seemed as if there was no one there. We discovered that one of the bathroom windows was open a little and I was the only person small enough to get through into the room.

I climbed up the wall and through the window. The room had been completely trashed – the marble table was shattered and paintings and ornaments had been ripped from the walls. I tiptoed through to the front door and let security in. Whatever the guest had heard going on was now clearly over, but there was still the locked-room mystery.

It was a crime scene without a body. No blood. Nothing. Security took photographs of the devastation. I stood on the veranda, perplexed, talking to the head of security when we heard a noise:

'Psss.' We looked up to see a half-naked guy on the roof. I called back, 'Who are you?' 'Has she gone?' he asked. 'There's nobody here Who's "she"?' I replied. 'That wild woman.' 'There's just us,' I reassured him.

We helped him down off the roof and back inside and then he explained. 'I was just taking photographs of her, that's all. But she… didn't want me to.' In fact she had shown her displeasure with unbridled rage.

(Above): It was a delight to welcome Sophia Loren to the Bel-Air. In her 50s at the time, she was still stunningly beautiful.

Surveying the room, I told him that it was going to be a hell of a bill. There was no denying it. Resigned, he agreed, but when the time came to settle, he refused to pay. When I made it absolutely clear that we would not back down and would pursue him for the costs, he relented. He was worse off by about $40,000 as we insisted he would have to pay for the room while it was out of commission.

Back in 1981, I remember I had been staying with my friend George Harrington at his parents' place in the Pacific Palisades when a call came through to his father Dr Harrington, that President Ronald Reagan had been shot outside the Washington Hilton Hotel. Reagan was seriously injured and three other lives were changed forever: James Brady, White House Press Secretary, Tim McCarthy, Secret Service agent, and Thomas Delahanty, a police officer. Secret Service men turned up at the house and George's father was meeting with Reagan's daughter Patti. I had no idea then that I would later encounter the Reagans in a professional capacity. I also never envisaged that I would be assuring the Secret Service that, if necessary, I would take a bullet for the President.

And yet, three years after the attempt on his life, the Fortieth President of the United States of America attended his daughter's wedding

To Geoffrey A. Gelardi – With Very Best Wishes & Regards.
Ronald Reagan

at the Bel-Air, Los Angeles. The *New York Times* of 15 August 1984 reported that the President and First Lady's future son-in-law was Paul Grilley, their daughter Patti's yoga teacher. 'He is the son of Mr. and Mrs. Terrance F. Grilley of Columbia Falls, Mont., who attended the ceremony and met President and Mrs. Reagan for the first time on Monday at the wedding rehearsal.' What the *New York Times* didn't say was how that meeting came about, or the arrangements I had made with Nancy Reagan.

The hotel's Swiss banquet manager had been there for thirty-odd years and was rather stuck in his ways. Aware of the enormous responsibility which the hotel now faced, I realised that I had to take over. The Bel-Air was one of the most popular wedding venues in the city and weddings formed a significant element in the hotel's portfolio of services: sometimes three weddings per day were hosted at the weekends. It was a well-practised and efficient process, the preparations and turnover from one wedding group to the next, perfected and seamless, even though we only had one function room.

(Opposite Page and Left): Security issues made the President's daughter's wedding a major event at the Bel-Air but it was not just the Secret Seervice who had to be kept happy. The First Lady Nancy Reagan knew exactly what she wanted and was an exacting client. However, our team ensured that it was a successful and memorable day and both President Reagan and Nancy wrote kind notes to me afterwards.

Such a day would begin with the first wedding on Swan Lake at 10am, move to the Upper Lawn for drinks, then to the Ballroom for the wedding lunch. The next wedding repeated the same process, which rolled smoothly because we made quite certain ther would be no crossing of the different wedding groups.

Planning was essential. There would be tables already stacked and ready to be moved into place for the next group to facilitate the smooth turnover. But when Patti Reagan was married, there was no other service, there could be no other service. And it had to be just so. The bride's mother would make sure of that – and she was a good friend of Caroline Hunt's so there was no question that we had to get every little thing absolutely right on the day.

If I'd been told, as a kitchen steward, that I would one day host such a wedding, I might have started planning it from that moment onwards. Determined to make it memorable for the newlyweds as well as a celebration of which the President and First Lady would approve, I put together with my team a bespoke menu, which included a choice of veal or *filet de boeuf* dishes. But as I described the intricacies of these dishes, Nancy asked for chicken as she didn't want to be seen as extravagant!

Surely such an occasion required choices beyond merely chicken? We met three or four times to plan the wedding, each time an opportunity to present a menu I felt would befit the occasion. But I pushed too hard. 'She wants chicken,' Caroline Rose Hunt told me in a telephone call. 'Stop it with the veal and beef. Keep it simple!'

Nancy was tough and formal, beautifully dressed, and polite to the point that she left one in no doubt that she was the First Lady. It was with some surprise that, when I finally met Ronald Reagan, he said, 'Nancy has enjoyed working with you.' It was a meeting that took three weeks to arrange, a Secret Service advance party visiting for an initial introduction to how it was all going to work. Security would be far more extensive and obvious on the wedding day when for around 100 guests there were over 200 Secret Service people on duty.

For the first meeting with Ronald Reagan, it was determined that he would not approach the hotel via the main thoroughfare over Swan Lake bridge, but through another parking area at the rear of the hotel. A room had to be set aside where Reagan could prepare with Secret Service personnel and his support staff. While I waited for the President's car, the Secret Service briefed me about where to stand –

in front of the president, to cover high velocity shots. 'If you don't agree to do this,' they said, 'you don't meet him.'

'Okay' I said jokingly, 'I'll take a bullet for the president.' The Secret Service also showed me how to walk with Reagan to cover a specific angle from the surrounding valley. The precautions were exceptionally detailed and careful. Everything – from the moment the President entered the hotel boundary, to where he would be standing and sitting throughout the day – was scrutinised and secured.

I had already taken the Secret Service to all the surrounding houses overlooking the valley, the occupants of which needed to be vetted by the Secret Service. They included a character by the name of Red Buttons who lived above Swan Lake and, after a particularly busy three-wedding day, decided to complain in a manner rather more public than a telephone call, about the fact that the ceremonies were disturbing his peace, shouting my name through a megaphone – 'Get me Geoffrey Gelardi! I need to get my sleep!' – along with a litany of expletives. My only recourse had been to visit Red and placate him

(Below): President Ronald Reagan, First Lady Nancy and Patti. Patti's wedding was held at the Bel-Air.

with a bottle of Dom Pérignon and an assurance that the hotel would, of course, keep the noise down to an appropriate level in future.

The surrounding area was further secured with snipers on all strategic rooftops and officers on every drain cover throughout the Bel-Air's grounds. Even the airspace was closed.

Thankfully, all the planning came good and the President arrived safely. I had welcomed Reagan and accompanied him to his suite, then we shook hands. 'If there's anything I can do Mr President.'

'Geoffrey, don't go. Take a seat, shoot the breeze! The guys say you've been so helpful.'

I sat to one side, Reagan and his security men at ease with each other now that he wasn't on the move. They knew each other's quirks, each other's families. The atmosphere was light, the wedding an occasion to savour amongst the remarkable demands of presidential office. The Secret Service and support staff shielded Reagan from all the day-to-day issues so he could concentrate on fixing the country while Nancy fixed the wedding.

When the call came through that their son-in-law's parents had arrived, I stood with the father and mother of the bride, two of the most elegantly dressed people in America, to greet them. The son-in-law's father arrived in an open-necked shirt, jeans and big-buckled cowboy belt while the mother, very much overweight, wore a skin-tight pink jumpsuit. Just out of their earshot, Nancy gasped. But in the end all went well: needless to say, the Presidential couple were their usual diplomatic selves.

This encounter with the President and the First Lady was just one of many I had with the rich and famous during my time at the Bel-Air. And it made me realise just what a great life the hotel business can offer to people who enjoy the company of others and who are dedicated to ensuring that their guests' needs are always met and if possible, exceeded. It's not just the stars and the international figures that makes ours such a great career – every day you get to meet new people, not all of whom are in the newspapers every day, but all of whom have their own stories to tell.

After three and a half years, I was to move on again, this time to Seattle. I had achieved what I set out to do, to make the Bel-Air once again one of the fabulous places in Los Angeles in which to socialise and stay. We had transformed it from a tired and shabby property clinging to its reputation as a one-time hangout for stars of Hollywood's golden age, to an elegant, swish and truly vibrant venue.

The hotel was outperforming the market and so it made sense to take on another project. My 'persuader' was Michael Malone, at that time part owner with Bob Burkheimer of the Sorrento Hotel, Seattle. Mike is one of the most charismatic marketing entrepreneurs I know and was a high-profile socialite in the city. He owned AEI music and eventually bought Muzak – the business which installed systems to play background music in different commercial companies and buildings. I'm not sure how he did it, but he coaxed me to leave the Bel-Air for the Sorrento by offering an equity position based on performance.

The Sorrento, which Malone had acquired in 1981, wasn't performing as well as he wanted it to. The idea was that once we had made the Sorrento one of Seattle's finest hotels, we would expand the brand into a management company by buying, renovating and operating other properties. With my own achievements, I had re-forged the key that had been passed on to me. I would arrive in Seattle at the age of thirty-two and single and leave four and a half years later married to Eileen and with two daughters. It was the best of times.

(Below): The wonderful city of Seattle, where I would spend four and a half memorable years.

# Chapter 10

# From Seattle to London

I had actually first met Eileen some years before, when I was still working at Resorts International in Atlantic City. I had arranged to meet my friend Barry Cregan, who was head of food and beverage at The Golden Nugget, but as he was dealing with a work issue when I arrived, he sent me down to the bar to join his girlfriend Dolores and her friend.

I spotted Dolores sitting with this gorgeous creature – it was Eileen. I was a little bit full of myself, I guess, and didn't hang about. When you meet someone that beautiful, you have to move fast!

I mentioned Johnny Mathis coming to the showroom at Resorts International. Eileen said she loved Johnny Mathis so I asked if she would like to go to the show. I didn't think she heard me correctly because she politely said, 'Thank you but no.' To say the least I was taken aback as I wasn't used to being turned down and she had just told me she liked Johnny Mathis. Maybe she thought I was offering to sell her a ticket?

I explained again that I was inviting her to come to the show with me. She apologised for the misunderstanding, but by then it was clear things were not going well. Eileen decided it was time to leave. I think she had had enough of this arrogant young British guy.

Not wanting to let Eileen get away, I invited myself to join her and Dolores at Harrah's Casino, where they had decided to go next – obviously I wasn't very good at taking hints at the time. Eileen was driving a Fiat and I followed in my Chevrolet. Trying to impress – though I am not sure how impressive a yellow Chevrolet actually was! – I overtook and cut her up. To my surprise she made an aggressive move, racing me down the road while a full moon shone on the bay.

We were clipping along at sixty to seventy miles per hour with a bridge

(Left and Below): Happy days dating Eileen in Atlantic City before the move to Seattle.

and a hairpin just ahead and Eileen just a couple of inches off my bumper. If I braked, she'd go right into the back of me. I pulled the car out of the hairpin and up against the nine-inch kerb, the wheels sparking spectacularly before coming to a halt on a sandy verge, with two tyres blown and badly damaged wheels. My car was in bad shape.

'I'm sorry, I'm sorry,' Eileen said, asking 'this wasn't my fault was it? Are you ok?  Shall I take you to a hospital?'

'No, no,' I said, 'we just got off on the wrong foot. I'd like to have a drink with you.'

So Dolores, Eileen and I went for a drink, after which Eileen drove me home in her little Fiat, and I invited her in.

My roommate appeared in his underwear! That was George Harrington and I discovered several months later that George was a potential blind date for Eileen that never happened as Eileen did not do blind dates.

Incidentally, a few years later, in 1985, The Golden Nugget where Eileen and I had first met became part of the business empire of

(Above): The Sorrento Hotel under construction on the corner of Madison Street and Terry Avenue in Seattle. It first opened in 1908.

the future forty-fifth President of the United States: it was known as Trump's Castle, then Trump's Marina. Since 2011, it has been known as The Golden Nugget again.

In that time, our three daughters – Piera, Georgina and Olivia – attest to the foundation on which our marriage was built after that first sparky encounter. Piera, who puts everyone ahead of herself; Georgina, who's my pea-in-a-pod equivalent; Olivia, a free spirit who has always marched to her own drum and continues to do so to this day.

Eileen has been a constant rock ever since she accepted my proposal shortly after I arrived in Seattle. We were married in Philadelphia, which is where most of her large family lived, then returned to the west coast to start our life together. In the hotel business I was often away and often working long and very unsocial hours but she never complained and I never had to worry about either the home or the children – she just quietly got on with looking after all that side of our life together.

I'll be forever grateful for the support she gave me – and I was always proud to have her at my side on the many social functions we attended together. Table plans were never a problem where Eileen was concerned, as she has the knack of being able to get on with just about anyone! Over the years she has sat next to so many different celebrities, all of whom seem to have got on with her very well indeed – including the late genius comedian Robin Williams, HRH the late Duke of Edinburgh, former UK Prime Minister John Major and the wonderful late British actor John Mills to name just a few of her favourites. As Piera did all those year ago for Giulio, Eileen and the three girls grounded me when I left the demands of a luxury property behind for some semblance of normal family life. I owe them so much.

But here I was in Seattle, working at a small seventy-six-room hotel despite all my experience and qualifications. Later on, many people have looked at my CV and wondered how that could ever have happened – even my mother described managing the Sorrento as a job for someone who was heading into retirement and slowing down, not a position for someone who was still making his way upwards in the world of hospitality! But what she and others maybe didn't realise was that I had high expectations of starting a small hotel chain of my own with the Sorrento's owners.

However I have no regrets. I had a lot of autonomy, I loved Seattle and I met some great people there. The city became familiar to many in the 1990s when its skyline was featured in the opening credits of the hit sitcom Frasier. But when I arrived in the mid-80s, the city's reputation for cool was already well established.

Seattle had relied on its enormous employer Boeing for its wealth up until the early 1970s, when the company was forced to reduce its workforce from 80,000 to 37,000 after the 1972 oil crisis which devastated the airline industry in particular. But a startling new industry was emerging in the city that would connect each of us in ways we had never imagined, even more than the company which had made our world smaller with air travel. The company; Microsoft. Its founders Paul Allen and Bill Gates created a company whose sales in 1985 were nearly $150 million, and when I left for London in 1990 they had reached $1.18 billion. Both frequented the Sorrento from time to time.

Seattle was also the birthplace of the Starbucks coffee shop chain. The first store opened in 1971 close to Pike Place Market in the city and there are now over 30,000 Starbucks outlets in over 70 countries around the world. Nordstrom is another company which started in Seattle and its founder John Nordstrom's grandson Jim was a regular visitor to the Sorrento. And it was in Seattle that Costco was founded – the first warehouse opened in the city in 1983 and there are now nearly 800 around the world which makes it the second biggest retailer in the world after Walmart.

The city was – and is – beautiful, and Microsoft, Starbucks, Nordstrom and Costco were savvy in basing their companies there because it was the most wonderful environment to attract the skilful labour force required. It was certainly the best place to be in the States at that time.

Although Seattle was not quite as exhilarating as Los Angeles as far as celebrity guests were concerned, it was exciting from a professional perspective, as the Sorrento was statistically the second-best hotel

(Below): The Rollout of the first Boeing 707 prototype at the company's Renton plant on May 14, 1954. The 707 was America's first jet airliner to go into production. (Opposite Page): The Sorrento Hotel.

in Seattle at the time, outperformed only by the Four Seasons, which had the advantage of being much better appointed and better located.

To the owners Mike Malone and Bob Burkheimer, I was a personality they could put out front, the man with the impeccable hotel lineage who had come from the world-famous Bel Air. There's nothing wrong with that, of course, and they treated me very well. I loved Seattle, the city, the people, the fact

SORRENTO HOTEL

that I could jump into a limousine to drive the forty-five minutes to Snoqualmie Falls to go night skiing and finish the evening off with a couple of bottles of champagne on the way back. This was also the time that I became interested in shooting, which became a lifelong passion. I have Bob Burkheimer to thank for that.

His main business was real estate in Seattle but he was persuaded by Mike Malone – I did say that Mike was a great salesman! – to invest with him in the Sorrento Hotel. At the time Bob had another offer on the table, which was to become one of the founder investors in that start-up called Costco. Unfortunately for him, he took the Sorrento! I hope it gave him a great deal of fun and satisfaction, but most importantly for me, Bob and I became, and still remain, the very best of friends.

Bob is a man's man, so to speak. He invited me to his ranch in northern Washington and kitted me out for duck shooting. First he put me into an old pair of waders and made me jump in a whirlpool

Though originally founded in 1975 by Bill Gates and Paul Allen in Albuquerque, New Mexico, Microsoft moved to Bellevue, Seattle in 1979. The company's rapid expansion resulted in another move to nearby Redmond in 1985 and it has remained headquartered there ever since. (Below): The main entrance to Microsoft's Redmond campus.

to check they were waterproof. My jeans became wet so Bob found whatever it was to waterproof the holes, ready for the next morning: quite scary when you know you are going to be wading into freezing water at 5am the following morning.

We got up at 3am to get to the waterfront before the ducks start coming in. It was a two-hour drive and when we arrived it was freezing – literally, as we had to break the ice on top of the lake so that we could wade to the blinds. The water came up to within four or five inches of the tops of our waders as Bob lead me to a spot under overhanging branches where the ducks wouldn't be able to see us. There we were, standing in freezing water above our knees. Near me I noticed a plank of wood across two branches and thought I would jump up on it just to get out of the water. At which point Bob's dog came swimming right at me to join me on the plank. His added weight made all the water run down the plank to my bum – now I know what it means to freeze your arse off. Bob laughed. 'That plank is for the dog,' he said.

(Above): Staff at Microsoft in 1978, just before the move to Seattle. Paul Allen is on the right of the middle row while Bill Gates is front left. Gates later described this picture as 'indisputable proof that your average computer geek from the late 1970s was not exactly on the cutting edge of fashion.'

(Left): The first Starbucks outlet near the Pike Place Market in Seattle opened in 1971.

I had never been so cold in my life but I was hooked. I now shoot approximately fifteen days a year in the UK with a matched pair of Holland & Holland sidelocks, made in about 1920 – they are beautiful examples of the gunmaker's art. Those who appreciate such things would understand my love of their weight and speed.

But back to the Sorrento: Bob sold his shares in the hotel to Craig McCaw who had launched McCaw Communications, one of the very early cellular phone companies in the USA, which was sold in 1994 to AT&T for a reported $11.5 billion. Craig was an amazing low key but high-flying businessman. I used to enjoy talking to him about business, not that I could always understand everything that he was saying. 'These technology companies buy the future,' he said as he tried to get me to understand how his company had sold for so much despite never having made any profits. This was a difficult scenario for a hotelier to get his head around.

For him this partnership at the Sorrento was small fry but his management knowledge was invaluable. I got quite excited when Craig became a partner because I thought it might also mean money for expansion. I put together a couple of possible acquisitions and presented them to the managing partners, but they didn't seem to have the appetite for the proposed expansion. Then I proposed the purchase of another hotel in downtown Seattle in which Craig McCaw's mother already had an interest. I had the price at approximately $9 million, which I presented to Mike and Craig, but they decided not to go with it. That hotel sold a few months later for $11 million.

I loved my time in Seattle, which is where I made a number of lifelong friends – people like Bill Baffert, who ran Baffert's Restaurant on Capitol Hill. It was part-owned by Mike Malone so in a way I was running his hotel while Bill was running his restaurant in the city. We

(Left): After being introduced to the sport by Bob Burkheimer in Seattle, shooting became one of my passions. This was some years later, back in the UK, after a successful day with Lord Ivor Mountbatten. (Below): Mike Malone is another with a passion for field sports, both shooting and here fishing on his ranch. (Opposite Page) Mike displaying his passion for classic sports cars – here racing his Ferrari 250 TR at Goodwood in 2012.

became great friends and also allies whenever Mike Malone was not in the best of moods! Bill is at heart a country boy from Arizona whose brother Bobby is one of America's leading racehorse trainers, having won six Kentucky Derbies, seven Preakness Stakes, three Belmont Stakes and two Triple Crowns. Bill has been a great friend of mine over many years, so much so that every year I still take a trip to Arizona to ride with him.

(Above) Riding with my good friends Bob Burkheimer (Centre) and Bill Baffert (Right) in Arizona - an annual outing that I always look forward to.

But however good my social life was in Seattle, my main focus remained on finding ways to expand the Sorrento name; however, it became apparent that neither Mike nor Craig really were particularly anxious to acquire more hotels. They liked to be in the hotel business but it didn't bring the returns that their other businesses did so expansion was never a high priority for them.

When I realised the expansion programme wasn't going to happen, and as I had no desire to run a seventy-six room hotel I started talking to people about moving. I soon got a call from Atef Mankarios, the man who had been general manager at the Mansion on Turtle Creek when I was at the Bel-Air. Our paths had crossed in the past and in recent years I had got to know him better: I sat on one of the selection boards of the marketing company Preferred Hotels, of which he was chairman, so we met a few times a year and had become quite friendly.

By this time Atef was president of Rosewood Hotels, having taken over when Bob Zimmer left the company. He said he needed my advice, telling me that Rosewood had made a presentation to the owners of a new hotel in London which was going to be called The Wellington. Although they had no hotels outside the US, they had won this management contract. He described the hotel and the commitments that had been made by Rosewood, which were substantial, not so much from a financial perspective but because they had promised unprecedented levels of service. This had been a sticking point for a number of potential managers who had baulked at accepting such a position because the expectations were so very great.

Atef went on to deliver the prerequisite: the nationality of the general manager had to be British, but also someone who understood American service acumen, and ideally someone who also understood the level of service expected by Rosewood. With a wry smirk I said, 'There's only one person who fits the bill and you can't afford him.' The rest is history.

(Below): St George's Hospital, pictured at the end of the nineteenth century when Hyde Park Corner was much quieter than today.

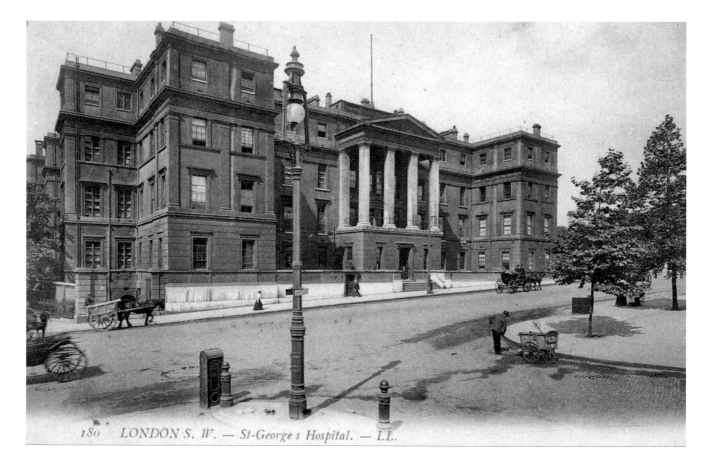

180  LONDON S. W. — St-George's Hospital. — LL.

The lease of the former St George's Hospital – one of London's best-known and most loved buildings which would later be known as The Lanesborough Hotel – was originally owned by Alan Bond, the brilliant Australian businessman who at the time was still revered for winning the America's Cup from the States with his yacht *Australia II* in 1983 – the first time in the 132-year history of the event that the Cup had left America's shores.

He negotiated a contract with Peninsula Hotels to run the hotel, then brought in the Abu Dhabi Investment Authority (ADIA) as his fifty-fifty partner in the venture.

Before work could start, however, Bond was facing serious fraud charges so ADIA bought him out and thus acquired 100 per cent of the 175-year lease from the Grosvenor Estate. This change of ownership gave ADIA the right to withdraw the management contract that had been agreed with Peninsula Hotels. Richard Ellis, the property consultants at that time, were instructed to hold a new competitive tender for the contract.

Initially, some thirty hotel operators and companies submitted expressions of interest but in the end it came down to a shortlist of just three – Rosewood, Rafael and Peninsula Hotels. Rosewood had come to the party late but despite having only a few days in which to put together a bid, Atef's team worked round the clock to prepare a beautiful presentation that spelled out the exacting service levels they envisaged, such as being the first hotel to implement butler service to every room in a hotel. It was a stunning success for Atef and Rosewood when the winner of the bid was announced. It was, after all, their first endeavour outside the USA and they had probably not seen themselves as front-runners in the contest. Fortunately Atef had worked his magic: 'Our presentation was inspired,' said Atef later. 'We did our preparations and put in the hard work, because success in this business is never an accident!'

The building was and is one of London's most prominent landmarks, the former St

George's Hospital right on the busy Hyde Park Corner, with views over Hyde Park to one side and over the gardens of Buckingham Palace on the other. The first mansion on the site was built in 1719 by James Lane, the second Viscount Lanesborough. After his death in 1724 the architect William Wilkins, who was also the architect of the National Gallery on Trafalgar Square and University College in Bloomsbury, was commissioned to enlarge the property and convert it into a new hospital 'for the reception of the sick and lame; a noble foundation, supported by voluntary contributions'.

The hospital's more famous students included Edward Jenner (1749 - 1823) the pioneer of the smallpox vaccine; Henry Gray (1827 - 1861), famed for *Gray's Anatomy*, the reference for millions of doctors and artists world-wide; Edward Wilson (1872 - 1912) who accompanied Captain Scott to the Antarctic and perished with him in their tent and Florence Nightingale (1820 - 1910) the 'Lady with the Lamp' who did so much to care for the wounded during the Crimean War and who later set up a nursing school in London.

And, of course, it was also where Dr Joseph Dudley Benjafield, married to Elvera Gelardi, worked for many years. It gives me a shiver to think of these men and women strolling through the building's doors generations before me, and what they would make of the luxurious accommodation we would create for the modern guest.

Calling the new hotel The Wellington was a non-starter as there were too many other establishments with the same name. We considered calling it the George or St George after the hospital it had once been, but there were too many places of that name also. Wilkins was considered next, after the architect who had designed the building. Eventually the idea of calling it The Lanesborough came up – which obviously referenced the grand house owned by Lord Lanesborough that had first stood on the site.

I wasn't overly enthusiastic when I heard it because I thought it could be a little too complicated for non-English speakers and guests might struggle with its pronunciation. But the PR company and Rosewood management liked it because it sounded English – though Lanesborough was actually an Irish title. But what was most important, and what finally swayed the decision was that it would be memorably different to anything else.

I arrived from the USA in June 1990 and began work on 1 July. Eileen and our children remained in Seattle until school finished. My plan,

(Above): When it opened in 1991 The Lanesborough was immediately recognised as London's leading luxury hotel. The Daimler pictured outside the front door was the first limousine I bought for the hotel.

which I had already explained to Atef, was that I would open The Lanesborough and remain in post for between three to five years. We opened an office on the third floor of the Bacardi Building right opposite on Grosvenor Crescent, and set to work.

The property had been stripped down to its bearing walls and floor plates. As it was a listed building, the exterior could not be touched. In the UK, there are a number of different grades attached to certain buildings that prevent them from being demolished or altered without special permission. The former St George's Hospital was listed Grade II*, which denotes it as a building of 'more than special interest' and which is why we could make absolutely no changes to the exterior – the name 'St George's Hospital' can still be seen carved into the stone over the former main entrance facing Hyde Park Corner. There were

(Above): The opening management team of The Lanesborough from Left to Right: Analisa Maduro, public relations manager; Bernard de Villèle, food and beverage manager; David Renton, head butler; Paul Gaylor, executive chef; Ciro Zalno, restaurant manager; Colleen Daniels, switchboard operator; Michael Bourne, head of security; Bob Gould, head concierge; Michael Naylor-Leyland, front of house manager; William Hope, chief engineer; Geoffrey Gelardi, general manager; Terri Shearer, Rosewood food and beverage manager; Alexandra Hurley, private dining manager; Amin Remtulla, director of finance; Markus Lehnert, food and beverage controller; Larry Jarman, purchasing manager; Sergio Gibeni, in-room dining manager; Michael Wills, director of human resources; Shirish Desai, assistant finance director.

(Right): Mrs Caroline Hunt, Rosewood owner.

also elements within the building which were protected by English Heritage so converting from the original hospital to a modern hotel was never going to be easy.

The only major changes we made from the original plans drawn up by Peninsular Hotels – and approved by English Heritage and all the other relevant official bodies – was to reduce the number of rooms as we felt some would have been too small in the concept we inherited. We reduced the keys by eighteen and increased the room-suite ratio to over 40 per cent.

The original design and construction of The Lanesborough made it one of the most expensive hotels in the world. In 1991, the budget was approximately £1 million per room, a staggering and unheard-of cost at that time. The bean counters and jealous competitors said it would never make money and would be a flash in the pan, especially when they heard that Caroline Hunt's Rosewood company from Texas was coming to run it. At that time I had lived in America for seventeen years and had begun to pick up a bit of a trans-Atlantic accent; even though I was specifically chosen because of my Britishness, many people would still call me a 'bloody Yank' endearingly – I hope!

But the bean counters were wrong. I carefully researched the competition and visited and stayed in most of the competitive set: Claridge's, The Connaught, The Dorchester, The Savoy and the Four Seasons. I was quite surprised at how the hotel industry in London had stagnated. For example, only one of those hotels had central air conditioning – the Four Seasons – which was statistically London's number one hotel at that time.

Our plan was to develop a hotel that had the American service philosophy and attitude but to execute it in a quintessentially British fashion. That sounds like a contradiction in terms, but I could see at the time that the British hotel sector needed a fundamental concept change. The service attitudes were anachronistic: stiff upper lip and look down your nose at anyone who was not how one would perceive a guest should be.

By contrast, The Lanesborough would be the first hotel in the ultra-deluxe category that did not have a dress code. Even in 1991, some of my more notable guests, especially those from the west coast of America, didn't own a suit and wore a jacket only if it was cold. It wouldn't do for such a guest to be refused tea – as I was in Claridge's – for not wearing a tie. In fact, the Ritz had that particular rule in place

(Opposite Page): The interior of The Lanesborough was stunning in both its design and execution. The entrance lobby (Top Left); the Library Bar (Top Right); the Conservatory (Bottom Left) and Royal Suite (Bottom Right).

until 2017, and a guest could walk to their room in jeans through the lobby only. As if to underline the issue, when the original Peninsula team held a management meeting at Claridge's, one of the managers turned up in a polo neck under a jacket and was told he would not be served without a tie.

The Connaught, if anything, was just as bad or worse. It wasn't even accepting credit cards in 1991. Even so, these hotels were still very successful. But none of them understood then what The Lanesborough meant for them and they would all be forced to adapt their culture in the years to come.

Firstly, there was the service element. We had in excess of three employees per room, which at the time was a UK industry high. Secondly, the technology we put into the rooms, which was far beyond any other hotels in the UK, and established The Lanesborough as one of the leading hotels in the field: from electronic keys to individual private phone lines for each guest, which allowed individual access to a direct line. This might not seem very impressive today, but at the time this was a first for the UK.

Early on in the development process we mocked up a suite on the first floor for Kalifa Al Maheri, the ADIA director involved with the development and design of The Lanesborough. When he examined the grey Carrara marble in the bathroom, he didn't like it. It didn't matter that this marble had already been bought for the whole project – the finished article had to be exactly as Al Maheri specified. He flew to Italy where he bought the side of a mountain containing a very special marble known as Carrara P. He then specified that it should be cut into $1m^2$ slabs and flown in to the UK.

No expense was spared to achieve the right look and feel. Designers were given strict instructions that the interior should be a timeless English design, so the overall approach was to maintain a Regency style reflecting the building's original heritage. Almost all the furniture was designed and constructed in the UK to the highest specifications and the fact that it remained in use for the next twenty-five years is testament to its intrinsic quality. All we needed to do was replace fabrics from time to time and maintain the vast amount of wood by employing an in-house French polisher.

At 10am on a cold January morning in 1991, on Hyde Park Corner, I turned my key in the door to one of the greatest hotels the world would ever know.

# Chapter 11

# One of the Best Hotels in the World

What I saw as I entered was exactly as our guests would experience. They would note the open fire in the vestibule and then the massive solid wood double doors and arch leading into the main reception area.

There, they would take in the richly marbled floor, the lavish textures of the sofas and chairs, and the stunning floral display that became almost a Lanesborough trademark, viewed through a second arch leading into the lift lobby. On the right-hand side were a pair of understated Regency-style desks where our guests were greeted, welcomed and then handed a small leather wallet containing their room keys and a supply of business cards with both the direct dial and fax numbers of their bedrooms or suites. Most importantly, there were no computers on those reception desks – because we wanted our people to look our guests in the eye, not be looking down at a computer screen.

The guests would then be escorted to their room, to be introduced to their butler for the duration of their stay. A key part of the original Rosewood concept of ultimate luxury involved this individual butler service for every client – and this was just one of the elements that made The Lanesborough experience truly unique at that time. The day we opened we had twenty-eight, including one of the first female butlers in the UK, all trained at the Ivor Spencer International School for Butlers, all offering that quintessentially British amalgam of tradition, dignity and service alongside the friendliness of American Southern hospitality.

Those age-old standards went hand-in-glove with the most modern technology that the early 1990s could provide. Every room not only had its individual telephone and fax lines, but also a CD player, a highly sophisticated touch-control lighting, heating and TV system (which some of our guests struggled with initially – but happily the butler was always available to help out), and state-of-the-art security and discreet

(Opposite Page): What set The Lanesborough apart right from the outset was the combination of individual service, the most modern technology and the very finest furniture and fabrics.

(Above): Construction of the Brighton Pavilion, built as a seaside pleasure palace for the future King George IV, started in 1787. Its exotic combination of Indian and Chinese grandeur directly influenced the design and aesthetics of the Conservatory restaurant.

monitoring systems which meant the butler knew when guests were in or out of the room, so they were never bothered unnecessarily by staff knocking on the door.

Because of the restrictions that were central to the design – we were not allowed to strip out the whole of the interior and build rows of identical rooms – almost every bedroom and suite was different. But all shared the same exquisite standards in terms of the Carrara marble bathrooms, the hand-tufted rugs that followed the design of eighteenth and nineteenth-century patterns and were even woven on looms that dated back to those times, the Empire-style chandeliers and bespoke bedroom furniture.

Open fireplaces were a feature of the public rooms too. The Withdrawing Room, off the main reception area, retained its original Wilkins fireplace below the window – a most unusual juxtaposition! There was another in the Library Bar, a stunning mahogany-panelled room, its walls covered in fitted bookcases and fine art pictures.

When The Lanesborough first opened there was a formal dining room off the vestibule at the front of the hotel and a second, more informal Conservatory restaurant created in a former courtyard now enclosed by a stunning glass roof. Its centrepieces were Chinese figurines and a pair of giant urns weighing some two tonnes apiece. Visually and aesthetically, the room was based on the Brighton Pavilion – the exotic seaside palace built for the Prince Regent. There was truly nowhere else in London anything like this stunning room.

But there is far more to a great hotel than décor and furnishings: the single most important factor is its people, and that is why the initial recruitment phase was so vitally important. My first task was to bring in the five people who would form the executive committee – all would have to be highly experienced, but more to the point, all would have to be absolutely service-driven and the sort of people who would always lead by example.

Helen Smith had been at The Dorchester and she came in as director of sales and marketing. She was a beautiful and charming lady who was also a great strategist whose key play was to get me to do her job for her! She saw straight away that Geoffrey Gelardi the managing director would get through more doors than Helen Smith the director of sales and marketing. And so she spent the next twelve years winding me up and sending me out. Together, we worked wonders and despite opening during Desert Storm, and the economy struggling, by 1993 we were breaking all records in terms of both rate and occupancy levels.

Our first financial controller was Amin Ramtulla, who at five foot four was not a big man physically but he was determined, aggressive and

(Left): When the hotel first opened we had a formal Dining Room as well as the more relaxed Conservatory.

a stickler for detail. His insistence that all operational procedures were carried out to the 'T' made him unpopular in some quarters but his demand for perfection made him a great ally of mine. Better still, despite being in finance, he clearly understood that bean counting must never get in the way of service levels. Sadly he passed away from diabetes far too early.

Bernard de Villèle was one of the best food and beverage directors I have ever worked with. He was a stickler for service acumen, always kept meticulous records and had an astoundingly good memory. He was at The Lanesborough for four years before moving to manage hotels in the Caribbean, Mexico and the Middle East. He is now general manager of the Ritz-Carlton in Bahrain.

Perhaps the most difficult position to fill was that of front of house manager. I needed someone whose social skills would present the hotel as a quintessentially British residence and I found that person thanks to my brother Michael introducing me to Lord Charles Spencer Churchill, brother of the Duke of Marlborough. Charles knew a great deal about hotels and restaurants as he had worked with Rocco Forte for many years and he unreservedly recommended one person: Michael Naylor-Leyland. He had an aristocratic background, was

(Below): Welcoming HRH The Queen to The Lanesborough. Michael Naylor-Leyland pictured right was the finest front of house manager we could ever have hoped for.

educated at Eton, was blond and six foot tall and described as one of the most handsome men in London. He also, said Charles, 'had had a little problem with drugs and alcohol' but he was in recovery and was looking for a position in the hotel industry.

Michael's front of house skills were the best I have ever known – if we ever had a guest who was upset about something, we'd put him or her in front of Michael and in no time they would be eating out of his hands. Our guests loved him, mainly because he went out of his way to make each and every one of them happy. And this made him a perfect fit because I have always maintained that we are not in the hospitality business, but in the happy business.

The final vital position to fill was human resources, a vital role as whoever became the director would have to recruit some 300 staff, all of the right calibre, all of whom understood our ethos and culture, and all of whom would have to undergo intensive training in the run-up to opening. Michael Willis was that man and he set about finding the people we would need – the best people would already be happy in their jobs so would not be trawling through advertisements. Michael understood that poaching will get you a better calibre of people than advertising and so he began a process of using all our existing contacts to identify those we wanted to attract to The Lanesborough.

There were other people who were equally important in taking the hotel work to the heights it achieved. Bill Freeman whom I'd originally met at Plazas of the America in Dallas where he was the HR director, had helped me open the Remington and the Bel-Air, trained my team at the Sorento and was a critical element in the training and motivation of the staff, getting them to believe this was going to be the best hotel in London and one of the best hotels in the world. Our first head concierge was Bob Gould who sadly fell ill shortly after the opening.

He was replaced by Colin Short, the quintessential concierge who kept his 'black book' very close to his chest, but who could open any door, find a table at any restaurant and find tickets for any show. He also got me innumerable upgrades when I was flying on business, even a couple of return trips on Concorde. He was difficult to manage and it was sometimes best not to enquire too deeply into how he performed his magic – but he provided an an unrivalled service for our guests.

Salvatori Calabrese also joined us a little after we opened to run the Library Bar. He arrived with a great reputation and when he left, that reputation was even stronger. He put together an unrivalled collection of cognacs and wrote a book, *Cognac: A Liquid History*. Salvatore's 'Liquid History' collection at The Lanesborough continued after he left in 2004 to open his own bar, most notably in 2008 when the hotel bought one of the oldest known bottles of cognac, distilled in 1770 and sold for £4,000 a shot. Today it would go for twice that!

How influential was Salvatore in London those days? One evening Stevie Wonder was in town and agreed to play a full thirty-minute set on the piano in the corner of the Library Bar. But once the applause for the great singer died down, so Stevie turned and applauded Salvatore for his own unrivalled showmanship when preparing cocktails or serving those precious cognacs.

Salvatore was the showman, but much of the hard work that went on behind the scenes was just as important to the hotel's success. The classic example was the housekeeper Janet Bamford who was with us for twenty-five years before her well-earned retirement. She had worked at Raffles and the Mandarin Oriental and so knew all there was to know about luxury hotels. It was said that she ran her department with the discipline of an army sergeant but with a heart of gold. She not only ensured a consistently high standard of housekeeping at The Lanesborough, but she was also a true expert on renovation and hotel openings and had the great ability to manage fabrics, carpets and the general maintenance of the guest rooms at a level that would be almost impossible to replicate.

Last, but most emphatically not least, is Paul Gaylor, the man who has held the position of head chef ever since we first opened. In fact his first major function was not in London but at the Mansion on Turtle Creek where Mrs Caroline Hunt hosted a party in August 1990 to announce the opening of The Lanesborough later in the year. Paul, who had only joined a month earlier, was thrown in at the deep end as he flew out to Dallas to prepare a 'Lanesborough Banquet' for Mrs Hunt and her guests.

But once the hotel opened, he was busy running both the formal dining room – imaginatively called The Dining Room – and the Conservatory. Earlier in his career, Paul was Anton Mosimann's number two at The Dorchester and he came to The Lanesborough from The Halkin. In my view he is one of the best, hardest-working and talented chefs in London and the fact that Chris Galvin, among others, were mentored by him in The Lanesborough's kitchens – chefs who have gone on to achieve great successes of their own – is testament to Paul's ability.

The first people that our guests meet tend to be the doormen, and since first impressions are so important, there could be no better ambassadors for the hotel than Dominic Mullen and Victor Radojevic and the rest of the front door team, all resplendent in their traditional bowler hats. Over the years they have welcomed royalty, celebrities, business tycoons, politicians, friends and family. In many ways they are the lifeblood of our hotel community.

These, and of course many others, were the people who made The Lanesborough tick in those early days. It was not a big hotel and with just ninety-five rooms it was actually one of the smallest luxury hotels in London in the 1990s. But although this obviously had an impact on revenues, it was also one of our greatest strengths because it meant we really could take care of each and every guest who came through the door. And once we had been open for a while, I would look at the list of arriving guests on any particular day and would know perhaps twenty per cent of them personally. That is why, for me, turning up at the hotel in the morning never felt like going to work – because so often I was greeting friends.

They kept returning because they loved the atmosphere that we created at the hotel and appreciated one essential aspect of the original concept of The Lanesborough – that it would be a residential hotel. This was partly because of practical considerations – there was no space for large corporate events – but more for cultural reasons. We wanted this to be a genuine home from home for our guests and so we

(Above): Salvatore Calabrese, the first manager of the Library Bar, started collecting old and rare cognacs, some selling for thousands of pounds per shot!

resisted the temptation to encourage too many business functions or even to allow shops or vitrines on site despite their revenue potential.

I am still convinced it was the right decision, but this did not mean that we got everything right first time. We didn't anticipate at first how important a spa would be to many of the guests who wanted to be able to work out or get a massage without having to leave the hotel. This we rectified by moving my offices down to the far less salubrious lower ground floor and using what had been the management suite for a compact but eminently workable spa and gym. Later, after the major renovations, we would construct a far larger bespoke spa and gym space of 18,000 square feet.

The other oversight in the initial design was potentially far more serious, particularly in terms of revenue. We had just one Royal Suite, which when we opened, it boasted the highest room rate in London at £2,500 a night – today it is £15,000! The problem was that there was only one and if it was occupied, others who would accept only the very best went elsewhere as our next best suite was considerably smaller.

For example, in the early days we had an Arab prince in the Royal Suite who had booked for ten days, after which a prominent American guest was due to move in. The prince then announced he would be staying a further three days and refused to be moved to another suite. What could I do? I called our American guest and offered him the smaller but still very fine Buckingham Suite – free of charge.

(Right): A private dinner with former Prime Minister Margaret Thatcher and Mrs Hunt coincided with one of the tabloid newspapers trying to concoct a story that our butlers were willing to procure 'escorts' for our guests!

He refused, insisting on having the Royal Suite that he had booked and we had confirmed. So to cut a long story short, I booked the Piano Suite at Claridge's and offered to pick up the room charges, as well as providing him with a Rolls-Royce and chauffeur and all complimentary meals he wished to take at The Lanesborough for the duration of his stay in London.

He reluctantly agreed to my offer and did in fact visit us regularly for breakfasts, lunches and dinners while staying at Claridge's. And although he did give me a bit of a hard time he clearly understood the impossible predicament I was in and three months later returned with his wife and took the Royal Suite for a full year! I remember that a month or so after they arrived, I gently requested that he settle his account up to that time; a couple of days later I took a call from our astonished financial controller who thought I should know that someone had just transferred £1 million into our bank account and he didn't know who it was from!

That little episode turned out well in the end but what we should have done up front was to have a second Presidential or Emperor suite. In time, around 2005, we did manage to craft a new Lanesborough Suite right underneath the Royal Suite and in some ways that original problem was solved – though some eleven years too late.

Nevertheless, the Royal Suite welcomed many heads of state, CEOs of top global companies, Arnold Schwarzenegger, Michael Jackson, Madonna, Bernie Madoff and many more. And many memorable parties were hosted there … though here it's time to be very discreet.

Discretion was our watchword, but there is no denying that The Lanesborough was the place to be in London in those spectacular times for the hotel. There are many wonderful stories that can be told – enough, in fact to fill a whole series of books! Often our problem was that others were trying to get those same stories – usually people from Britain's notorious tabloid press.

I remember once not long after opening having dinner with the former Prime Minister Margaret Thatcher and Mrs Caroline Hunt in the Conservatory. That very same evening a journalist from the *News of the World* – then the UK's biggest-selling Sunday newspaper and one notorious for muck-raking stories – checked in, obviously hoping to manufacture a scandal at our expense. Basically he asked first the concierge and then one or two of our butlers to supply him with a 'lady of the night'. Naturally they refused but he kept asking so to placate

him our head butler went to his room and gave him a copy of *What's On* magazine, a rather downmarket version of *Time Out* that provided visitors to London with information about what was going on but which also had a contacts section at the back. 'Everything you need is here,' said the head butler before leaving the room.

Needless to say, the very next morning the *News of the World* ran a splash claiming that The Lanesborough's head butler was supplying guests with hookers while Margaret Thatcher was having dinner with the general manager in the restaurant!

I suppose we have to be grateful that the *News of the World* didn't check in on one of the days that Prince Philip, Prince Charles, or even the Queen was in the building. Both Prince Philip and Prince Charles visited in the early days; Prince Philip was interested in what we had done to the old St George's Hospital, while Prince Charles was fascinated by the architectural and design elements we had introduced. The Queen hosted a private dinner in the St George's Room for the Duchy of Lancaster which was established in 1399 by Henry IV to provide an income for the Sovereign and which now owns nearly 46,000 acres of farming land, mainly in the north of England, but also some properties in the Strand in London, including the land on which the Savoy Hotel sits. I suppose it means that in a way my grandfather Giulio was a tenant of the Duchy in his time! The Queen's sister Princess Margaret visited on a number of occasions and Princess Diana was also an occasional visitor, usually to attend a charitable event, and it was always a great pleasure to welcome her to the hotel.

We also enjoyed welcoming a host of international stars, people like Larry Hagman who tipped staff with $100 dollar bills – though sadly with Larry's portrait where Benjamin Franklin's should have been. Patrick Swayze was a favourite guest, not least because he got on so well with the staff. Other favourites were Jay-Z who stayed regularly and Beyoncé who tended to stay at the Mandarin on her London visits, but who always came to The Lanesborough when Jay-Z was in town. Both were such good people who always had time for the staff and it was a great pleasure to have them in residence.

We were fortunate to welcome a host of royalty and celebrities to The Lanesborough including HRH Princess Diana (Below Left); Patrick Swayze (Below) and David Frost (Bottom).

(Opposite Page Above):
With Bill Elliott and Bill
Feldstein, two Lanesborough
guests who became close
friends. This was on a skiing
trip to Courchevel which
explains the red faces!
(Opposite Page Below):
Another memorable trip
with guests who became
friends, this time shooting in
South Africa. From left: Benji
Mavros, Patrick Mavros,
Martin Derrick, Bill Elliott,
Bill Feldstein, Joe Clark, Bill
Belzberg and me.

An important American travel agent called to make a booking for Madonna which I initially turned down as in the early 1990s we were flying high and had close to 100 per cent occupancy. She – or more accurately some members of her entourage – had a reputation for being noisy and disruptive in hotels and I didn't want our other guests disturbed. However, the agent had earlier booked his clients Arnold Schwarzenegger and Cher to stay with us so he persuaded me to change my mind, though I did warn him that if there were any problems with either guests or staff I would have to ask her to leave.

When she arrived I went to greet her and she made her feelings absolutely clear by walking right past me! But eventually I took her to her room and all was okay. She stayed with us a number of times after that and there were never any problems.

The first time Michael Jackson came to The Lanesborough he was with the record company Sony and before he arrived they made all sorts of preparations including installing a juke box, games and pinball machines in his rooms. They also said that when he arrived, they wanted me to hand over to someone else at the guest floor to take him to his suite. They had positioned a remote control toy car driven by a clown and fitted with some sort of walkie-talkie mechanism right outside the lift. As the door opened, it appeared to be the clown saying 'Welcome to The Lanesborough Michael, follow me to your suite.' The car then set off down the corridor to the suite with an absolutely delighted Michael Jackson in its wake. It was strange to see a forty-year-old so entranced by toys and childish paraphernalia, but Michael Jackson became a regular guest and in fact had booked a whole floor for a planned appearance at the O2 in the summer of 2009, but sadly he died shortly before. At that time he was managed by Dr Tohme whom I had originally met during my time at the Bel-Air.

I also well remember Geri Halliwell, the former Spice Girl, who stayed at the hotel for a long time. While she was trying to negotiate her rate she kissed me full on the lips in the main lobby, which caused a bit of a stir with the staff. Did she get a preferential rate? Discretion prevents me from remembering!

But it wasn't just the superstars who made life at The Lanesborough so rewarding because we welcomed so many guests from so many walks of life. Granted, the hotel was an expensive place to stay, so the people who stayed with us tended to be very successful in their own lines of business, but it was the sheer breadth of human experience that made working there so rewarding – for me and for most of our staff too.

I particularly remember my very good friend Bill Feldstein who used to stay with us around nine months of the year – whenever he was not away shooting. Bill Feldstein was responsible for introducing me to the shooting fraternity in the UK and inviting me to some of the best shoots in the country – ever since, shooting has remained my number one sport. Joe Clark, also a great friend from my Seattle days, who owned an immensely successful aviation company in the city, also stayed with us regularly from the day we opened – often flying himself to London in his own Gulfstream G5 jet. Bill Elliott, another character from the aviation world, lived at The

Lanesborough for five or six years, first in one of our suites and later in the mews apartment that we created behind the hotel. After he moved to Monaco to live on his yacht with his new wife Catharina, they asked me to be Godfather to their twins Nicholas and Sabrina, along with Joe Clark and Stelios Haji-Ioannou, founder of EasyJet. I often visited them in Monaco and enjoyed meeting Prince Albert and Princess Charlene with whom Bill and Catharina had a very close relationship.

(Below): Well-deserved awards for our fabulous kitchen staff. (Opposite Page Above): In 2011 I was presented with a Hotelier of the World Award at a wonderful presentation ceremony I attended with my ever-supportive wife Eileen (Opposite Page Below).

There was Clive Jacobs, the highly-successful publisher who also loved to shoot and who for a while had his own driven shoot in Devon; and Erik Fällström, an entrepreneur who stayed around 100 or more days a year with us and who, along with Bill Feldstein, actually stored a full wardrobe at the hotel which the butlers would retrieve and put in his suite whenever he arrived, quite a daunting task when one saw the amount of clothes in storage. He too is part of the shooting fraternity. Georg Kaehny, an investor based in Switzerland, who was previously a guest at the Remington in Houston many years before, was also a regular guest at The Lanesborough, taking a junior suite almost every month. Georg's greatest love is show jumping and he owns some of the world's leading horses. He is such an interesting character and remains a close friend and confidante.

Above all, it was the daily interaction with people like this that makes the hotel world such a great life and why I'd encourage anyone to come into the business. Every day is different; you never know what's around the corner or who you're going to meet – it's a truly glamorous, stimulating, interesting, rewarding and fulfilling career.

# Celebrating Jaguar's 60th Anniversary

The Lanesborough was the chosen venue for numerous prestigious events but one I remember very clearly was when we hosted an event as part of Jaguar's 60th anniversary celebrations.

The guest of honour was Sir Stirling Moss, though for many the greatest attraction was the line-up of fabulous classic Jaguar cars outside the hotel. Sir Stirling turned up on the three-wheeled scooter that he regularly used to get around London, then after the event, treated me to an exhilarating drive around London and Hyde Park in the prototype D-type Jaguar – the very car which was developed by the company specifically in order to win the Le Mans 24-Hour race and which was taken to the circuit and immediately broke the lap record by some five seconds in May 1954.

(Below): With Sir Stirling Moss just before he cut the cake our chef had created for the event. (Opposite Page Above): Jaguar C-type which competed in the Mille Miglia in 1953; the original 1954 prototype D-type from which that year's Le Mans 24-Hour cars were developed; and the 1950 XK120 which won the Tulip, Alpine and RAC rallies in 1951. (Opposite Page Below): a memorable ride as Sir Stirling drove me around London in the D-Type.

# Chapter 12

# Beyond the Golden Years

(Below): Afternoon tea was extremely popular, thanks in part to our innovation of developing the world's first tea sommelier – Karl Kessah (Below Right).

The first eighteen years were, I suppose, the golden years for The Lanesborough. Both socially and statistically, it led the London hotel market by a wide margin. We had the highest occupancy rates and were maintaining the highest room rates at the same time. Part of this was down to aggressive and innovative marketing methods which were fully supported by both Mrs Caroline Hunt and Atef Mankarios at Rosewood: Rosewood didn't own The Lanesborough but it was absolutely in their best interests to support it to the hilt because it would help the company establish an international base from which to expand outside the USA.

The Lanesborough's recognition and exposure right around the globe was extraordinary and very quickly we were acknowledged as one of the top hotel companies in the world in terms of quality of service. Maintaining that reputation was made easier because we had very little turnover in staff, and virtually none within department heads for the first few years. When it came to recruitment, everyone wanted to be a part of the hotel's success. We made sure we selected the right individuals, looking particularly carefully at their attitude and suitability for the environment. The restaurant, though, did have some turnover, but that's quite usual in the hospitality industry. Overall, however, on an annual basis, turnover of staff was below ten per cent, which was clearly due to the status the hotel had established.

But nothing stands still. We continued to upgrade the hotel's technological features – so that, for example, the original push-button switches for the lighting, heating and entertainment in the rooms were upgraded to tablets that controlled every feature, from the physical and lighting environment to personal communications. The Lanesborough was the first hotel to put laptops in every room.

We introduced new features, such as developing the world's first tea sommelier, Karl Kessah, who ensured that tea at The Lanesborough was not just a meal, but a truly memorable experience.

(Above): The Conservatory was transformed into Apsleys, a new restaurant overseen by Michelin three-star chef Heinz Beck. Just five months after opening, Apsleys had won its own Michelin star, the fastest any London restaurant had ever achieved that accolade.

The Conservatory restaurant was completely redesigned by Adam Tihany, the famous New York-based designer and re-born as Apsleys under the watchful eye of Heinz Beck, a highly gifted three-Michelin Star chef from La Pergola in Rome – his first foray outside Italy. No-one was surprised when just five months later, Apsleys was itself awarded a Michelin Star, the fastest any restaurant in London had ever gained that accolade.

One of our smartest moves of all came in 2007 when the UK banned all smoking in pubs, bars and restaurants. Thanks to the pioneering work of first Salvatore Calabrese and later Giuseppe Ruo in the Library Bar, we were doing a very big trade in vintage cognac, cocktails and fine cigars – in fact we were the only hotel, for example, to sell Cohiba Behike cigars individually. They were produced in a very limited edition of one hundred humidors holding forty cigars each to mark the fortieth anniversary of Cohiba, with each individual cigar rolled by Norma Fernandez – Castro's personal cigar roller – in the company's El Laguito factory in Havana, Cuba. We were selling them at £1,500 each, though today they sell for £5,000-plus for each stick.

And so a total smoking ban was going to make a massive dent in our revenues, as well as depriving our guests of one of the great pleasures in life. As I paced back and forth, I was determined to find a creative way around this ban. I could not have my guests standing on Hyde Park Corner smoking a Cohiba.

On one of my inspections of the property, I had spotted a door to an unused sunken terrace which turned out to be the answer to my prayers – here was a potential area for a smoking shelter. We got to work, for time was of the essence and number one on my list of essential works was to remove the unwanted guests who currently occupied this terrace space…mice! Off to Harrods, I bought some big umbrellas, garden furniture and outdoor electric heaters and rented a portable bar. We set this area up with a large humidor and thus the Garden Room opened for business.

At the same time we applied for planning permission for a more permanent shelter but initially we were turned down flat. We kept persevering with different designs and eventually got permission to build a solid-roofed structure that was a metre away from the walls of the main building, then to protect our guests from the elements we fitted louvres which filled most of the space to the walls. With underfloor heating, electric blow heaters and radiant heaters we created an amazing space that most visitors never realised was

(Above and Left): The Garden
Room that allowed our guests
to continue to enjoy their cigars
after the ban on indoor smoking
came into effect in the UK.
Especially at night, it was almost
impossible to know that this was
technically an 'outside' area!

'outdoors'. It was not very green, but it was highly effective and gave us a venue that was so busy that we were turning over some £1.3 million a year in a forty-five-seat bar – and all from a space that had never before been utilised!

Alongside these improvements we were making at the hotel itself, there were changes on the management front too.

First of all, the Hunt family decided to bring in partners. These were Flip Maritz and Lou Wolf of Maritz-Wolf who already owned hotels in the USA – a couple of Four Seasons properties – and who had funds for future hotel investment.

They also brought with them a development arm – Martin Foxon, and they promoted me to executive vice president of operations for Europe, the Middle East and Asia. In that role, I opened the Al Faisaliah Hotel and the Abha Palace in Saudi Arabia and the Dhamawangsa Hotel in Jakarta. I also oversaw Badrutt's Palace in St Moritz, Switzerland and Seiyo Ginza in Tokyo.

Back in London, The Lanesborough did fantastically well for about eighteen years. There really had been no new luxury hotels opened in London prior to our arrival in 1991. The old established hotels had been resting on their laurels and had been doing so for many, many years. But now they realised that they had to spend money not only to catch up but to keep up. To some extent, that's exactly what happened and the distinction between London's luxury hotels was lessened as others invested heavily in their own buildings and adopted new marketing methods and service culture, in an effort to compensate for the disparity in the market.

Rosewood was also changing somewhat, mainly due to the influence of Flip Maritz and the man he brought in as chief operating officer, Jim Brown. He had been with Four Seasons for twenty-three years and was known to be a no-nonsense numbers man, which was quite contrary to the original Rosewood philosophy that, prior to the partnership with Maritz-Wolf, had always focused on quality, even at the expense of profit. It was abundantly clear to me that Atef and Jim, my two bosses, did not have the same focus.

Bob Zimmer and Atef had created this company and due to the on-going changes in company philosophy, Atef started to look at opportunities to allow a management buyout from Maritz-Wolf and the Hunts. He had put together a team which was loyal to him and had a

(Above): The Rosewood senior management team.

plan backed by some wealthy developers based out of Florida. It was around 1998-1999 that he attempted to buy out the Hunts to operate Rosewood as a private company, taking his executive team with him, all of whom were *au fait* and in favour of going in this direction. The team consisted of Scott Blair - financial controller, George Fong - development director, Andy Anderson - vice-president of marketing, Jim Brackensick - head of purchasing, and me.

But there was an informer in our midst who told the owners behind Atef's back: Jim Brackensick. Atef was told that a buyout was out of the question and the episode marked Atef's demise at Rosewood Hotels. This was a colossal shame since he had extraordinary vision and he had given me great encouragement and support.

I needn't have worried about Atef though. He was very highly regarded and was quickly hired by the chairman of Starwood, Barry Sternlicht, a visionary in hotel investment, who has since left Starwood Hotels but maintained Starwood Capital, the investment company he started. To this day he is still very much involved in high profile hotel investments and developments.

Atef had a very good rapport with Sternlicht and persuaded him to agree to develop the St Regis brand as Starwood's ultra-deluxe division. He needed bilateral international control of all these hotels, which wasn't popular with the other Starwood Europe, Asia and USA division presidents, because they would lose control of their best assets. However, Atef and Sternlicht could see that these assets were being sold by the same sales force as Sheraton, Aloft, Western, Meridian and Four Points: not good for an exclusive brand.

Ultimately Sternlicht decided that a new division should be created for St Regis, separate from the rest of the Starwood hotels, with all the St Regis branded hotels reporting to Atef.

At Rosewood, once Atef departed, Jim Brown was made president, a completely different character to either Bob Zimmer or Atef. Zimmer was a great design visionary and Atef had the knack of getting on with all those around him, Jim Brown was a smart man, technically very sound but had a tendency to upset people even if he didn't mean to.

About a year before the Rosewood management contract was due to expire, I was approached by one of ADIA's representatives and asked what I thought about changing management companies. I didn't think it was wise, believing that Rosewood represented The Lanesborough better than anyone else I could think of in the market.

(Below): Flanked by doormen Victor and Michael, welcoming Atef Mankarios, now president and CEO of St Regis Hotels and Resorts, back to The Lanesborough after St Regis took over the management contract from Rosewood. 'This hotel is my child,' he said, 'and the role of parent is one you don't walk away from. I am back and returning to the family after a brief absence.'

After a long discussion about other management companies which might or might not be able to maintain the hotel's profile and service levels, it became clear that they were trying to get me to support a change in management from Rosewood to St Regis.

At first I was taken aback by the fact that they were even considering putting The Lanesborough into such a corporate environment, unaware of the Mankarios-Sternlicht agreement to make St Regis a separate and stand-alone brand. I was aware that Atef had joined Starwood as St Regis president and in one sense I had loyalty to Atef as he had always treated me so well; I also had a strong sense of loyalty to Rosewood, however.

I discovered that Rosewood had already been talking with ADIA regarding renewal of the management agreement and had been met with a polite but frosty response. This was perhaps because they had sent Martin Foxon to Abu Dhabi to renegotiate the contract but the powers there expected the most senior executive Flip Maritz to come to see them. At least, this was their feedback to me; I could never quite tell whether this was just an excuse to undermine Rosewood and push through the change.

Throughout this process I tried to remain neutral, although I had serious doubts about working for St Regis and Starwood. If it had been my decision, I would have stayed with Rosewood. But eventually the decision was made and much to the surprise of Rosewood and the rest of the industry - we would become a St Regis hotel.

Rosewood simply couldn't believe ADIA would put the future of The Lanesborough in the hands of a corporate identity like Starwood but clearly Atef's relationship with ADIA had paid off - and he had assured them that it would be business as usual with The Lanesborough being run as an independent concern within the Starwood umbrella.

The first few months with St Regis were interesting, much to the chagrin of all Starwood's corporate sales and marketing offices because they were all told to take their hands off The Lanesborough - the new jewel in their crown. This was absolutely the right thing to do because Rosewood had done an outstanding job in creating The Lanesborough as a stand alone hotel, as this was their philosophy at the time. Those in the industry knew it was a Starwood Hotel but to the greater world and most guests, it was stand-alone and unique, talked about in the same vein as Claridge's, The Connaught, The Dorchester and The Savoy, despite being only a decade old.

The newly-formed St Regis upmarket division was successful for the most part even though Sternlicht left about two years into The Lanesborough's ten-year contract. Within Starwood, the separation of St Regis from the other entities was very unpopular, and I suspect that because of those tensions, Atef also left shortly after.

Now I was potentially in trouble. My protection was gone and I could well have been helpless in the face of that corporate steamroller Starwood. I'm not for a moment suggesting that there was anything monstrous about Starwood or the way in which it did business – it is a great global organisation running many very fine properties – the danger for me was its sheer size which could have swamped The Lanesborough had it been forced to operate the way Starwood's mass-market hotels did, thereby losing its individual identity. But thankfully, Roland Voss, president of Starwood Europe, Asia, Africa and the Middle East, and later Michael Wale, recognised that The Lanesborough was successful in its own right and maintained a hands-off protocol for the rest of the contract.

(Below): Other luxury hotels in London were upping their game but in 2011 The Lanesborough and I were still getting recognition in the industry for maintaining the highest standards.

It was around 2010 when the hotel started to lose traction as the premier property on the market, as many new hotels had been developed and a significant number of existing hotels had invested in extensive renovation projects over the previous twenty years. It was clear that The Lanesborough had to raise the bar once again, both in service and design innovation. We could clearly see how the industry was evolving as both the new hotels and the existing luxury properties all sought ways of meeting and even exceeding The Lanesborough's design, technology and service levels.

It was an inevitable development and I suppose in a way, we were blinded by our own success, and could and perhaps should have seen it earlier. I raised the possibility of a renovation with ADIA and was summoned to Abu Dhabi to give a presentation about what needed to be done.

I told them that the property was now about twenty years old and some of its infrastructure was becoming weak. I requested a budget

of £17 million. ADIA had a new executive director of strategy and planning, Majed Al Romaithi, who was a creative thinker looking to develop his reputation by recreating The Lanesborough in a totally different manifestation, mainly by expanding it into the office building next door. At first this was an intriguing idea and with a simple concept behind it: if you take a successful one hundred-room hotel and add another hundred, it means you're doubling the revenue and doubling the success – but only accountants think like this.

A huge team of architects, designers, project managers and structural engineers was put together to look at the feasibility of this new concept. On two occasions, this included flying over thirty people to Abu Dhabi to give presentations which seemed to me to be overkill. I've always held very strong – and rarely positive – views on consultants as their modus operandi seems to be to come up with ideas, many of which add cost but not value. And here was a classic example of a project that was sane, rational and sensible at the outset but which now was going from the sublime to the ridiculous.

Suddenly people were talking about taking out the existing restaurant and turning it into a driveway, having a reception each side of this, losing the drive-in garage which would be replaced with an lift system, and developing two more restaurants and a ballroom. By the time everyone came to their senses, £2 million had been spent on investigating the expansion. It was an interesting process, but the *coup de grâce* was the first cost estimate: £340 million.

Once the expansion programme had been discarded and most of the consultants had been eased off the project, we set about writing specifications on what was needed in the existing property. The first plan was for a complete renovation of the rooms and partial renovation of the public areas, excluding the restaurant, which had only been redesigned a few years earlier by Adam Tihany, one of the world's greatest restaurant designers.

The renovation also excluded the bathrooms because of the quality of the original marble. In the final analysis it was decided by Majed Al Romaithi that all areas of the hotel – including the bathrooms – should receive a complete renovation.

An issue brought to light was the cost of the public area ceilings coming in at a whopping £9.3 million. While I couldn't agree more that the original ceilings were pedestrian at best, the thought of spending such a stratospheric amount on ceilings irked me, especially as budgets were being cut in areas in which the hierarchy showed no great interest – technologies such as phone systems, security systems, lifts and lighting systems.

Considering the ever-increasing sweep of changes, which eventually included all the building's infrastructure and taking every bathroom back to its risers wherever practicable, it became apparent that the renovation would not be able to take place without closing the hotel. Even air conditioning and lift systems were to be replaced. The work could not take place while the property was functioning without major disruption to its guests and another important factor was that to do so while keeping the hotel open would mean the renovation would take three years as opposed to eighteen months if closed.

The repercussions of closing the property would cut deep, however, especially for our long-term staff. We looked at all options to retain them. At one point, I was informed that we could retain 60 per cent

(Below): Looking rather wistfully at the front door key after I'd locked up for the duration of the major renovation programme. (Opposite Page): The whole of the exterior was covered in scaffolding and cladding while the interior was stripped out.

**THE LANESBOROUGH**
**LONDON**

Our doors are now closed for renovation, reopening in the final quarter of 2014.

For further information, please visit
www.lanesborough.com

of staff on full wages. But the harsh reality was that most of the line staff relied on cash tips to supplement the industry-weak salary structures, and so although this sounded a generous offer, it was clearly not one that would satisfy most of the people I wanted to retain. As a result, it was decided to opt for a reasonably generous redundancy programme. At the time of closing, about 30 per cent of staff had been there for over twenty years.

The loss of many of these employees would make reopening a difficult process, although I was able to hold on to some core staff members, including the two faces who had been greeting guests at the door for nearly fifty years between them, our senior doormen Dominic and Victor. We trained them as drivers and offered a complimentary chauffeur service to our regular guests when they were in London. I also managed to retain the key positions of executive and assistant head housekeeper – both key roles in the renovation – the head butler, who did administrative work when the hotel closed, and accounting, sales, marketing, and engineering staff.

We found temporary offices in Victoria through Clive Jacobs – a regular guest at the hotel over many years – who owned some of the most influential magazines in the industry, such as *The Caterer* and *Travel Weekly*, and that became our base for the eighteen months that The Lanesborough was closed.

In 2014 the management contract with St Regis, which had already been extended by three years, was about due. Starwood were in negotiations with ADIA and to my knowledge, the owners were considering re-signing with Starwood as a Luxury Collection hotel. It should be remembered that The Lanesborough had only become part of Starwood Hotels because of Atef and his

personal close relationship with ADIA. Having had that discussion with the owners, I couldn't recommend another extension to the St Regis contract. I believe the owners were also holding discussions with a number of other big players in the hotel business including Hilton at one stage, but in my view none of these companies suited the unique profile of The Lanesborough.

At the time, I had introduced two companies: Cheval Blanc – owned by LVMH – and Oetker – owned by the Oetker family. At the 2014 Travel Mart convention held in Las Vegas, one of the USA's top travel agents – Bob Watson who later joined Valerie Wilson Travel – introduced me to Frank Marrenbach, boss of Oetker.

(Right): The original plan was that the hotel should reopen towards the end of 2014 but in the event the opening was delayed until summer 2015 – by which time The Lanesborough was under new management.

After that, Oetker and ADIA had meetings without me present and everything seemed to be progressing very smoothly. Sure enough, later that year a contract was signed.

And so, when The Lanesborough re-opened in the summer of 2015, it was under Oetker management. During the eighteen months or so when the hotel was closed, it had been totally transformed and once again reached the very pinnacle of service, technology and luxury. The two major changes were the new Céleste restaurant to replace Apsleys in what even earlier had been the Conservatory, and the brand-new purpose-built spa which was actually located next door in the office building at Number One Knightsbridge. This was largely thanks to Graham Cox our architect who was also a close friend and with whom I have worked for many years. Graham was able to achieve the unachievable when it came to planning and permissions. He was the person responsible for getting planning for the Garden Room; he was granted planning for the new Lanesbrough Suite in an area that was originally protected by English Heritage, and he found a way of transitioning our guests from the hotel into the spa without them realising they were in a different building.

(Above): The new Céleste restaurant's chef patron was Eric Frechon. Within a year, he and executive chef Florian Favario had been awarded a Michelin star.

Céleste's chef patron was Éric Fréchon, the Michelin-starred chef at Le Bristol in Paris since 1999. It took just a year before he and executive chef Florian Favario were awarded a Michelin star for Céleste – a great achievement. But sadly the restaurant was never as successful as it had been in the past – perhaps it was now a little too formal for modern tastes.

The new spa was a discreet and luxurious haven consisting of a spacious fitness room, treatment rooms, sauna, thermal suites and a hydrotherapy pool. In addition there was a tranquil space in which to relax before or after treatments – and a restaurant and bar. Hotel guests are welcomed, of course, but it's also run as an exclusive members' club. The spa was very well received, described by *Condé Nast Traveller Spa Guide* as 'the best in town' in 2018 and crowned England's Best Hotel Spa in the World Spa Awards the following year. Despite this, it always struggled to meet its membership goals.

The 'fit' between The Lanesborough and the other Oetker hotels looked very good indeed on paper. Among the fine hotels they ran were Le Bristol in Paris, Brenners Park Hotel in Baden-Baden, L'Apogée in Courchevel, one of France's most chic ski resorts, Château Saint Martin & Spa and the Hotel Du Cap Eden Roc in Cap d'Antibes on the French riviera, the Eden Roc on St Barts in the French West Indies and Fregate Island in the Seychelles.

Oetker were hoping for significant cross-pollination with guest and management practices. What I didn't know was that they had offered ADIA substantial revenues and guaranteed profit, a decision which would eventually come back to haunt them.

Evolution in any business is inevitable and there were certainly changes in management style once Oetker held the reins. ADIA was also a very different organisation to when I had first started working with them some twenty-five years earlier. Then, the department at ADIA I dealt with consisted of just eight or nine people; now there were about three hundred. Things were not the same and it gradually dawned on me that it was time for another move as my relationship with Oetker and the new ADIA was not going well.

The soul of The Lanesborough which took years to develop was disappearing before my eyes under Oetker's management. It was a sentiment expressed time and time again by long standing guests and employees. The introduction to Frank Marrenbach, boss of Oetker, at the 2014 Travel Mart Convention and my subsequent decision to introduce Oetker to the new AIDA, was coming back to haunt me.

After an initial renovation investment of £60 million, followed by another £20 million on the spa, The Lanesborough was at its physical peak; it was therefore a good time for me to part with one of the most wonderful hotels there has ever been. At a meeting with Frank Marrenbach at Frankfurt airport, we negotiated my departure. Frank came well prepared, with a twenty-six-page letter carefully crafted by lawyers. I signed and I left The Lanesborough in the summer of 2018.

My twenty-eight years at The Lanesborough were, I think, the best of my life so far and they went by like lightning. The honour of running one of the most successful hotels in the world was what kept me there for so long and I can't adequately express my gratitude for the support of the owners and management, and almost all those I have worked with over the years.

The Oetker Group consisted of a number of very fine hotels including Le Bristol in Paris (Below Left) and the Brenners Park Hotel in Baden-Baden (Below Right).

At the time I think I was the longest standing hotel manager in London and I doubt there are very many in the industry who have survived under three management companies – Rosewood, St Regis and finally Oetker – all under the ever-watchful eye of ADIA. Their support over the years has been tremendous and it is that support that ensured the success of The Lanesborough.

I'm proud that a significant number of now quite high-profile people have achieved great things after working in hotels under my direction. To mention just a few, there's Roland Fasel who worked with me at Badrutts Palace in St Moritz and went on to be the general manager and area manager of The Dorchester Collection and is now the CEO of Aman Resorts, Hotels and Residencies. Duncan O'Rouke opened the Abha Palace Hotel in Saudia Arabia, went onto be COO of Kempinski Hotels and is now CEO of Accor, Northern Europe.

Jeremy Goring, who worked for me at The Lanesborough, is now running his family hotel, The Goring in London. Other Lanesborough alumni include Bernard de Villèle, now general manager of the Ritz-Carlton in Bahrain; Knut Wylde, now general manager of The Berkeley Hotel, London; John Scanlon became general manager of 45 Park Lane, London; Chris Galvin is now running Galvin restaurants with his brother Jeff and is one of the most successful chefs in London; Ajaz Shieke is now CEO of The Arts Club, Dubai; David Cowdery became general manager of The Bentley Hotel London, general manager of The Westbury Hotel and is now COO of The Calvary and Guards Club; and John Frazer became director general of The Marbella Club Hotel in Spain and is now general manager of the John Lewis Partnership.

Luis Fernandes became managing director of the Dharmawangsa in Jakarta, managing director of Las Ventanas, Mexico, executive vice president of Viceroy, COO of Chileno Bay Golf and Beach Club Mexico and is now running a boutique hotel company called Grand House Collection in Portugal. This is to mention just a few of the grerat people I have had the privilege of working with during my career, there were of course very many more and sadly space here doesn't allow me to list them all.

When I left The Lanesborough I was sixty-five but had no plans to retire and I still have no intention of leaving the industry I love just yet. Since leaving I have remained busy. So many people in the hotel business approached me asking for advice and wanting to make use of my experience and contacts on a myriad of new luxury hotel projects, in London and around the world and then, of course writing this book

has been a much more time consuming project than I ever expected!

And so I have set up Gelardi & Associates. I can't quite believe this myself ... but I have become a consultant, one of that breed for whom I have expressed nothing but contempt throughout my working life. Who knows how long it will last?

For the time being, the future is certainly truly exciting as I'm working on some substantial projects that in the coming years will see London home to some incredible new high-end luxury hotels. Projects such as the redevelopment of the In and Out Club on Piccadilly which is now called Cambridge House, and the transformation of Admiralty Arch and the Old War Offices – both of these are projected to have a significant impact on the ultra-deluxe 5* market in London.

During my career I've been fortunate to meet and work with so many visionaries, forward thinkers and influencers in my career. I return to Giuseppe, Gustave, Giulio and Bertie. The advice given by César Ritz in 1897 to Giulio that set him on a path of hard work and the lessons of going 'through the mill' which proved to be invaluable in his understanding of hotels. This work ethic was woven into Bertie by the

(Above): The Lanesborough was always mainly about its staff and I remember fondly the very many highly talented people I had the pleasure of working with.

example and close relationship that he shared with Giulio, and in turn was entrusted by Charles Forte to help him create his hotel empire.

That same work ethic was imbued in me, who like Giulio, as a young man 'took a huge step' and went off to a different continent with that 'feeling of fear' but excited to work hard and to learn. Hard work came naturally to me due to the example set by the previous generations and as I began to develop skills my confidence grew. I found joy in my work regardless of the task that was set; I was fortunate that this joy turned into a passion which stayed with me my entire career. And so, it was my turn to be entrusted by Mrs Caroline Hunt to help develop the beautiful Bel-Air and what turned out to be the iconic Lanesborough on Hyde Park Corner.

So what is the one thread that runs from Giuseppe to Gustave and Giulio, then on to Bertie and finally to me, Geoffrey? I think that, like my great-grandfather, my grandfather and my father, I lived up to that Gelardi motto: *Avanti Sempre Avanti*. Forward, Forever Forward. Along the way, there was hard work and diligence; there is so much more, however – honesty, trustworthiness, discretion and fairness, but perhaps the most important is respect. Respect for the guests and just as importantly, respect for the army of people who truly ran the hotels I directed. I hope that I will be most remembered for these values by those that I served and by those who worked alongside me.

# Index